CHARLES CARROLL OF CARROLLTON

CHARLES CARROLL OF CARROLLTON
By Sir Joshua Reynolds

Charles Carroll

OF CARROLLTON

BY

ELLEN HART SMITH

NEW YORK / RUSSELL & RUSSELL

THIS BOOK IS FOR

MARGARET

Preface

I<small>T HAS</small> always seemed to me a shame that — a well-written life being, admittedly, almost as rare as a well-spent one — the two almost never happen together. I had hoped that they might happen in Charles Carroll's case. That is why the new material for this biography waited several years in my notebooks, before finally I made up my mind to use it. I wanted somebody else to write Charles Carroll's life — somebody who would do it the way I knew it ought to be done, even though I couldn't achieve that excellence myself.

But the ideal person never happened along. The newest original-source biography kept right on being the one published in 1898. And finally my patience came to an end. I was tired and worn out with reading book after book about the American Revolution, biography after biography of the men with whom Charles Carroll worked for independence, in which his name was not even mentioned. And when a historian did condescend to spare him a sentence it was worse. More often than not, he made a mistake about him. One of the most brilliant modern ones said, for example: "Most of the colonies denied the right of suffrage to Jews and Catholics; this proscription was overlooked, however, if the Jew or Catholic happened to be wealthy. Catholics could not vote in Maryland, for instance; but Charles Carroll, who was one of the wealthiest men in America and an ardent Catholic, represented Maryland in the Continental Congress, and was a signer of the Declaration of Independence." It was enough to upset anybody, but especially somebody who — on Charles Carroll's behalf — could beat on the table as hard as I could.

I was not ever thus. Before I had to read, in the course of

other research, the eight thick quartos of Carroll correspondence in the Maryland Historical Society, I should never have
thought of writing a biography of Charles Carroll of Carrollton. Jonas Green, maybe. Robert Eden — some day, surely.
But a biographer has to move right in and live with his subject, and so a biographer has to be careful. Because I had been
much in Maryland — where dabbling in research about
Charles Carroll of Carrollton is as well-recognized a hobby
as taking pictures or collecting stamps — I was not quite so
vague about him as is the average outlander; instead I was fully
prepared to be bored with the plaster saint I'd heard Charles
Carroll was.

I wasn't bored. I found out for myself that the Carroll
charm, as famous among his contemporaries as the lifelong
Carroll ability to make prejudiced people change their tune,
was still as strong as ever. And while I have never come to like
everything about him (as some of his earlier biographers did,
or pretended they did) I do like him so much that I feel I owe
him an apology; and I have developed for him an enormous
sympathy. Charles Carroll of Carrollton had a hard time.
But as the result of it he grew into the man whom I consider
the most interesting, in certain ways the most outstanding, of
the patriots of his day. That's a startling statement, I know.
But I make it carefully. I'm not forgetting Washington or
Jefferson or any of the great men and good patriots most
people would mention far ahead of him. From the very first
Charles Carroll wanted independence, a free country — and
Washington didn't. He had a reason, not just a theory, for
wanting independence and a free country. And Jefferson
didn't. He was always magnificently consistent in what he
believed and wanted and fought for; and some of the founding
fathers weren't, as we find when we look closely into their
records.

Our history is not so overcrowded with great men — or so
it seems to me — that we should fail to know the primary facts
about them. You may not agree with me about Charles
Carroll of Carrollton's comparative status; perhaps I am as

prejudiced on his behalf, now, as I used to be against him. I have been so long and so intimately in his good company. But I think you will find him a great man. By his own definition, if you like. "Who are deserving of immortality?" he wrote in his thoughtful old age, deprecating some elaborate verses a rising poetess had sent him. "They who serve God in truth, and they who have rendered great, essential, and disinterested benefits to their country." Charles Carroll did all of that, and his country has repaid him by being vague about who he was, anyway, and what it was he did.

I have written this book in a pleasant missionary glow.

It is the first book I ever did write, and I didn't know just how to go about pleasing the reading public. And I knew before I started that I had no chance of pleasing myself. So I have tried to make it the sort of book that Charles Carroll himself would have liked. At that, I started with a decided handicap. I remembered how he hated "ye little Levities" that kept bubbling up in his young wife Molly; I could imagine what he would think of me, who had not Molly's charm to offset them. But I have tried to cancel off that and other natural disabilities by giving this book the "Sollidity" I know he liked. It has a good solid background, for I know Charles Carroll's home town far better than I know my own. It is a conscientious book. It deals exclusively with facts. (Many biographers nowadays fill in their own colorful unimportant details, but I don't like that and I don't believe Charles Carroll would either.) Where it has been quite necessary to draw conclusions I have tried to draw only the most obvious ones. Wherever possible, and always on controversial points, I have let him speak in his own words. I haven't had an axe to grind. I haven't tried to build any Cause around him; I haven't used him as a peg to hang a literary effort on, nor yet as an excuse to write a history of the American Revolution. Great as I think Charles Carroll was, he interests me not as a Statesman or a Catholic or an Ancestor but as a person. And that is the way I have tried to write about him.

Because of that I have devoted what many people will consider too much space to the part of his life when he was not in the public eye. It would have been more conventional, I know, to start with a chapter called "Ancestry and Early Years," end with a chapter called "Retirement and Later Years," and fill the intervening space with a more detailed account of his political career. His public contribution is the part of his life that matters to outsiders. But all of it mattered to him. He lived it, day by day. Ninety-five years of it! That is one of the reasons why his life rather than his times has had my best attention. Quite aside from the fact that I dreaded having this biography turn into "one of those eighteenth-century mezzotints in which the humanity of the chief figure cannot compete with backgrounds," I couldn't have squeezed any more social and political and military history into the one-volume life of a man who lived to be ninety-five.

And it would develop into a five-foot shelf if I included a list of all the people who — not knowing, any more than I did, that they were helping with a book about Charles Carroll of Carrollton — made my research easier and more pleasant. I have dedicated it to the person who helped me most — who made me try it in the first place, who worked as hard as I did on it, and who has unblushingly insisted throughout that it was beautiful — but the others are too numerous to mention by name. I am no less grateful to them all: the librarians and assistants in various manuscript departments, the people who have given me access to their private collections, my friends in Maryland, and finally the strangers-across-the-table toward whom I have pushed many of the letters in Charles Carroll's terrible handwriting and said: "Please, can you make anything at all of this word?"

ELLEN HART SMITH

MAY 1, 1942

CONTENTS

ILLUSTRATIONS

CHARLES CARROLL OF CARROLLTON

CHAPTER I

An Hawk Uprising

1688–1737

IT IS IMPOSSIBLE to begin a book about him by saying abruptly, "Charles Carroll of Carrollton was born September 19, 1737." So might begin, very properly, the biographies of most of the great men he knew: Benjamin Franklin, inventive genius born of a long line of laissez-faire dullards; George Washington, military genius born with a nice respectable background of peaceful country squires; Thomas Jefferson, genius of revolution whose very existence was an anachronism in his unrevolutionary family. It is not often that a man, and more particularly a great man, is so entirely molded by tradition as was Charles Carroll of Carrollton; and, therefore, the matter of his background is important.

Socially that background was unimpeachable. Unlike many of the colonial aristocracy's, Carroll's ancestors in Ireland were quite as creditable as his more immediate ancestors on this side of the water. They had, indeed, been kings. It is true enough that they reigned over very small realms, for Ireland in her great days was full of simultaneous kings; in fact a king in Ireland was neither more powerful nor more important that the head of a Scottish clan. His title was simply a matter of racial hyperbole. Nevertheless, these paltry kings were unquestionably Irish gentlemen, and there is nothing paltry about an Irish gentleman.

The Carroll family — originally calling themselves O'Carroll — had lived for several centuries in King's County without experiencing the slightest desire to live anywhere else. By remaining in Ireland they had, however, been forced to share in the misfortunes and persecutions of their country, and the latter part of the seventeenth century found them pitifully stripped of lands and titles. They still married into the best families in the kingdom and they were still as proud as the devil, but from the financial point of view it seemed indicated that young Charles Carroll, second son of Daniel of Litterlouna, go out into the world to seek his fortune. There was nothing for him at home.

This young Charles interests us chiefly as an ancestor. He was the grandfather of Charles Carroll of Carrollton. Yet it would be hard to imagine anyone inherently less like an ancestor. He was the kind of person who never gets old and tired, no matter how long he may live; who cannot be thought about as dead, no matter how long ago he may have died. He was always younger than his more illustrious, more dignified grandson. Young and high-spirited and big-talking and fun to be with; stubborn, too, with a temper that was never far below the surface and a ruthless, driving ambition that warred constantly with certain loyalties and prides.

Charles was in his twenty-fifth year, and had just graduated from the French University of Douay, when King Charles II died and his brother ruled in his place as James II. This seemed great good news to the Carroll family along with the rest of the Irish, among whom even potential good luck had been rare for some time. The Irish Catholics — "Irish" and "Catholic" were nearly synonymous words — had not found life under a succession of English Protestant kings either very pleasant or very safe. The crowning of a Catholic king meant not only that there would be no more confiscations and massacres, but that the Test Act would not be employed to exclude Catholics from the holding of public office. Matters of religion aside, the King's County Carrolls were not without influence, and the circumstances seemed to justify sending brilliant young Charles, who as the younger son of a younger son needed to choose some calling, to prepare for the law and

for a career in statesmanship. They found the money somehow. Charles Carroll left Ireland for London and was admitted to the Inner Temple May 7, 1685.[1]

Sure enough, when the young man left the Temple he
promptly secured a place at court. He became secretary or
confidential clerk to one of King James's ministers, who
spelled his name Powis, Powys, or even Powice, as the spirit
moved him.

The Carrolls were, of course, pleased and proud. It was a
good, enviable post, with what were called "emoluments."
But these did not include that feeling of security which young
Carroll had thought would be so pleasant a change. King
James had built his government on shifting sands. His genius
for saying and doing the wrong thing, his personal and religious stubbornness, and finally his lack of any of that Stuart
charm which might have helped balance the faults, made even
his friends realize that he was heading for trouble. Lord
Powis' young secretary could not avoid hearing of the mutter-
ings and discontent in kingdom as well as court. He may
even have mistrusted the filial affection of King James's son-
in-law, the Stadholder of Holland.

In any case, he began to think seriously about a career outside of England. He had no love for England anyway, nor
for Englishmen. He was unmarried and unattached; he was
ambitious and at an age when Adventure is spelled with a
capital letter. So, naturally, he thought of America.

Among the English colonies which stretched along the east
coast of North America there was one which made a particular appeal to the young man who was not unfamiliar with
oppression and who had learned to value liberty. Maryland
was fundamentally unlike the other colonies. Strictly speaking, it was not a colony at all, but a palatinate under the
hereditary rule of the Barons Baltimore. It had been granted
to the first baron some fifty years before, with the understanding that he would divide with his king any gold and silver he

---

[1] Carroll Papers, VI, 557C. He is mentioned as "Carolus Carroll Secundus
filius Danielis Carroll de Ahagurton in Reg Comitatu in Regno Hiberniae."

happened to dig up on the premises and that he would in any case pay tribute of two Indian arrows every Easter Tuesday. These obligations aside, he was free to do with Maryland as he pleased. As palatine he was as absolute as many kings.

Lord Baltimore had his own ideas of government, too. He died too soon to put them into practice, but he handed them down to his son. Cecilius, the second Lord Baltimore, was a rather remarkable man, and would have been so considered in any century. Against the intolerant backdrop of his own century he assumes heroic proportions. He was interested in his property less as a source of revenue than as a field for sociological experiment, and he planned a Utopia in which everyone might worship God as he chose, without prejudice and without fear.

The most respectable historians still allude to Maryland as a Roman Catholic province, because Lord Baltimore happened to belong to the Catholic Church. They say he planned it for the benefit of his fellow Catholics, who at that time were not allowed to worship freely in England.

Like most historical misconceptions this is partly true. Lord Baltimore did want to found a province where Catholics might worship freely. But he also wanted that province to be equally a haven for the persecuted members of other sects — Puritans, Presbyterians, Lutherans, Anabaptists, Brownists, and so on. He listed these and many others in his famous Toleration Act, which he issued as early as 1649 and which said as plainly as possible that "noe person or psons whatsoever within this Province . . . professing to believe in Jesus Christ, shall from henceforth bee any waies troubled, Molested or discountenanced for in respect to his or her religion." [2] And while many Roman Catholics did emigrate to Maryland, Lord Baltimore's governors also extended special invitations to Protestant people — to the Puritans, for example, who were being persecuted down in Virginia — and these Protestant people flooded into Maryland and far outnumbered

[2] *Archives of Maryland: Proceedings and Acts of the General Assembly . . . January 1637/8 — September, 1664*, pp. 245-6.

the Catholics. Some of them were not cast in the same tolerant
mold as the Lord Proprietary, and religious affairs in Maryland did not always proceed with smoothness and brotherly
love. Even so, the contrast between Maryland and England
was sufficiently striking.

Thanks to the Toleration Act, the differences between
Maryland Catholic and Maryland Protestant never got beyond unpleasantness. But England still followed the discreditable pattern of the last hundred and fifty years. There was
not much choice among the politico-religious sects of the day:
Puritan, Church of England, Roman Catholic, and the rest.
Every one of them that was strong enough to gain political
control was guilty of persecution in the name of religion.
When the Catholics were in power, Protestants were mas-
sacred or imprisoned or deprived of their property and political rights. When the Protestants gained the ascendency,
Catholics suffered in their turn. At the time Maryland was
chartered, and until the crowning of James II, Protestants of
one kind or another had been on top; now the Catholic
James was, it seemed, trying to change England into a Catholic country as quickly as Henry VIII had changed it from a
Catholic to a Protestant one. Parliament was packed with
Catholic members; the court swarmed with Jesuits; the Bloody
Assizes disposed in short order of hundreds of Protestants
who were accused of aiding Monmouth. King James sent to
the Tower seven Protestant bishops who had refused to publish a Declaration of Indulgence setting aside the Test Act.

He found his missionary work very uphill work indeed.
The English people, or the greater part of them, had been
Protestants now for several generations, and fear and hatred
of the politics of the Roman Catholic Church were strong in
them. They made it plain, too, that they had no idea of proper
meekness. The seven bishops were acquitted (the Declaration
of Indulgence being held illegal) and the resulting celebrations
alarmed even the thick-headed king. There were bonfires in
every London street; the Pope was burned in effigy; threatening crowds surrounded the houses of prominent Catholics;

private citizens were stripped naked and branded with the significant initials "R.C." And, while all this was going on in England, William of Orange was not idling his time away on the other side of the North Sea. Perhaps King James was not smart enough to see around the corner and know what was likely to happen, but there were numbers of smarter people who could.

One of these was Lord Powis' young Irish-Catholic secretary. Charles Carroll was not given to discussing his soul, and we have no way of knowing, particularly at this distance of two hundred and fifty years, how much his Church meant to him. We do know that he had no idea of becoming a martyr for that particular brand of Catholicism which was so mixed with political interest that it scarcely deserved the name of religion. That was to the credit of his good sense. We know also that he was personally very ambitious, no matter how genuinely religious he may have been as well. He knew that in Maryland he would have a better chance than in England of pursuing a career without interruption; the Act proclaiming religious freedom would be his safeguard. And there were many material advantages attached to Maryland. The proprietary — who in Charles Carroll's time was Charles Calvert, third Lord Baltimore — had within his power of gift thousands of acres of fertile farming-land, on which might be established manors after the good old British system. He had too the appointment of many well-salaried offices in connection with the government of his province. Finally, his lordship was eager to offer these inducements to people who would go out to Maryland. He especially preferred settlers of English or Irish descent.

Lord Powis may have recommended Carroll to Lord Baltimore as a promising and well-educated young man, or the two may already have been personal friends. They were certainly friends later, when we find Lord Baltimore directing that Carroll be given lands "as near as possible to one of the Proprietor's Manors, for the benefit of his society." [3] At any

---

[3] Kate Mason Rowland, *Life and Correspondence of Charles Carroll of Carrollton 1737–1832* (1898), I, 6.

rate, Charles Carroll soon resigned his secretarial job for something better, and set out for America. Though he was only twenty-eight years old, he carried with him Lord Baltimore's commission as Attorney-General for the Province of Maryland. There was not the slightest doubt in his mind that he was going to become a personage and found a dynasty. Pursuant to the latter, he made certain changes in his family coat-of-arms. For the passive, stay-at-home bird that perched unadventurously atop the crest he substituted "an Hawk uprising," symbolical of his flight to America; and he took as his new motto, *Ubicumque cum Libertate.*

Anywhere, that means, *so long as it be free.*

The new Attorney-General reached Maryland the month before the Protestant Revolution took place in England — that is, in October 1688. On the thirteenth of the month he presented to the council then sitting at St. Mary's City, the provincial capital, a commission stating that Charles Carroll was to act as Lord Baltimore's "Attorney Generall for and throughout our said Province of Maryland For us and in our name to prosecute and defend all and all manner of suites and accons whatsoever anywaies relateing to us or our Interest in the said Province," and that he was to receive a salary of twelve thousand pounds of tobacco "over and above all manner of Fees Perquisites and advantages whatsoever which doe belong or ought to belong unto the said place in as large and ample a manner as any Attorney Generall of the said Province hitherto received or ought to have received the same." [4] This official routine over, Charles Carroll settled down to what he had every reason to believe would be a long career as Attorney-General of Maryland — for was he not fully resolved to represent Lord Baltimore faithfully and gratefully and did his commission not say that the post was his "For and during his good behaviour in and dilligent and carefull management of the said Imployment"?

A few weeks later his world turned upside down. Along with the rest of Maryland, Charles Carroll heard with mixed

[4] *Archives*, VIII, 48.

feelings how the plot against King James had finally climaxed: how one by one his most trusted officers and friends, his daughter Anne and his military mainstay John Churchill, had deserted to the standard of Prince William of Orange, the ambitious husband of his elder daughter Mary; how King James, panicky, had dropped the Great Seal in the Thames and fled to France; how William of Orange had marched a triumphant army into London; and how, as the result of all this, "King William" and "Queen Mary" must now be recognized as the "True & Lawfull Rulers" of all the British dominions.

Every British subject who had normal good sense knew quite well, of course, that William of Orange was no more the true and lawful ruler than he was. The true king was still ineffectual, stupid King James, out of a job for a number of good reasons including the fact that he was a Roman Catholic. It was equally plain to the average mind that little would be done about it. William had behind him all the power and most of the people in England; he had come to stay.

Maryland waited apprehensively to see what stand Lord Baltimore would take. It was assumed that he would recognize the new king and queen, as almost everybody else in England was doing. He could hardly do less if he wanted to keep Maryland, and King James, in spite of the divine right of the Stuarts, was an unattractive, unadmirable person to suffer for.

But time passed and there was no word from the proprietary. The council hardly knew what to do. They consulted Mr. Carroll, the Attorney-General. Nobody saw better than he the dangers of delay, yet he could only tell the council what they already knew — that they had no authority to proclaim William and Mary except at the command of Lord Baltimore. Maryland, he reminded them, was not an ordinary colony but a palatinate; it was responsible to the Crown of England only in the sense that it was responsible to a Lord Proprietary subject in his turn. He was right; the council quite agreed with him. Yet, in the meantime, the people were growing more and more restless. There was a group of reactionaries who hated the proprietary. Nobody could know, of course, that Baltimore had long since sent a messenger with instructions to the council to proclaim William and Mary — nor that the messenger had died on the voyage, without revealing his mission, and that much valuable time had been lost before the proprietary could hear about it and send another messenger. So it was very easy to convince the masses that Baltimore had thrown in his lot with the exiled king and hence with the feared and hated Catholic party. It was going only a step farther to say that the Maryland Catholics were in league with the nearby Indians and would certainly massacre all Maryland Protestants unless the Protestants moved first.

So the Protestants moved first. Their leader was John Coode, a one-time Roman Catholic priest who enjoyed the reputation of being the most irrepressible hell-raiser in Maryland. If he had any virtues they have been writ in water. He had already been a leader in one revolt against the proprietary government, in 1681, and would survive to try another in 1696. He had hated Lord Baltimore ever since the latter had removed him from the St. Mary's County bench, on account of his debauched behavior; he had been waiting ever since for just such an opportunity as now presented itself. In July 1689, when there was still no word from the proprietary, Coode led about seven hundred Protestant Marylanders against the capital and seized control of the government. In the name of the King he brought about the election of a new Assembly — an Assembly very much to his liking. Then he sat down and wrote a letter to William III. His motives and purposes, and the situation of the Maryland Protestants, he explained in a masterly dish of lies mixed with just enough truth to make them go down easily; but in any case William was in no position to criticize the motives and purposes of other people. He chose to approve. Ignoring Lord Baltimore's explanations and protestations of loyalty, he sent his own representative to act as governor of Maryland. Lionel

Copley arrived in 1691 and took his orders directly from the crown. Though Lord Baltimore continued to receive his revenues from Maryland, he was stripped of all power to govern there.

Lord Baltimore lost a number of friends overnight. But among the most loyal of those who remained was Charles Carroll, no longer Attorney-General of Maryland but simply a private gentleman who had left home to find a land of liberty and who had been sadly disappointed.

He was Irish and had an Irish tongue in his head. He either could not hold it or did not want to. He left nobody in doubt as to what he thought of the whole business. He spoke freely of the "wicked instigations" of the ringleaders; of their "illegal proceedings," "inhuman actions," and "evill speritts." To Lord Baltimore he wrote: "Certainly your Lordship's Charter is not such a trifle as to be anulled by the bare allegations of such profligate wretches and men of scandalous lives, as Code, Thurling, Jowles and such fooles as they have poysoned by the most absurd lyes that ever were invented." [5] He was as indiscreet as he was loyal, and finally he went to jail for it.

The charge was "high misdemeanours." His captors, indifferent judges of character, let him out on bond and soon found that Carroll had no intention of keeping on what they called good behavior. He was quoted as "saying he valued not Bonds for that was a small matter he could procure a Noli prosequi out of England & that for a pottle of Cyder or some such inconsiderable value he would clear Mr Batson his fellow Bondsman. . . ." [6] Nor was this his only impudence. He continued to say exactly what he thought, and in 1693 they put him in jail again, "charg'd and accused for uttering several mutinous & seditious speeches in derogation to the present

---

[5] *Archives*, VIII, 124-5. Both Charles Carroll, writing this letter, and Lord Baltimore, reading it, were of course considerably upset; so it cannot be determined which one made a mistake in the date. The letter is dated September 25, 1689, and endorsed as having been received just four days later.

[6] *Archives*, VIII, 509.

Government scandalously reflecting upon affronting and abusing the same and the Authority thereof. . . ." [7] This time the authorities had learned wisdom and refused to "set the said Carrol to Bayle thereby giving him further opportunity of doing mischief. . . ." [8] On the contrary, they ordered him "closely Confined" and were quite unmoved by what the prisoner called "the great detriment which my present Confinement brings not only upon myself but likewise the Orphans whose Concerns I have in Charge," [9] as well as by the fact that they were interrupting his honeymoon. He had married romantically on Valentine's Day and was back in jail the next month.

By the time Carroll finally did get out he too had learned a little wisdom. His loyalty to Lord Baltimore was unshaken and he still considered King William an upstart and a traitor. As for that traitor Marlborough,[10] who had been consistently defeating the loyalist Irish. . . . But the victories of Marlborough had established William very firmly upon his usurped throne; Carroll might be loyal to King James, an exile in France, but he had too good an estimate of his character and resources to believe that he would ever cross the channel again. Nor was he optimistic enough to think that Lord Baltimore would ever get his palatinate back. King William, who liked to hear himself spoken of as the Protestant Champion, would never return the government of Maryland to a Catholic, and Baltimore was as thoroughly Catholic as the Holy Father himself.

In the meantime there was not much point in Charles Carroll's spending his life in jail for an outworn cause. Loyal as he was, he had sense enough to realize that. So he tried very hard to put a bridle on his tongue and in a measure succeeded. He never did come to speak highly of King William and he stubbornly refused to renounce in any particular his Catholic faith; but at least he stopped airing his views about religion

[7] *Ibid.*, VIII, 496.   [8] *Ibid.*, VIII, 508.   [9] *Ibid.*, VIII, 508.
[10] John Churchill, created Earl of Marlborough as a reward for turning his coat.

and the Stuart Succession before anybody and everybody. Though anti-Catholic sentiment remained, the anti-Catholic hysteria had worn itself down, and Charles Carroll was a personable and entertaining young man whom Maryland society still welcomed if Maryland politics did not. Out of jail in 1694, apparently without prejudice, he immediately went into the private practice of his profession — partly because he was still ambitious, partly because he needed the money. He was a good lawyer, perhaps the most capable in Maryland; and even people out of sympathy with him politically thought it best to swallow their pride and ask his advice. The royal governor, for example, consulted him several times on points of law, ignoring the less brilliant gentleman who had succeeded him in the office of Attorney-General.[11] When the provincial capital was moved from St. Mary's to a place on the Severn later called Annapolis, Charles Carroll moved too, knowing that the best legal pickings were to be found, inevitably, in whatever town politics and fashion and business converged — though a lawyer could make a good living anywhere in Maryland, for it was an age when litigation was as popular and as well-recognized a sport as horse-racing. His best client continued to be Lord Baltimore, who paid him well for looking after his enormous personal interests. This was a trying job as well as a big one, for the new Maryland officials were quite out of sympathy with the ex-executive's pretensions to Maryland revenues and tried to balk his agent at every turn. More often than not, however, Lord Baltimore's agent succeeded in balking them.

In addition to making money at the law, Carroll was rolling up a sizable fortune in other lines of endeavor. He kept a store in Annapolis and sometimes stayed in it himself, though he also employed a storekeeper.[12] Doubtless he imported his dry goods himself, from England, and sold them at enormous profit as the other merchant-importers did. He was, too, a successful planter. Lord Baltimore had made him a number of grants of land, and he added to them whenever he could. He had a

[11] *Archives*, xx, 314, 439, 590.
[12] *Archives*, xxvii, 133.

passion for land. Finally he owned about sixty thousand acres in Maryland. (He named his manors after the family estates back in Ireland — Ely O'Carroll, Litterlouna, and so on. His favorite manor he called, with characteristic grandiloquence, Doughoregan, or House of Kings.) Most of his land was good tobacco ground and under the management of capable "overlookers" brought in good money. Carroll was too excellent a business man to let this money lie idle. He loaned it out to his less enterprising neighbors and it brought in still more money. It goes without saying — Carroll being Carroll — that he loaned it at a very nice rate of interest; and a committee of the Lower House once cited "as an Aggrievance that Charles Carroll and Amos Garrett and others of the City of Annapolis ask, require, take, demand, and extortionately receive of her Majesty's Good Subjects of this Province ten Pounds p Cent more than their Debts due upon Bills of Exchange under Pretence of Exchange of Money and that directly openly and avowedly in Contempt of this House useing reproachful Speeches against it telling the People to thank their Assembly Men for it in making the Act for ten p Cent and that they have writ for England to get the said Act and the Act for Relief of poor Debtors disassented to by her Majesty protesting that let the Assembly make what Laws they please it shall not effect them they having Money and Interest enough at Home to procure a Disassent to any Law that pleases them not. . . ." [13]

Most of the official recriminations against Mr. Carroll have to be taken with a grain of salt, but this quotation sounds too much like him to need seasoning. He probably said just that. He behaved himself pretty well, on the whole, but it was not his nature to be discreet and the good Lord never intended an Irish gentleman for a doormat. Every once in a while he would break out in a new place, and how he kept out of jail is a wonder only to be explained by the fact that many people could not help liking Charles Carroll even when they deplored the sentiments that — for all his efforts — sometimes rolled from his impudent tongue. Also, many people owed him money and had to be more polite than they really wanted

[13] *Ibid.*, XXVII, 435.

to be. His secure financial position made him cocky — and he had been born cocky to start out with. Anyway, he was not afraid to act as attorney for the two Catholic priests who were arraigned in 1704 for the crime of performing the rites of their religion.[14] He was grossly impudent to more than one royal governor, and did not hesitate to threaten him when he felt like it — Governor Hart complained of being "Even Insulted on my sick bed, at a late hour of the Night when in a Dangerous State I was making my Will. . . ." [15] He signed the officially objectionable "Petition of the Roman Catholicks" in 1706.[16] He quarreled over a period of years with Sir Thomas Lawrence, the influential Secretary of the Province, because they would "both demand the full fees for patents." [17] He was always being called up on the official carpet for something or other and in spite of the tremendous odds against him he usually managed to make fools, single-handed, of the entire House or the entire Governor's Council.[18]

He was a magnificent fighter because he never knew when he was beaten. He was incorrigibly optimistic. Circumstances could not defeat him. He always kept hoping for a turn of the wheel.

When he was fifty-four he thought the turn had come. Princess Anne, younger daughter of the exiled James, had succeeded to the English throne on the death of her brother-in-law William, who in his turn had ruled alone after the death of Queen Mary. When it became apparent that Anne would leave no child to succeed her, the question of the succession attained the dimensions of a major political issue. Weak and sentimental Anne inclined toward her young half-brother, who according to the Jacobites should have had the throne in the first place, before Anne or Mary either. Her ministers, however, were quite sure that he would not do, for he was a Catholic like his father before him. Unfortunately,

[14] *Archives*, xxvi, 44.
[15] *Ibid.*, xxxiii, 482.
[16] *Ibid.*, xxvi, 543.
[17] *Ibid.*, xxii, 30.
[18] E.g., *Archives*, xxx, 395–7.

the best Protestant relation they could produce, in substitute, was a distant cousin in unimportant Hanover — a fat, uninteresting gentleman who could not speak a word of English and who would certainly not make a brilliant appeal to the English people. Both factions, therefore, had arguments against them, and it seemed to the Jacobites that James III, as they faithfully called the Pretender, had as good a chance as George of Hanover.

In the midst of the speculation about the succession, Lord Baltimore's son and heir cast a bombshell by renouncing the Church of Rome for the Church of England. He did this, he said, because he had at last perceived the error of his ways and wished to make what atonement he might. The fact that his apostasy made it pretty sure that, after his father's death, he would get back the palatinate of Maryland had of course nothing to do with his decision. Or so he said. His poor old father, who had his faults but was quite incapable of religious hypocrisy to gain a material end, nearly had apoplexy and did cut off his son's allowance. But the son did not greatly mind. He promptly began drawing another allowance from the Crown.

No wonder Charles Carroll's hopes skyrocketed. He had much to gain in either of the two eventualities. If James III succeeded as such, he would be in the enviable position of a faithful adherent who had suffered civil persecution for their common religion, and to whom the new king would in common decency feel that he ought to make amends. If, on the other hand, the Protestant George got the throne, he would doubtless return to the fourth Lord Baltimore (as soon as he followed his sick old father in the title) the government of Maryland. In the latter case, it was not to be supposed that the new Lord Baltimore, whose conversion to the Church of England had been so obviously from interest rather than conviction, would continue to persecute Catholics; and matters of religion aside he would surely recognize the fact that in Charles Carroll his family had had a most loyal and capable representative.

In 1714 Queen Anne died and George of Hanover succeeded her as George I of England. Old Lord Baltimore was
in a dying condition. Always an opportunist, Charles Carroll
decided that, what with one thing and another, he would do
well to take a trip to England.

He was there when Lord Baltimore died, and acted as
attorney for his widow. The recently converted son duly
succeeded as fourth baron, but he too died promptly thereafter, neither Catholics nor Protestants mourning overmuch
the loss to humanity. He was succeeded in turn by his son
Charles. The fifth Lord Baltimore was a minor, and Lord
Guilford acted as his guardian. The signatures of both of
them were appended to the "remarkable Commission" (dated
March 24, 1715) with which Carroll returned to Maryland
and which he complacently presented to the governor.[19]

This new commission was not received with the graciousness of twenty-seven years before. The governor — Captain
John Hart, who had come to Maryland as the representative
of royalty and now remained to take his orders, under the
changed state of things, from the Baltimore family — was stiff
with fury when he finished reading the parchment. But not
speechless. He was, on the contrary, "pleased to say That,
that Commission being Granted to any other Person but himself, especially to a Papist is such a lessening of his Power &
Dishonour to his Character that He has desired to be recalled
unless He can be Restored to the full Authority he held under
the Crown." Governor Hart also had his opinion as to how
Mr. Carroll had happened to be given these extensive powers
and did not hesitate to air it: "Mr Carrol has deceived the
Lord Proprietary in his tender age & also his Guardian in imposing upon them to grant him such a Commission contrary
to the afd Acts of Parliament and his Duty to his Lordship
the Lord Proprietary." He meant the law violated by "the
said Mr Carrol having refused to take & Subscribe the Oath of
Abjuration Enjoined by the Laws of Great Brittain and this
Province." Further, "His Excellency was pleased to inform

[19] *Archives*, xxx, 375–6.

the Board that the sd Mr Carroll by Virtue of his sd Commission had required of his Excellency an Account of the 3d
p hhd appropriated for the purchasing Arms & Ammunition
for the defence of this Province to which He had returned
that He would as soon give him up his Hearts Blood" [20]

Governor Hart's outrage was understandable. Carroll's
commission in many ways cancelled his. Whereas he had been
under the crown a governor in fact, he was now expected to
surrender a good deal of his authority to a man whom he honestly mistrusted and feared on account of his religion. He
realized that the Calverts were getting neatly around the difficulties of the ex-Attorney-General's Catholicism. They were
gratefully appreciative of his handling of their interests up to
this time, and they would gladly have let him supersede Captain Hart as governor if that inconvenient religion had not
been in the way. They did not dare do that — they were,
after all, subjects of a Protestant King who was king because
he was Protestant — but they did the next best thing. Carroll
was not only appointed "our chief Agent Escheator, Naval
Officer, & Receiver General" but was authorized to conduct
all of Lord Baltimore's business, not merely his private business as he had done before the restoration of the palatinate.
Obviously this infringed upon the governor's prerogatives
and duties. Finally the commission said in very plain words:
"And We do hereby ratify confirm & hold for good Effectual
& Valid whatsoever the said Charles Carrol shall lawfully do
or cause to be done in the Premisses notwithstanding any In-
sufficiency or Defect in the Words Expressions Clauses or
Sentences of this our Commission And altho every particular
Matter Strictly requisite be not therein particularly mentioned
& Expressed." [21]

Charles Carroll had been irrepressible enough with no commission to back him up; now he proceeded to make the governor's life one long misery. Nobody knew better than
Governor Hart that Carroll was more than a match for him,

[20] *Archives*, xxx, 377-9.
[21] *Archives*, xxx, 376.

or indeed for the other officials individually or collectively, when it came to a battle of wits; but he was quite as stubborn as Carroll was and never tired of trying to trip him. Mixed with his hatred for this impudent Roman Catholic Hart felt an enormous respect for him. He could never quite understand how such a brilliant man could believe in the Transubstantiation. The problem honestly baffled him to the end of his days.

Governor Hart has obliged posterity with a very clear and unintentionally amusing résumé of his difficulties with Mr. Carroll. Since this is not the Attorney-General's biography but his grandson's, it is much too long to quote here; the incident of the Pretender's birthday, however, was quite typical. A number of young Annapolitan Catholics had celebrated June 10, 1715, by sneaking up on State-House Hill and "fireing the Great Gunns" sacred to the birthday festivities of the Hanoverian dynasty. Some of the culprits were caught and thrown into prison, but Charles Carroll's first act under his new commission was to let them out, "Giveing a line to the Sherr that the Lord Proprietary was Satisfied as to the fine Imposed." This in spite of the fact that Governor Hart found it "more than Unreasonable that a profest Papist should sett Criminals att Large who were Convict of so great Crimes agt our Sovn. . . ." [22]

Carroll died in 1720, stripped of position again but far from beaten. It was the same year which saw his old enemy Governor Hart succeeded by a Governor Calvert with whose interests there would have been no conflict. It would have been a restful change for Carroll; but perhaps he would not have liked that, after all. He was a born fighter, a rebel to whom rebellion was the very breath of life. But he was more than that. He was a link between two men important beyond the bounds of Maryland. One of them was Cecilius Lord Baltimore, the author of the Toleration Act. The other was his own grandson, Charles Carroll of Carrollton, the signer of the Declaration of Independence, the man who got religious freedom for Maryland and helped to get it, later, for the new

[22] *Archives*, XXXIII, 477–85.

United States. It is extremely doubtful that the Attorney-General was as good or as great as either of them; he spent thirty years fighting for religious freedom, but he was fighting quite as much to avenge Charles Carroll as he was for the principles of the Toleration Act. He does not sound like a pure pale martyr. His flaming defense of his civil and religious rights was, very probably, more Irish stubbornness than anything else. But in any case he left a significant heritage to the Carrolls who came after him: a heritage of disappointment and frustration and prejudice, a tradition of loyalty to his own people and his own conscience and his own faith. He had put up — nobody could deny it — a good fight for the motto that he had been the first to write under the crest of the Maryland Carrolls: *Ubicumque cum Libertate.*

Charles Carroll the Attorney-General (why on earth history has ever fastened that title on him, the title he wore only a few weeks after he came to Maryland!) left behind him four children, all of them by his second wife. He had married, first, Anthony Underwood's daughter Martha; but she and their baby had both died and the young widower consoled himself with Mary Darnall, whom he married in 1693 between jail-terms. She was the daughter of that Colonel Henry Darnall whom Carroll succeeded as "his Lordships Agent in Land Affairs"; she bore him ten children and lived on in Annapolis many years after his death, an old lady in "Leather Rimed Spectacles." [23] It must not be supposed that she was a poor mother because she succeeded in bringing only half her family to maturity — that was about the average proportion for the Good Old Days. The girls as well as the boys were carefully educated in France, because of the oppressive anti-Catholic laws which made it impossible for them to receive in Maryland instruction in their own faith; and both parents made the long sea-journey to visit their children at school. Even when he was three thousand miles away the Attorney-General tried to be a good father. "I would have

[23] Rowland, *Life*, I, 15.

you Stile your Self in your Theses — Marylando-Hibernis," he wrote to his boys; and "I . . . desire you will Vigorously prepare for the defence of your Universal Philosophy, if the Rector and your Professor approves thereof, who shall be furnished with the necessary Expense, but if they do not think, that you can go through it with applause, it is better lett alone, for a dunce in a pulpit makes but a very awkward appearance." [24]

All three of the Carroll boys were educated at the College of St. Omer, which since the Attorney-General's time had succeeded Douay as the fashionable school for the sons of Catholic gentlemen. The eldest son, Henry, studied law at Gray's Inn in London; it was the last of Charles Carroll's misfortunes to hear that Henry had died at sea on his way home to Maryland, when he was only twenty-two years old.

Thus when the Attorney-General died, the following year, it was eighteen-year-old Charles who took over the family burdens. His younger brother, Daniel, was able to stay in Europe and complete his education, but Charles, the student of the two, had to leave school when he had no more than finished his philosophy. All his life he was bitter about the frustration of his plan to study law. He wrote many years later: "I have from the time I came from school, in the year 1720, to the year 1757, been a constant servant of my family." [25]

Along with one of the biggest fortunes in the American colonies, Charles Carroll the Second — Charles Carroll of Annapolis, he called himself later, so as to be distinguishable from several cousins of the same name — had inherited a somewhat ambiguous social position. Nobody doubted that the Carrolls were cultivated people of breeding and background, and money is money and helps even in Maryland. But there was still that matter of religion. Of course educated Marylanders did not really believe, as the common folk did, that all

[24] To Charles (of Annapolis) and Daniel Carroll, July 7, 1719; *ibid.*, I, 10–11.
[25] To Clement Hill, 1761; Rowland, *Life*, I, 17.

Catholics were in league with the Evil One and that inside the shoes of even the high-born and richly-shod there were hairy cloven hooves instead of the more conventional toes. Still there was no denying the fact that cordial relations with Catholics frequently led to social complications. People were always drinking toasts, for instance, and the one offered first of all was usually "Long life to the King and confusion to the Pretender!" Rather awkward to ask a Papist and a Jacobite to drink that one. It was equally awkward in the dining-room after the ladies had left and the white cloth had been taken off the table. Gentlemen were supposed to discuss politics over their wine and walnuts, and how could you discuss politics with a disfranchised Roman Catholic without asking for a quarrel? You couldn't. Nor was it altogether desirable to excuse your Catholic guest so he could join the ladies in the drawing-room. Females were notoriously brainless and bore watching — first thing you knew one of your daughters might take a notion she wanted to marry a Roman Catholic, and, of course, you'd sooner see her married to a stableboy. . . . So reasoned every good Church-of-Englander, and every Catholic knew it as well as anybody.

Even Catholics had their pride. And Charles Carroll of Annapolis, specifically, was the Attorney-General's own son, born with the same be-damned-to-'em outlook on life. He was irrepressibly high-tempered and strongly opinionated; he could see a real or fancied slight around the corner and was always willing to meet it more than halfway. The Jesuits at the College of St. Omer had failed to teach him to turn the other cheek. Nobody who had known his father was unduly surprised when, not long after he attained his majority, the second Charles Carroll managed to get himself into jail. He had challenged James Hollyday to a duel, and since Hollyday was a member of the Assembly then in session, Carroll was brought "before the House to answer for his Contempt therein." It was accordingly "Resolved that the said Carroll ask the pardon of the House for such an Offence, And that he remains in the Custody of the Sergeant untill he give

Security himself in the Sume of One thousand pounds Sterling And two Securities in five hundred pounds Sterl Each to keep the peace &c. And pay to the Clerk and Sergeant Ten Shillings Each

"The said Carroll asks pardon of the House but chooses rather to Continue in the Custody of the Sergeant than give the Security required." [26]

Very much like his father, too, was the talent for antagonizing one Maryland governor after another. Carroll of Annapolis was impudent to three of them that we know of.[27] He had even less control over his temper than his father had had. He knew it and deplored it; in later years he was always advising his own son to be circumspect about what he said in front of other people, and always telling him that the best way to get along in the world was to submerge his own opinions for the sake of politeness and social harmony. He would have been at better business if he had stood in front of the mirror and addressed himself.

But the same traits that had redeemed his father the Attorney-General stood him in good stead. He was intensely likable in spite of having been born with a chip on each shoulder — good company, witty and well read and, everybody had to agree, brilliantly intelligent in spite of his stubborn adherence to the Catholic faith. Also, he had enough money to command anybody's respect. The great fortune of which the Attorney-General had died possessed had been divided and only a part fell to the eldest surviving son; but Charles Carroll of Annapolis had inherited also his father's ability to make money. By the time he was middle-aged he had amassed probably the greatest fortune in all the American colonies. Most of it proceeded from lending money out at interest. His account books show that about two-thirds of the population of Annapolis, high as well as low, were at one time or another in his debt; and all reports agree that Carroll was not a lenient creditor. The moneylenders of this world have, however, never been spoken of highly. There seems no good reason to

[26] *Archives*, xxxv, 557.   [27] E.g., *Archives*, xxviii, 162–4.

credit the stories which have grown up about Carroll's mean-
ness and hard business dealings. It is true that he was not inclined to mix business and charity; he could not afford to, and
not only from the pecuniary point of view. He realized
shrewdly that money, plenty of money, must serve as the bar-
rier between him and an administration which was becoming
more and more hostile to Catholics. Catholics might not, in
Charles Carroll of Annapolis' time, either vote or hold public
office. They might not practice law, even though they were
trained lawyers. They might not hold church services, even
though they were consecrated priests. They might not instruct young children, even though they were well qualified
teachers. There was every expectation that Catholics would
soon be forced to pay a double tax, simply because they were
Catholics. They were already having to support two churches
instead of one, for they were taxed for the support of the
Church of England. Because most of them were violating the
law in one way or another — by having their children educated as Catholics, for instance — they knew that they were
constantly liable to extortionate fines. So even a Protestant
could see why Charles Carroll of Annapolis wanted money
and more money. He needed all he could get to keep his
head above water. Other avenues of achievement being closed
to him, wealth was his only hope for influence and prestige.

Civil oppression on religious grounds made Charles Carroll
of Annapolis furious, just as it had the Attorney-General.
But there was less that he could do about it. His hands were
in greater measure tied. He had not even a semi-official position which gave him an excuse for entry into quarrels over
the rights of Catholics. He could not, as his father had done,
make his own opportunities by taking the cases of Catholics
and Catholic priests who were in danger of being meted out
legal injustice, and blowing off more or less steam before his
honor's gavel crashed down to cut him short. He could trade
on no personal bond of friendship between himself and the
Baltimore family. The Attorney-General, who had had position and power in his time, was always sure that he would get

them again some day. Carroll of Annapolis had never had position or power and did not know what they felt like. Where the Attorney-General was incurably optimistic, his son expected the worst. Nobody can blame him. The Attorney-General was too busy fighting to have time for bitterness; his son had all the time in the world.

He was as bitter as a man can be when he is intensely religious and really believes that this world does not matter. Charles Carroll of Annapolis believed that. But sometimes it slipped to the back of his mind, and then the slights and inequalities of life in eighteenth-century Annapolis seemed terribly, heart-breakingly important. There were black moments when he hated Maryland and everybody in it.

He was hypersensitive and mistrusted the men who in other circumstances would have been his friends. The logical thing would have been for him to bury himself in the country and mix only with his Catholic relatives, but this Carroll was unwilling to do. He liked cities. The busy atmosphere of a social and an intellectual center was the wistful breath of life to him. But when he determined to build a house of his own in Annapolis he did choose a site a little removed from the center of town, down by the edge of Spa Creek. There he would have a view, and plenty of space for "green Gardens"; there he could live apart from his neighbors actually, as spiritually he already lived.

Remembering the eleven children begotten by his father the Attorney-General, Charles Carroll of Annapolis built himself a big house while he was about it. It still stands, massive, red-brick, severely plain but not unbeautiful. To it Carroll brought as his wife his cousin Elizabeth, the daughter of Clement and Jane Sewall Brooke; she was seven years younger than he and one of the famous beauties of her day. And there, on September 19, 1737, their only child was born. It was a boy, thank goodness, to inherit the great Carroll fortune and carry on the Carroll name. They called him Charles, after his father and his grandfather the Attorney-General. When he grew up other people called him Charles Carroll of Carrollton.

CHAPTER II

The Twig is Bent

1737–1757

H IS EARLY CHILDHOOD was happy and uneventful. Tradition has provided us with no such violent episodes,
indicative of future greatness, as George Washington's little hatchet or James Watt's tea-kettle. Though he
was an only child, he seems not to have been a lonely one; and
if he sometimes lacked the companionship of white boys his
own age he did not greatly mind. Never in his life was he
dependent on his friends. He had many of them; he enjoyed
their company immensely; and he got along very nicely when
they were somewhere else.

Conversely, he learned to depend a great deal on the society
of his parents. "Mama" and "Papa," he called them, accenting
the titles in the French fashion. He adored both of them, and
they, in their turn, were hard put to it not to spoil him, for
besides being their only child he was always a delicate boy —
"puny" was the expressive eighteenth-century word for it.
Years later, in writing of his mother, Charles Carroll said,
"Now all those occurrences of my infancy, those happy days
spent at Elkridge in her sweet company, our lonely retirement
and mutual fondness, pass in remembrance before me. I shall
never see such happy days again." [1]

The little boy growing up in the big brick manor of
Doughoregan, which was his father's favorite country seat as
it had been his grandfather's, or in the town house in Annapo-

[1] To Charles Carroll of Annapolis, June 10, 1761; Carroll Papers, I, 67.

lis where he had been born, was too young to realize that his own peculiar situation must soon bring these "happy days" to a close. His father and mother, however, were all too aware of the fact. Obviously the sole heir to the Carroll fortune — which was growing as rapidly as he was — must have a proper education, and this he could no longer receive at home. His mother had been quite adequate to the elementary situation; she had not had, like his father, a French education, but she was a great reader and her writing was so fluent and easy and her spelling so excellent that the ladies of her acquaintance doubtless considered her a bluestocking. But her son, at ten, was getting too old for female instruction. He could have had a tutor, of course (though Catholic tutors for Catholic children were forbidden by law), but both parents realized that this only child particularly needed the experience of school life and the companionship of other children.

There were several objections to sending the little boy to any of the recognized schools, though there were four or five in Annapolis and many more throughout the province. Most of these schools were, in the first place, extremely poor. Their curricula were sketchy and superficial; their masters were not among the best representatives of their profession, being too often convict servants, brilliant drunkards with unsavory pasts back in England, or the poorly educated and sometimes morally lax rectors of their day and age, taking pupils purely for the extra money involved. Besides, these Maryland schools were no place for a Catholic child. Charles Carroll of Annapolis was no bigot. Under other circumstances he would have had no objection to his son's receiving his secular education side by side with the little Protestant boys of the neighborhood. But the whole difficulty lay in the fact that it was not possible to secure a purely secular education in any of the Maryland schools. Most of them, whether privately conducted or chartered under the Crown, were definitely pro-Anglican and anti-Catholic. Repudiation of the doctrine of transubstantiation was as much a part of the course of study as Latin or "little figures"; it was expected of every student, just as every

German schoolchild, under the third Reich, is expected to start the day right with "Heil Hitler." A Catholic child might attend one of these Maryland schools only at the price of his faith; only parents who were courting his proselytism would have been foolhardy enough to send him to one.

In protest against this prejudiced state of affairs, Catholic sentiment in Maryland had caused to spring up a number of little Catholic schools, surreptitiously conducted in mortal fear of the law. They did have the advantage of teaching Catholic tenets to the children of Catholic parents, and the Jesuits who ran them were usually well-educated men, but the disadvantage of their being outside the law was a formidable one. The law provided that children whose parents so attempted to have them educated might be removed to the custody of persons who would see that they were properly brought up in the Anglican faith.

The best of these little sub-rosa schools was Bohemia Manor Academy, conducted by the Society of Jesus on Augustine Herman's old plantation. We know very little about this school, for the Jesuit fathers were too wise to set down records which, if found, would circumstantially sentence them to life imprisonment; but there are other indications that it was started about 1744, and that it closed and opened spasmodically after that. Its activity was regulated much like that of another Maryland institution of a bygone day, the speakeasy. As long as the official attention was fixed on something besides the enforcement of anti-Catholic laws the little school discreetly flourished, as nearly wide open as might be. During minor campaigns against the Roman Church a few extra precautions were taken for secrecy, but in periods of true official zeal the school was closed completely, the boys sent home, and nobody knew a thing in the world about it.

Naturally, a school operated under these disadvantages could not provide a complete curriculum or compete with the Jesuit schools of similar plan which operated under normal conditions abroad. Bohemia offered only an elementary and a preparatory department; still, for the time being it would suffice, and it was here that Charles and Elizabeth Carroll decided to send their little boy, ten years old in 1747. It was dangerous, yes. But it would put off the day that they had been dreading ever since their child was born, the day when he must cross three thousand miles of water, and stay ten or fifteen years, in order to get a proper education.

Among Charles's schoolmates at Bohemia were boys from some of the most aristocratic families in Tidewater — Brents and Heaths and Neales — and also there was his cousin John Carroll, whom Charles spoke of disrespectfully as "Jacky," not knowing that he was to become the first American bishop, and Archbishop of Baltimore. Jacky was two years older than Charles and was ahead of him in his studies, but the two boys became very good friends. Both of them were preparing at Bohemia for entrance into one of the Catholic European colleges, and it was decided that when they were ready they would go together to the famous Jesuit college in French Flanders, St. Omer, where the elder Charles Carroll had received his own education. They proved to be such good students that about a year later they finished their preparatory course and together took ship for France.

We know very little about the first years of Charles Carroll's student life abroad. He himself dismissed them in a few words: "I left Maryland to be educated in ye college of English Jesuits at St. Omer, where I continued 5 1/2 years. . . ." [2] Like most normal boys off at college, he was prompted by neither homesickness nor filial affection to write many letters to his family. His father had exacted from him a promise to write "at least twice a year," [3] but though Charles obeyed the "twice a year" part, the "at least" seems to have glanced harmlessly off his conscience. Left to his own devices, he wrote exactly two letters a year, no more, no less. Because his

[2] To the Countess of Auzoüer, September 20, 1771; "A Lost Copy-Book of Charles Carroll of Carrollton," *Maryland Historical Magazine*, xxxii (1937), 207.
[3] Charles Carroll of Carrollton to Charles Carroll of Annapolis, *c.* March 22, 1750; Carroll Papers, I, 5.

father had made the mistake of letting him draw on his London agent, Mr. Philpot, for what he needed, Charles did not even have to write home for money.

The semi-annual bulletins were, however, fairly satisfactory. Even as an eleven-year-old, Charles had the makings of a good correspondent. "I am very happy, my master is very good to me, and he says he will always be so If I continue to be a good boy, and I am resolved to be so," he wrote fluently. "If" is capitalized as though Charles wished to indicate that at this point his master stressed the important word and looked him straight in the eye. "I believe Cousin Jack Carroll will make a good scholar, for he is often first. Most of our Marylandians do very well, and they are said to be as good as any, if not the best boys in the house." [4]

Though he professed himself happy in his new school, Charles was not without his troubles. He liked Latin, but mathematics appealed neither to the mind nor senses. He viewed with alarm the prospect of leaving "little figures" for the uncharted wastes of "great figures," and he received "with the greatest joy imaginable" his parents' permission to put off the evil hour. Buoyed by the prospect of "staying in little figures another year," he hoped "either to be 1st or 2nd." [5]

To this desirable state of affairs he was indebted to "Cousin Carroll," who in another letter was spoken of warmly for having "got me to stay in little figures and I believe it is better for me." [6] This was Antony Carroll, a cousin from the Irish branch of the family who was, on occasion, his young relative's tutor. His presence and the real interest which he obviously took in "Charley's" studies no doubt contributed greatly to the ease of mind of that young man's parents. Cousin Antony could be depended on to break the barren six-month periods between Charles's letters with nice long letters of his own, and he also obliged by prodding Charles, from time to time, to take his pen in hand. "Cousin Antony

[4] *Circa* March 22, 1750; Carroll Papers, I, 5.
[5] September 4, 1749; Carroll Papers, I, 2.
[6] *Circa* March 22, 1750; Carroll Papers, I, 5.

forced me to write to you," Charles would tell his father, with more candor than tact. "I have very little to tell you only that I am very wel. . . ." [7]

The elder Carroll had reason to be well satisfied with the progress his son was making at school. Charles, who besides mathematics studied "greek latin and the maps," [8] was, he learned, always ranked at least among the first six in his class, though most of the boys were much older than he. Cousin Antony saw to it that, outside of school hours, he also applied himself to "the Maps . . . not so as to hinder his other studies, but amuse him some half hours and quarters, which otherwise would be spent unprofitably." [9] He went every day to the writing school at the college, trying hard to improve the script his father had criticized, and he began to take dancing lessons. This regimen must have left him very little time for play. The eighteenth-century school assumed, naïvely enough according to modern standards, that boys had been sent there primarily to learn; and it therefore put them through a course of study which, again according to modern standards, was nothing short of mistreatment. Instead of presenting to the child-mind in its most retentive period the saga of Lambkin's rolling downhill in a drumkin to escape the big bad wolf, these old-fashioned schoolmasters gave their boys the story of the wooden horse outside the walls of Troy, and taught them to read, in the same cogent Latin in which he had set them down, the philosophical works of Cicero. Eighty years later Charles Carroll's favorite books were the same ones which he had first read as a little boy at the College of St. Omer, the little boy who wrote home to his father: "I am extream glad to hear that you are pleased with me & I assure you I will do all my endeavours that you may continue in the same sentiment. I can easily see the great affection you have for Me by sending me hear to a Colege, where I may not only

[7] March 23, 1751; *ibid.*, 1, 8.
[8] September 24, 1750; Carroll Papers, 1, 7.
[9] Antony Carroll to Charles Carroll of Annapolis, February 26, 1751; *ibid.*, 1, 4.

be a learned man, but also be advanced in piety and devotion." [10]

Charles completed his studies at St. Omer when he was not quite seventeen years old. This was not unusual; boys frequently graduated from college at sixteen or even fifteen years of age. But though he had finished one college course his student life was far from being over. His father, whose own education had been cut short by the Attorney-General's death and who had never ceased to regret it, was determined to send him to the excellent French Jesuit college at Rheims. "You will there enter upon a new stage," he wrote to his son, "and enjoy a greater degree of Liberty than you have hitherto had." [11] The wise father realized that the cloister would not prepare the richest young man in America for the kind of life which he would inevitably lead; and the son's own words endorsed his judgment. Speaking of a young man who, though possessed of all the virtues, seemed unprepared to cope with the complexities of the world around him, Charles Carroll of Carrollton commented: "It was ill Judged to keep him so long at St. Omers. That education is only fit for priests." [12]

Leaving St. Omer meant parting with Jacky Carroll, who had decided to take holy orders. But Cousin Antony Carroll accompanied his pupil to Rheims. Father and son considered themselves very fortunate to have secured the services of this gentleman, who remained with Charles for three more years and whom he found an entertaining companion as well as a capable tutor. Charles was "entirely persuaded he had allways my interest and wellfare at heart," [13] while his father, according to Cousin Antony himself, was the first person he had ever heard of who seemed "completely content" with his son's tutor.[14] *Rara avis in terris*, Charles would have said it neatly.

[10] Undated, but obviously late 1750 or 1751; *ibid.*, I, 3.

[11] September 30, 1754; Rowland, *Life*, I, 22.

[12] To Charles Carroll of Annapolis, December 19, 1761; Carroll Papers, I, 74.

[13] To Charles Carroll of Annapolis, February 11, 1758; Carroll Papers, I, 28.

[14] To Charles Carroll of Annapolis, February 10, 1758; *ibid.*, I, 27.

He had learned by this time to sprinkle his letters and his conversation with scraps of Latin (and that without looking up the words in his dictionary) and did so on all occasions. It was one of the marks of the eighteenth-century gentleman.

Young Charles Carroll remained in Rheims for a year, or so he said. But here the account of his schooldays becomes somewhat confused. This is his own summarization of his education: "In 1747, I left Maryland to be educated in ye college of English Jesuits at St. Omer, where I continued 5 1/2 years, from thence I was removed to a college of French Jesuits at Rheims, from which place after a year's residence I went to Louis-le-Grand at Paris, & continued there two years. . . . From Paris I went to Bourges to study ye civil, or Roman law; in 18 months I returned to Paris & after ten months' stay, set out for London toward ye close of ye year 1758. I lived in London near 4 years and embarked ye 20th of Septr 1764 at Gravesend for Maryland." [15] Now it is obvious to anyone who does not share Charles Carroll's difficulty with "little figures" — a difficulty which seems still to have existed when he wrote this summary at the age of thirty-four — that there is something wrong. In the first place he surely did not leave Maryland until 1748, not 1747. (He wrote on March 22, 1750: "I have not been much above eighteen months out of Maryland.") [16] In the second place, if he went to London in 1758 and left in the autumn of 1764 he had lived there not "near 4 years" but nearer six.

This contradiction about dates, which is one of the reasons why his biographers to a man glide gracefully over Charles Carroll's schooldays, cannot be straightened out in the obvious manner because the records of his various schools are not fully available. Many college records failed to survive the sack of French towns during the first World War. The Carroll correspondence, however, makes it fairly plain that young Charles went to Louis-le-Grand, in Paris, about the time that, accord-

[15] To the Countess of Auzoüer, September 20, 1771; *Maryland Historical Magazine*, XXXII, 207.
[16] To Charles Carroll of Annapolis; Carroll Papers, I, 5.

THE CHARLES CARROLL HOUSE
ANNAPOLIS, MARYLAND

ing to his later version above, he set out for London ("I arrived at Paris ye 8th of January 1759," he announced in a letter stating that he was "lodged in ye College of Louis le Grand" and dated January 17, 1759); [17] reached London some eight months later (he announced his safe arrival there in a letter dated September 27, 1759); [18] stayed there five years instead of nearly four, and did sail for Maryland in the autumn of 1764.

But all this is getting ahead of the story. Certainly it was in Paris that father and son met on August 10, 1757, for what Charles called (further to confuse the issue) "la 1re fois apres 8 ans d'absence." [19]

He had expected his father earlier, hoping that he would arrive in time for the college exercises of June 21st, when he was supposed to "sustain his universal Philosophy." [20] The elder Carroll too was disappointed not "to be present at Charley's public appearance"; [21] but he had been delayed, he explained, by the important business which, rather than the unaccompanied desire to see his son, had brought him to Europe in wartime.

He explained the business to his son. They talked together as adults for the first time and found to their mutual satisfaction that their minds met amazingly. This in spite of the fact that Charles found it hard to comprehend the peculiar situation which made his father, explaining it, grow red in the face and pound with his fists upon the table.

Up to this time Charles Carroll had known only vaguely why he was being educated in France instead of Maryland. He had been told that it was the custom for Catholic parents, English as well as American, to send their children abroad to school; he accepted it as a custom, not bothering about the underlying cause. He knew also that he had been sent to the

---

[17] To Charles Carroll of Annapolis; Carroll Papers, I, 38.
[18] To Charles Carroll of Annapolis; ibid., I, 43.
[19] To Charles Carroll of Annapolis, August 10, 1758; Carroll Papers, I, 33.
[20] Antony Carroll to Charles Carroll of Annapolis, June 6, 1757; Carroll Papers, I, 11.
[21] Ibid.

College of St. Omer because it was his father's school. No other reasons had been given him, for Charles and Elizabeth Carroll had been wise enough not to plant bitterness in their child's mind. If anybody had suggested to young Charles that he had been sent away from home because the government did not consider his parents fit persons to bring him up he would have been sadly bewildered. Papa not a fit person, Papa who was all kindness and understanding, Papa who was the fount of all wisdom? As for Mama, she was so beautiful and so good that a little boy might have said his prayers to her without committing much irreverence.

Now at nineteen he was hearing family history he had never suspected before. All about the O'Carrolls in Ireland, who had been born so high and been brought so low. About his grandfather the Attorney-General, who had expected freedom in Maryland but who had never achieved it. About his own father, disfranchised, mistrusted, fifty-five years old now, and still an onlooker in the affairs of the province where he had been born.

Charles Carroll of Annapolis brought the history up to date with an account of the French and Indian War. Though the Seven Years' War had only recently broken out in Europe, France and England had been fighting since 1754 for the mastery of the American continent. It was the old question of boundaries, which the Treaty of Aachen, in 1748, had failed to settle satisfactorily. Both countries claimed the vast unsettled region west of the thirteen colonies that outlined the Atlantic coast, and both had certain points in favor of their claims. There was a good deal of bitterness between the French and English and, as is usual in time of war, a good deal of propaganda launched by both sides. The chief talking-point of the English was the same one which during two centuries of hard use had never failed to prick Protestant Englishmen to fear and resentment and hatred of their neighbors of France: the French were Catholics.

In Annapolis the Reverend James Sterling, loyal rector of the Church of England, coöperated with the government

which his church had kept in power since the Protestant
Revolution. The war with France was, he asseverated, a holy
war. Addressing both Houses of Assembly on December 14,
1754, he called on every loyal Englishman to defend his faith
against the popery, perfidy, and arrogance of the Catholic
French. "The Enemy are at our Doors!" he shouted: "They
are intrenching, and fortressing our Borders. . . . They have
. . . by the vilest artifices render'd us cheap and suspectable
in the Eyes of our ally'd Indians; . . . They have perverted
multitudes of honest heathen Clans into *christen'd* Demons.
Their *Rome-imp'd* Priests have refin'd simple Savages into
human Tygars and to enlarge their Creed have totally cor-
rupted whatever they knew of Morals before. . . . Ye Sons
of the *Reformation*, confirm'd by the Death of so many bright
Martyrs, guard your holy Religion from *Papal* Persecution,
Idolatry, *Irish* Massacres, Gun-Powder Treasons, and worse
than *Smithfield* Fires! . . ." [22]

Now the Reverend Mr. Sterling was a gentleman outside
the pulpit, and, according to his lights, a good man. Also he
considered himself extremely broad-minded. For some one
of these reasons he incorporated in this sermon a truly mag-
nanimous concession: "I am satisfy'd there are some *Roman*
Catholic Gentlemen of Fortune and Family, both here and in
England, who do not swallow implicitly all the Impositions of
that Church, though they hold external Communion with it."

He meant Charles Carroll of Annapolis just as surely as if
he had mentioned him by name. His hearers, and later his
readers (for he had his sermon printed to insure wider circu-
lation) were touched by the Reverend Mr. Sterling's charitable assumption. They wondered why on earth Mr. Carroll
should get mad.

Mr. Carroll not only got mad but stayed mad. When he
visited his son in Paris in 1757 he had been mad for three years
straight.

---

[22] James Sterling, *A Sermon, Preached Before His Excellency the Gov-
enor* [sic] *of Maryland, and Both Houses of Assembly, at Annapolis, December 13, 1754* (1755), pp. 41, 45.

Quite imaginably, Annapolis had not been a pleasant place of residence for him since the war started. All the things the official propagandists were saying about the French were applicable to him too. That little touch about the *"Irish Massacres,"* for example. And everybody knew that he had been educated by the Jesuits in France — Jesuits were worse than any branch of the genus Catholic — and that his son was at the moment in their fell clutches abroad. Only his wealth, and the fact that half his neighbors owed him money and had to smile politely when they met him on the street, had made his residence in Annapolis bearable. He held his temper in leash most of the time — like his father, he had learned that one cannot always tilt at windmills — but he had a new access of fury every time he wrote a letter and sealed it with the new version of his family coat-of-arms: the hawk uprising, and the motto, *Ubicumque cum Libertate.*

So when the law came imposing a double tax upon Catholics it was the last straw. Charles Carroll of Annapolis was sensitive anyway, in the region of his pocketbook. He broke off all friendly relations with Governor Horatio Sharpe, who had signed the bill, and who now wrote his brother in honest puzzlement: "We were on good Terms till I incurred his Displeasure by assenting to an Act which I thought equitable & which you say appears to you in the same Light. . . ." [23] And he took ship for Europe.

He related all this to his son, adding that he had had enough. Too much. So he had decided to leave Maryland for good. He would dispose of all his plantations there, call in his loans, turn everything he could into cash. He had already sold some property — at a considerable loss, which hurt him. He would need every cent. His Maryland affairs in order, he would lead a group of rebellious Catholics in the formation of a new colony somewhere. They had been meeting secretly ever since the war and its attendant anti-Catholic activities had broken out; now they had authorized him to come to France and ask King Louis for a grant of land, somewhere in Amer-

[23] To William Sharpe, July 6, 1757; *Archives,* IX, 46.

ica. They hoped that they would be allowed to settle in part of the Louisiana territory, lying along the Arkansas River. There, damn it all, they could enjoy the religious freedom that Lord Baltimore had meant for everybody to enjoy in Maryland.

Charles Carroll of Annapolis had arrived at his own personal decision after considerable travail of mind. He and his wife had both been born in Maryland and, except for its oppressive laws, they liked everything about it. By eighteenth-century standards Carroll was at fifty-five a rapidly aging man; certainly he had passed the period when emigration can be a great adventure. He had never lived the life of a pioneer and he did not relish the idea of exchanging for it the gaiety and polish of Annapolis or the quiet luxury of manorial life. But he had had, he repeated, enough. Too much.

He had expected his son to agree absolutely with his point of view. In most respects Charles did agree. He quite understood why, under existing circumstances, Maryland was no desirable residence for a Roman Catholic; he was quite willing that the Carroll dynasty be transplanted to a new French colony or wherever his father thought best. But it did seem a shame. Could the Carrolls never take root anywhere, must each succeeding generation leave its home to escape oppression? Was it the only solution? He had so wanted to return to Maryland when his "Exile," as he called it, was over. He was homesick for the big house on Spa Creek; he wanted to see the improvements they had made at Doughoregan Manor, to enjoy his parents' companionship among the old scenes, to renew his childhood friendships. Though he agreed that Maryland's discrimination against Catholics was cruel and unjust, many instances of it could not affect him personally. He had no ambition to become a lawyer, for instance, and shine at the Maryland bar or any other bar. He certainly had no idea of wanting to hold political office. His dearest ambition was to lead the life of a private country gentleman, farming and reading most of the time, coming up to Annapolis for the races and the theater.

This casual piece of news was a hard blow to Charles Carroll of Annapolis. Why, one of his chief reasons for wanting to leave Maryland was to give his boy a chance for a public career. He had always wanted one himself, for he had the Attorney-General's own driving ambition. Surely this important ingredient had not been left out of the Attorney-General's grandson? And he could not understand Charles's lack of interest in the law. Didn't he want to study law at the Temple, as his grandfather had done, as his father had always wanted to do? Of course he did. His ambition simply needed to be developed. It would have plenty of time to develop in the course of several years' law-study, on which, he told his son, he expected him to enter immediately.

Young Charles protested in his turn. For the first time in his life he questioned his father's judgment. No, he certainly did not want to study law, or practice it either. He wanted to go home. Having seen his father, he wanted more than ever to see the gay pretty mother whose health was no longer of the best. He wanted to live at the Manor, read, farm, go into Annapolis for the races. . . . They went over all of it again. Back and forth they argued the question, between visits to the Tuileries and the Palais Royal, up and down the corridors of the Louvre, during the little sightseeing trips they took into the country around Paris.[24] But finally — all this being back in the Good Old Days, when parents told their children what to do and the children did it — Charles Carroll the Younger set out for Bourges to begin the study of civil law.

From some branch of his family — not the Carroll branch — he had inherited an instinct to save the surface, to seem to give in gracefully, when it was necessary, and to bide his time. He was his father's own dutiful, obedient son, and was commended as such; but his thoughts were his own. It was all very well to flee oppression and go to a new colony, as his grandfather had done and his father was planning to do.

[24] Charles Carroll of Carrollton to Charles Carroll of Annapolis and Elizabeth Brooke Carroll, August 10, 1758; Carroll Papers, 1, 33.

Unless — wasn't it running away from the responsibility of a citizen? But Catholics weren't citizens. It was all very mixed. An impossible situation, as his father had said. The cards were stacked against Catholics in Maryland, as they had been stacked against them in the England of his grandfather's day; but something ought to be done about conditions *there*. What would Cecilius Lord Baltimore say, if he could see what a shambles had been made in Maryland of his favorite theory — equal rights for everybody, regardless of his religion? It was a fine theory and there seemed to be no good reason why it should not work. It was certainly worth trying again. Everybody had a right to be free. Somebody ought to do something about that situation in Maryland, not evade the issue by going somewhere else to live. He'd like a try at it himself, some day when he had finished his education and was ready to take a man's place in the world. Some day. . . .

CHAPTER III

Law and First Love

1757–1764

YOUNG CHARLES CARROLL arrived at Bourges with a very definite prejudice against it and against the study of law. He had parted from his father in Paris and, having parted from Cousin Antony as well, found himself entirely alone for the first time since leaving Maryland. By this time, however, he was used to making new friends in new places (he had already attended four different schools) and soon began to make a niche for himself. In this he was undoubtedly helped by the fact that he was the son of his father, and therefore probably the richest young man in America. It was only a few days after his arrival that the Intendant invited him to dine; and the Intendant, who, Charles wrote home, was "like a little king," put himself out for very few young law-students.[1] Also other people, quite strange people, began to invite him here and there. "I went a few days ago to a ball," he recorded on February 4th, ". . . but did not danse. I was a perfect stranger and not well acquainted with their danses. I believe I shall take a dansing master for 4 or 5 months or thereabouts." [2] Evidently his dancing did not require such thorough remedying, however, for he wrote just a week later: "I went masqued to a ball. . . . I had the pleasure of accompaning and danseing with one of the most butifull young ladies I ever saw." He hastened to add: "Don't be affraid now

[1] To Charles Carroll of Annapolis, January 1, 1758: Carroll Papers, 1, 20.
[2] To Charles Carroll of Annapolis; *ibid.*, 1, 26.

that I am fallen in love with her there is no danger; she is going in few day's time to Paris to be married there to a handsom gentleman of a pretty fortune: her's is but very inconsiderable." [3] As far as we know this was the first time he had ever gone places with any young lady, safely engaged or otherwise.

Unfortunately for Charles, who loved to dance, Bourges gentry spent far less time at balls than at playing cards. It seemed impossible for company to gather anywhere without somebody's suggesting a game of ombre or faro; and Charles, who thought card-playing the lowest resource of the human mind, was very much out of his element. "You must Conforme to their amusements and learn to Play at Cards," [4] his father admonished him; but Charles replied frankly that he would far rather "live quite retired, see little or no company . . . there is no instruction to be reaped in those companies where they do no thing but play at Cards. . . . If I go to one I shall be invited to another and can't absent myself without committing an impoliteness. . . ." [5] So whenever he could he pleaded a pressure of work.

He really was busy. He went three times a week to Mr. Champion, his tutor, and in the intervening periods he had much studying to do. He was not finding civil law at all easy, and he could not tell his father often enough how "dry and tedious" it was. The only ray of hope was the fact that, if he studied hard, he could probably finish it in about two years.

He was "lodged in a very discreat and regular family," [6] whom he liked at first; he had plenty of money to spend and, for the first time in his life, complete control over his leisure hours. But he simply would not play cards and most of the time when he was not busy with his law-studies he was sitting up in his room reading. "I find," said this twenty-year-old, "no conversation more agreable than that of a Horace's a Virgil's

[3] To Charles Carroll of Annapolis; *ibid.*, I, 28.
[4] January 1, 1758: Thomas M. Field, *Unpublished Letters of Charles Carroll of Carrollton, and of his Father, Charles Carroll of Doughoregan* (1902), p. 26.
[5] February 4, 1758; Carroll Papers, I, 26.
[6] To Charles Carroll of Annapolis, January 1, 1758; Carroll Papers, I, 20.

a Racine's &c." [7] Alarming symptom! His parents were no doubt relieved by the admission that "These and such like amusements are now and then interrupted by others of a quite different nature," [8] even though the example he gave was nothing less educational than a sightseeing trip from Bourges to Sancerre on which the young man had surely taken notes, for he described the beauties of nature in detail which was ample even for the eighteenth century.

It was on that trip, however, that he happened to visit the button factory of "Mr. Alcock an Englishman" at Chanté, of which he recorded his impressions concisely: "His method of making 'em is curious and amusing; but not half so amusing as his young, pretty, witty daughter." [9] This was all he said about Miss Alcock in June; but in August, when by the strangest coincidence he again happened to pass through Chanté, it became apparent that the affair was serious — to Charles at least. He wrote home with an effort at casualness that she "n'a d'autre bien que son esprit et sa beauté. . . . cependant il etoit dans le dessein de l'epouser si elle avoit voulu, et même sans le consentement de son Pere." [10] Translated from the French which Charles occasionally showed off to Papa and Mama, it became startlingly clear that their cherished only son, who had never given them a moment's anxiety in his life, had been ready to make up for lost time. Although Miss Alcock was dowerless except for intangibles he had fully intended to marry her even without the paternal consent — punctiliousness going overboard along with practicality. The only thing that stopped him was the fact that the young lady proved unwilling.

Simultaneously with this disappointment, young Mr. Carroll discovered "Bourges commence a m'ennuier un peu." There was nothing to see, nowhere to go, ". . . . il y faut Jouer aux cartes, ou ne voit personne; j'aime mieux vivre en hermit ou comme Diogene dans un tonneau que de perdre tant

[7] To Charles Carroll of Annapolis and Elizabeth Brooke Carroll, June 14, 1752 (undoubtedly should be 1758); *ibid.*, I, 32.

[8] *Ibid.*   [9] *Ibid.*

[10] To Charles Carroll of Annapolis and Elizabeth Brooke Carroll, August 10, 1758; *ibid.*, I, 33.

de tems a Jouer aux cartes." [11] For quite a number of weeks the world was dust and ashes. The incident was as unpleasant a part of his education as civil law.

In the latter part of 1758, Charles Carroll's tutor in law died suddenly. We have Charles's word for it that he looked, and looked thoroughly, all over Bourges, for a master who could adequately replace the excellent Mr. Champion — but he found none, and back he went to Paris with his heart as light as his heels.

He arrived there January 8, 1759, and "lodged in ye College of Louis le Grand." [12] Here he would have far less liberty than he had had at Bourges, his pleasures would be more restricted, and he knew from experience that the college food would not be very exciting. But he could put up with more than these — and gladly — for the privilege of being back in his beloved Paris.

He soon found an excellent master to tutor him in the civil law, in which, under Mr. Champion, he had already made considerable progress. He also enrolled at the riding-academy, and found himself a master of design, for he enjoyed drawing even though he did not "expect ever to be a Michel-Ange or a Raphael." [13] These extra items, with the fact that Paris was more expensive than Bourges (where he had lived nicely within an allowance of £130) made him determine to try to get along without his servant. "I own I cost you a deal of money, more than ever I shall be worth," he wrote his father about these financial problems. "For supposing you had the power of ye Ancient Romans *Jus vitae et necis in Liberos* and consequently of selling them I am certain you wou'd never get more for me than 10 or 12 pounds sterlin at most for if I remember right a good lusty strong nigro only costs 30. Be it as it will I endeavour to manage with as much economy as is consistent with decency." [14] He was developing a good idea of the value of money but his ideas of decency were still

[11] *Ibid.*
[12] To Charles Carroll of Annapolis, January 17, 1759; Carroll Papers, I, 38.
[13] To Charles Carroll of Annapolis, June 22, 1759; Carroll Papers, I, 41.
[14] To Charles Carroll of Annapolis and Elizabeth Brooke Carroll, February 17, 1759; *ibid.*, I, 40.

youthfully high-flown. When he ordered new shirts he did it twenty-five at a time.[15]

Civil law did not grow more interesting under the new tutor in Paris, but by fall, after something less than the two years which he had expected these studies to take him, Charles was again ready to push on to greener academic fields. He was now prepared to begin the last and most important part of his education, the study of English common law. The best lawyers of the time were educated in the Temple or other Inns of Court in London, and it was therefore to London that Charles now went. His father had written to his friend Mr. Perkins to engage chambers and have them in readiness for him, so the move to a strange country was accomplished smoothly, if not without the usual bitterness on the part of the traveler about the heavy duty he was forced to pay on his books.[16]

If Charles had liked Paris he was even better satisfied with London, from which place he wrote enthusiastically to his father, a few weeks after his arrival: "I have been happy in all ye different Scenes thro' which I have passed, yet my present sejour promises to turn out ye most agreable of all: my Chambers are genteel and convenient and in ye most wholesome pleasant part of ye Temple. The choice of good company is the most difficult & yet ye most important article, in which ye temple appears to be deficient, tho' extremely convenient in every other point. few young gentlemen are here to be found of sound moralls. . . ."[17]

This was just the kind of thing his father had been afraid of. His own letter crossed his son's on the way: "If this meets you in London, it will meet you in an open and wide Ocean of danger: hitherto you have had friends to advise with, and good Example constantly before you; now you can only rely on God's grace, your own prudence and ye good principles instilled into you by a virtuous Education: I beg you will never

[15] To Charles Carroll of Annapolis, January 1, 1758; *ibid.*, I, 20.
[16] To Charles Carroll of Annapolis and Elizabeth Brooke Carroll, September 27, 1759; Carroll Papers, I, 43.
[17] November 13, 1759; Carroll Papers, I, 44.

fail daily and sincerely to implore ye first, without which ye other two can be of no Service. In your Situation ye greatest Resolution will be necessary to withstand ye many Temptations you will be exposed to: so abandoned will you find most men as to be ashamed of even appearing virtuous. I do not desire to seclude you from Society or innocent pleasures, but I advise you to be very circumspect in ye Choice of your Company, and to watch so that your amusements may not have any ill tendency. . . ." [18]

"That my present situation is the most dangerous of any I have hitherto been in is evident," the son replied: "advice is necessary but most of all a sufficient resolution to put good advice in execution. . . . Young person's passions are strong of themselves & need no outward encouragement; but when roused by occasions, strengthened by example, fired with wine and Jovial company, become almost irresistable. Tis therefore with the greatest prudence and forecast you recommend to me the choice of my company, a matter really difficult in London, but most so among young men. . . . That the greatest resolution, prudence & virtue are requisite to protect me from . . . . contagion is undoubted. . . . I never like to promise unless morally certain of being able to fulfil my promise: and who can promise to others even to himself to remain always virtuous. I am now in an open sea, hitherto I have rode triumphantly. . . ." [19] If he intended this letter to reassure his father it is doubtful that he succeeded.

He was in his twenty-third year and he had never sowed a single wild oat. But we should not dismiss him, on that account, as an Alger hero too good for this troublous world. Without reflecting in the slightest upon Charles Carroll of Carrollton, who really was one of the best men America has produced, as well as one of the greatest, it must be respectfully submitted that up to this time his opportunities had been negligible.

But certainly now he was in the open sea, as he and his

---

[18] October 6, 1759; Field, *Unpublished Letters*, pp. 32–3.
[19] January 29, 1760; Carroll Papers, I, 47.

father agreed. London in the eighteenth century had a reputation for wickedness which made Paris seem innocuous in
comparison, and which made the Methodists wonder audibly
about the double standard which had failed to spare Sodom
and Gomorrah. The primary vice was gambling at cards, and
from this at least young Mr. Carroll was safe as long as he
retained his preference for living in a tub. But wine that
flowed like water was also characteristic of fashionable London, and wine was Charles Carroll's favorite beverage, though
he had never overindulged. He disliked the taste of malt
liquor and cider made him sick at his stomach [20] — but whoever heard of going wrong on cider anyway? Then too he
was susceptible to women. (His parents recalled with dismay
the precipitate incident of Miss Alcock.) This circumstance
probably proceeded in part from the fact that women in his
life had been about as rare as giant pandas. They were not
part of the Jesuit curriculum. But whatever the reason,
Charles wrote solemnly to his father: "I can't close this letter
without touching on that part of yours precautioning me
against too great familiarities with women. A most necessary
precaution indeed; for what so decieving, what so engaging
as women! I have often wondered why Providence has bestowed such art, such sagacity on that sex, and at the same
time so much beauty. However set aside the charms of beauty,
all their alluring enveigling arts will avail them little; for I
have frequently remarked, that the most beautiful are always
the most powerful, at least with me. I wou'd defy an uggly
woman endowed with all the sagacity of a Sphinx ever to
entrap me." [21]

That wasn't very reassuring either.

But at least his studies still kept him reasonably busy. He
had a tutor, a Mr. Twinkio, who was introducing him to the
complexities of the common law; this Charles Carroll found
rather awful, no improvement whatever over the civil law he
had struggled with in France. "However neither its difficulty

[20] Charles Carroll of Carrollton to Charles Carroll of Annapolis, February 30, 1760; Carroll Papers, I, 48.
[21] January 29, 1760; ibid., I, 47.

or dryness frighten me," he wrote bravely to his father: "I am convinced of its utility and therefore am resolved at all hazards to plunge into this Chaos. I expect to meet with no smaler difficulties than attended Satan on his voyage thro' the primeval one." [22]

Ironically enough, about the same time that his son thus announced his conversion to the point of view that a legal education was desirable for him to have, Charles Carroll of Annapolis was meeting disappointment of his own hopes for the founding of a free colony. The project had been hanging fire these several years, awaiting the royal pleasure; now it was pretty clearly indicated that France was not interested in giving the Maryland Catholics a colony on the Arkansas River or anywhere else. The elder Carroll was bitterly disappointed at the miscarriage of his plans, but his son thought that perhaps things had worked out for the best. His study of the civil law in France had confirmed his conviction that a colony under the jurisdiction of France would not be a final solution of the *Ubicumque cum Libertate* problem. "Religious persecution, I own, is bad, but civil persecution is still more irksome," he concluded, and he knew of no Catholic country or colony where "that greatest blessing civil liberty" might be enjoyed. At the same time he could not "conceive how any Roman Catholick especially an Irish Roman Catholick can consent to Live in England or any the British dominions, if he is able to do otherwise. . . . Now where is the man of spirit that can behold the rod lifted up, tremble, and kiss the hand of him that holds it?" That was the Attorney-General's grandson speaking. But the ability to see both sides of a question, the tolerance inherited from somebody besides the Carrolls made him add: ". . . Notwithstanding my natural aversion to all such oppressions, and to an humble, silent, groveling submission, I cou'd even rather bear all this, than be deprived of the pleasure and comfort of living happily together." [23]

He was contradicting himself, and knew it. He was think-

[22] January 29, 1760; Carroll Papers, I, 47.
[23] To Charles Carroll of Annapolis, December 10, 1759; Carroll Papers, I, 45.

ing on paper, trying to formulate the theory that lurked in the back of his mind.

Charles Carroll of Annapolis found his son's point of view irritating. This thing of wanting to wait until circumstances were more favorable, to settle the issue somehow, some time, in Maryland instead of by going somewhere else (for this was what his son was trying to say) did not appeal to him. He was fifty-eight years old and all his life he had done nothing but wait for things to get better — and instead they were getting worse. He had, no doubt of it, a one-track mind; but we should say in fairness to him that in the matter of religious persecution it was he who was suffering, while his son, on the other side of the ocean, was merely hearing about it and could afford to theorize. The young man's ignorance of the state of affairs in Maryland is amazing; he was nearly twenty-three when he wrote asking his father to send him a copy of the provincial charter, and as "I am perfectly ignorant of the Maryland government, its laws, & power of the Proprietary" to make these matters "ye subject of your next Letter." [24]

Charles Carroll of Annapolis, naturally, did not pay much attention to a young whippersnapper who knew no more about the situation than that. He kept on making plans for his colony, if not on the Arkansas River, somewhere. He was still disposing of his Maryland property, still stubbornly determined to leave the province. He had made up his mind about this thing — he was going to live in a free country before he died.

All his planning came to an abrupt end, however, with Elizabeth Carroll's serious illness. She had always hated the idea of leaving her home, and worry over that, as well as the twelve-year separation from her only child, had no doubt hastened her declining health. She and his father had conspired to keep from Charles any hint of her illness, but as always in such cases there were busybody friends who took it upon themselves to break the news to him. "I am overjoyed to hear her swelling has abated without impairing her health," he

[24] April 10, 1760; Carroll Papers, I, 49.

CHARLES CARROLL OF ANNAPOLIS
BY JOHN WOLLASTON (THE YOUNGER)

wrote anxiously home; "tho' if I may credit some private in-
formations, she was once in great danger; this I suppose you
concealed from me de industria. Pray don't deceive me for
the future. In all your letters you mention her being in good
health and that she sends me her blessing: why can't she tell
me so in her own handwriting? if tis but a line or two." [25]

His fears were only too well grounded. On March 12, 1761,
Elizabeth Carroll died at the age of fifty-one. Her son had
not been told, until he had the news of her death, that she had
been confined to her room for several months and to her bed
for three or four weeks. "If 4 Physicians could have saved
her I shd still be blessed with her," the elder Carroll wrote to
his son. "Our Loss is as great as such loss can be, to you she
was a most tender Mother, to me ye best of Wives being a
Charming Woman in every sense, remarkable for her good
Sense evenness & Sweetness of her temper. She bore her tedious Sickness with great patience & Resignation, & had all ye
Spiritual helps ye Church can bestow in such Cases. Hence, &
from ye Regularity of her life we have ye solid Comfort of a
well grounded hope yt her Death was precious in ye Sight
of God. . . ." [26]

Charles did not hear of his mother's death until June, three
months later. This was the first real grief that he had ever
experienced, and he was overwhelmed by it. He could not
share it with any of his friends, however intimate, for none
of them had known Elizabeth Carroll; instead he poured out
his feelings in letters to his father, asking for the details of his
mother's last illness, begging to know if she had mentioned
him, and how — until his father had to answer, adding: "I
could not say less as you desired to be informed as to those
particulars, I cannot say more ye Subject being too moving.
. . . For ye future let us mention her as seldom as possible, we
can never cease to think of her & pray for her. . . ." [27]

More than ever, now, Charles wanted to return to Mary-

[25] September 16, 1760; Carroll Papers, I, 54.
[26] March 22, 1761; Carroll Papers, I, 61.
[27] November 10, 1761; Carroll Papers, I, 72.

land. From his point of view there was no reason why he should prolong his reluctant "Exile" abroad. "I loved my Mama most tenderly," he wrote Charles Carroll of Annapolis, in a letter notably lacking the characteristic reserve of which even his father complained; ". . . the greatest blessing I wished for in this life was to see to enjoy my Parents after so long a separation to comfort to support them in an advanced age. one is for ever snatched from me. May God almighty, Dr Papa, preserve yr health & grant you a long life. . . . I wish you would permit me to return to Maryland in the next fleet. I am only doing here what I cou'd do as well at home. I am persuaded I can apply as closely to ye Law in yr house as in the temple. . . ." [28] Anyway, he was impatient with his father's persistence that he should go on studying law at all. What was the use of it? — for Charles Carroll of Annapolis was telling him, now, that he personally had lost much of his interest in finding a land of freedom. Elizabeth's death had been a bitter blow to him; he felt like an old man. He would go on putting his affairs in order, in case Charles should decide he wanted to leave Maryland (Charles could tell him, right now, that he never would), but he himself no longer felt like taking the initiative. Well then, argued Charles, why study law? His religion precluded his admission to the Maryland bar — though his father thought that "a gratuity properly placed" might be of service in overcoming this difficulty [29] — and he hated it anyway. After nearly four years' study the young law-student's considered opinion was: "The books I read are so dry that they seem to have communicated their secheresse even to the reader. . . ." [30] But his father, pressed for a good reason for insisting that Charles finish his legal education, settled the matter by replying: "I have always told you I never intended you should practise ye Law; will, therefore, ye knowledge of it be unprofitable to you? would it not be of infinite advantage to England if every man of property who

[28] June 10, 1761; Carroll Papers, I, 67.
[29] To Charles Carroll of Carrollton, July 1761; Field, *Unpublished Letters*, p. 60.
[30] To Charles Carroll of Annapolis, May 15, 1761; Carroll Papers, I, 66.

serves in Parliament were a sound Lawyer and well acquainted with the Constitution? Will not ye knowledge of ye Law enable you to transact your affairs with ease and Security? Will it not enable you to state your own Cases, to instruct those you employ; and, if you find them ignorant, knavish or conceited, direct you to employ others? It is true, I have met with some of these Characters, but had I been a Lawyer, or deemed such, it's more than probable they would not have ventured to have imposed on me. Although other occupations here will hinder you from such an application to ye Law as to give you a knowledge of it, yet, certainly, after four years' study and close application to it in London, some spare hours here may conduce to improve your knowledge; your Path will be beaten and easy, and you will certainly know how to turn to proper books and Cases upon occasion, or your time and money must be wasted to no purpose. I endeavour to convince, I would always avoid ye hardness of a command, and I hope you will be persuaded that your wellfare, Interest and happiness only induce me against my natural fondness and propensity to see you and have you with me, not to alter my Resolution in this Respect." [31]

Charles stayed where he was. He felt himself very much injured, but really, in spite of his law books and his home-sickness, the young man genuinely liked being in London. He had made more friends there than he had ever made in France, mostly young law students or lawyers who enjoyed settling the world's political and economic problems over a social glass, just as earnest young students do today. Their favorite meeting place was the Crown and Anchor Tavern and Charles admitted that the tavern bills, on the evenings that these sessions were held, were "pretty high." [32] Most of these young gentlemen were not too serious-minded to enjoy the races, too — Charles certainly was not — and the strong meat which was the current theatrical fare. Because he still loved to dance,

---

[31] December 29, 1762; Field, *Unpublished Letters*, pp. 75-6.
[32] To Charles Carroll of Annapolis, December 8, 1763; Carroll Papers, I, 101.

Charles occasionally stepped out of this circle into the larger and more glittering world of fashionable London, to which his wealth and family connections gave him the entree, but he was youthfully disgusted with its superficiality. Besides, he had not yet learned how to be at ease when he was out of his element. "I never was fond of great companies," he confessed. "I am naturally timid & bashful: this timidity may occasion my dislike to company; my forbearance may have confirmed this timidity & propensity to silence & retirement. . . . I own I am too stiff & reserved I can only be free and open with an intimate friend. . . ." [33] Always, after such an excursion into high society, he returned with relief to the good company at the Crown and Anchor.

His best friend was a young master in chancery named William Graves; but almost as intimate were Daniel Barrington ("my lord Barington's brother and one of the welch Judges"), Christopher Bird, William Perkins, and Edmund Jennings. Mr. Jennings was a fellow Marylander, an Annapolitan at that. He also saw a good deal of Mr. Maure, Mr. Hutton, Doctor Hay, Mr. Hussey ("attorney general to the queen"), Mr. Pratt, and Mr. Ludwell of Virginia; Mr. Russell, in spite of the fact that Charles Carroll liked him particularly, had to be visited less often than the rest because "too great intimacy in a family where there are young ladies may give room to idle reports & familiarity with ye sex is immediately construed into love." [34] Young Mr. Carroll was still putting up a good fight against the temptations of London, which, as far as he was concerned, meant women. Most of the time he kept strictly away from them, though he did condescend to recover from smallpox at the country house of Mr. Bird, whose family circle included — the saints defend us! — an unmarried sister. [35] But even then he managed to play a great many games of chess with Christopher Bird's father, and to converse at length with his safely married and middle-aged Aunt Esther Browne.

[33] To Charles Carroll of Annapolis, July 15, 1761; *ibid.*, I, 68.
[34] To Charles Carroll of Annapolis, July 15, 1761; Carroll Papers, I, 68.
[35] To Charles Carroll of Annapolis, May 14, 1763; *ibid.*, I, 92.

Generally speaking, his father was very well pleased with the way Charles conducted himself. But though the danger of a *mésalliance* was one of his recurrent bad dreams, there were times when Charles's overexertions to resist female temptation annoyed him. For example there was the incident of Mr. Bladen of Maryland.

This Mr. Bladen was the gentleman who, on the strength of his having married Lady Baltimore's sister, had been made governor of Maryland in 1742. He had so few other qualifications for the post that he was removed several years later, and had been living in London ever since. The Bladen and Carroll families had been on friendly terms in Annapolis, in spite of the former's prominence in politics, and nothing was more natural than that young Charles Carroll should call upon the Bladens in London. Charles, however, objected. He inferred surprise that his father should want him to cultivate the company of such a notorious gambler, former Maryland governor or not. Besides, he hinted darkly, there were other reasons why he should avoid the Bladen acquaintance. That was all he would say. His father, bitten by curiosity now as well as by social conscience, persisted: "You say . . . yt you do not desier to be acquainted with him as he is a Gamester, & yt that is not yr only Reason for declining his Acquaintance. this is misterious What other Reason have you? He was Civill to me when in London I have been long acquainted wth him, & his & my Father were neighbours & Acquaintances I am intimate with Mr. Tasker who Married his Sister, therefore if he makes the 1st advances be Polite & Civill, not Intimate." [36]   And Charles Carroll the Younger wrote back: "A certain gentleman's being a gamester is, I think a sufficient reason to decline his company. I meant no more by saying *that was not the only reason* than that by frequenting his house I might fall a victim to his daughter: she is remarkably handsom; in a stricter acquaintance I might discover qualities wh have more influence on a man of sense than beauty." [37]   The elder Carroll was, quite properly, disgusted.

[36] July 14, 1760; Carroll Papers, I, 53.
[37] October 13, 1761; *ibid.*, I, 71.

His son would never make a man of the world at this rate. He sent him peremptory instructions to cultivate the Bladens at once, and Charles accordingly accepted an invitation to dine there the seventh of January. He found to his horror that the hazard was doubled: there were two Miss Bladens instead of one. "I am astonished two such fine young ladies have remained so long and still remain single," Charles wrote to his father the day after the dinner-party: "if beauty and sense improved by the best education, command esteem & inspire love, no lady was ever better entitled to both than the Miss Bladens; very few of our young gentlemen, if any, are deserving of them: They themselves are not sensible enough of their own worth, to entertain such a thought; possessed of every advantage; every amiable endowment of the fair, they are without that almost common fault of all, a too great sense & opinion of their own charms." [38]

Fathers are hard to please, and Charles Carroll of Annapolis now found his son a bit overenthusiastic. He began to write in his mind a letter on the important subject of matrimony.

When he finally got it on paper it was more the size of a package than of a letter. If he and his son had been on the same side of the ocean he probably would have stammered and got red in the face, like any other normal father talking to his son; as it was he had the satisfaction of knowing that he had left little unsaid. He had held forth on family, fortune, beauty, religion, virtue, in-laws, education, health, disposition, economy, industry, and intelligence; his standards were high, for he could not imagine, much less had he seen in the flesh, a young lady too good for his only son. Also, he was frankly thinking about his grandchildren. He was of good family himself and he had bred race-horses for a number of years; he knew that matters of heredity "are seriously to be weighed, for you will not geather Grapes from Thorns." He was desperately afraid that his susceptible young son was going to lose his head one of these days and marry for nothing but

[38] January 8, 1762; *ibid.*, I, 78.

beauty: "Beauty is not to be undervalued," he wrote, "But it is too transient & lyable to too many Accidents, to be a Substantiall Motive to Mariage & yet it affects our Propensity to last so strongly yt it makes most Matches & most of these Matches Miserable, unless when Beauty is gone Virtue good sense good Nature Complaisance & Chearfullness Compensate ye loss: An Agreeable Genteel & neat Woman wth these Qualities is therefore to be sought by a Man of Sense But how is she to be found? first of all by not being in love yt is by not letting our Passion Blind our understanding By not letting her know you have ye least designe on her as a wife untill you know her, the Sex are ye Most Artfull Dissemblers But Nature will shew itself. . . ." [39] And so on, and on.

Charles Carroll the Younger, receiving this dissertation, threw up his hands. "A Chearful sensible virtuous, good natured woman is rara avis in terris a Prodigy, a miracle, a deviation from the general & fixed laws: not one in 10000 is endowed with all those good qualities." Besides, he knew very few ladies, none of whom he could reasonably expect to follow him "to a barbarous uncivilised country" — that was how he thought of Maryland, making a nice connection between civilization and toleration — "what lady of family will be prevailed upon to make so great a sacrifice. I mention not fortune that is quite out of the question." But the whole point of the matter he summed up concisely: "I have never as yet seen the woman I shou'd chuse to marry. I have never been in love & hope I never shall be. . . ." [40]

Evidently dismissing *l'affaire Alcock* as a slip of the tongue. He had lived to be glad that the button-maker's daughter had not been swept off her feet; his more adult opinion found him "frightened at the clinking of matrimonial chains: those are never to be broke!" [41] But his father took all these sweeping statements with relief, if with a grain of salt: "I Plainly see

[39] September 1, 1762; Carroll Papers, 1, 84.
[40] February 19, 1763; Carroll Papers, 1, 89.
[41] To Elizabeth Brooke Carroll, August 12, 1760; Field, *Unpublished Letters*, p. 50.

you do not at Present think of Matrimony (*I have never been in Love & hope I never shall be*) I shall not therefore press it upon you. . . ." [42]

From this complacence father and son were soon to be rudely shaken. Recuperating from his attack of smallpox, Charles had decided to take a trip through Belgium, Holland, Germany, and France, in the company of William Graves. They left Dunkirk the latter part of July and were in Paris when, on October eleventh, Charles found occasion to sit down and write his father a very long letter. In fact, he wrote two of them, practically alike, in case that one should go astray.

Charles Carroll of Annapolis must have frowned through his spectacles when he read the heading. His usually methodical and level-headed son had forgotten that the year was 1763, and had plainly dated his letter 1761. This was surprising enough, but the body of the letter was more so. "Dr Papa," it began, "In my last letter from Rotterdam I promised to write to you again from Paris. At that time I little thought of writing in the following subject. Mr Crookshanks" — Mr. Crookshanks was a Jesuit living in Paris, and an old friend of the Carroll family — "has lately introduced me to a young lady of 17 of an agreeable person & good tempered if I may rely on Mr Crookshanks who I am confident wou'd not deceive me in a matter of this importance. She is the only daughter & sole heiress of a west India gentleman of great fortune his name is Baker; Mr Crookshanks is not acquainted with his circumstances but Judge he must be a man of great wealth by the unlimited credit he allows his daughter: She is now in the Convent of the Ursilin nuns in this city: if upon better enquiry the Father really turns out to be a man of great fortune there is one point gained: I only am to except to her person & temper: you can have no objection to her education: I therefore flatter myself If I can obtain the Father's and the lady's consent you will not refuse me yours. . . ." [43]

---

[42] June 22, 1763; Carroll Papers, I, 96.
[43] October 11, 1761 [sic]; Carroll Papers, I, 99.

And he was very sure of his own success. Going on to discuss the practical side of the matter, "supposing that my wife's
fortune amounts to 30000 then the interest wou'd be 1800 ss.
annum. . . ." he scratched out the word "wou'd" and substituted "will."

His proposed method of approach is interesting. He planned
to secure Mr. Baker's consent in London and, returning to
Paris, "pay my addresses to ye young lady & strive to make a
conquest of her heart: her youth & inexperience will I hope,
smooth the path of victory: the first addresses of a young
lover may make some impression on a heart unpractised in the
wiles & artifices of worldly women. . . . Miss Baker no doubt
will have stronger objections than her Father to my settling in
Maryland: but when once the knot is tied & her affection
fixed, my interest will prevail over her inclinations to remain
in Europe. . . ." No, not an Alger hero. Here is our high-
minded statesman-to-be deliberately setting out to profit by
the young lady's "youth & inexperience" to hurry her into
marriage; and he shows no scruples at all about waiting till
after the wedding to bring out the point that he expected her
to move to America.

He ended his letter: "That you may see me happily married,
enjoy your health & be happy is the sincere & ardent wish of

"Dr Papa　　　　Yr affectionate Son
　　　　　　　"Cha: Carroll."

Note the order. The lady with the shears had, apparently,
attended to another young misogamist.

There were on the face of it no objections to Miss Louisa
Baker: she seemed to have all the virtues as Charles Carroll of
Annapolis had set them forth himself, and he rose nobly to the
occasion. Not only did he "long to see Miss Baker with you
as you paint her in so Amiable a Light" [44] but he had the wild
idea of welcoming her father as well into the bosom of the
family: "Should Mr Bakers Objection be agst his Daughters
leaving him, if he be a good natured sensible man, he may

[44] January 9, 1764; Carroll Papers, II, 102.

come with his Daughter & retire with me to Elk ridge where we may pass the remainder of our lives in an easy retirement becoming & I think agreeable to old men. In yt case I shall surrender my house in Annapolis to you. . . ." [45] Still, the father's feelings were a little hurt to have the erstwhile home-sick young "Exile" write him: "If I meet with success in this enterprise it will be absolutely impossible for me to return to Maryland this next Spring. I am affraid that my voyage must be put off to the spring following: nothing I assure you can be more contrary to my own inclinations; but in all we do there is a mixture of pain and pleasure." [46]

The progress of his affair with Louisa bore out these wise philosophies. The eager suitor wavered between high hope and the direst apprehensions. He agonized over everything from the possibility that Louisa might conceive a prejudice against Maryland to the fact that his fashionable wig, which he had had to wear ever since his attack of the smallpox, was not quite as becoming as his own hair. [47] He could not get his mind on his law books; the theater, the races, even the daily horseback rides palled; the excessively male conversation at the Crown and Anchor seemed insipid. He hurried back from Paris to London, where he had been told he would find Mr. Baker, the wealthy West Indian gentleman. But Mr. Baker had gone to Southampton. Nor did he stay there long enough to be followed, but proceeded to Bath. From there he wrote acknowledging the letter that Charles had written him. He would, of course, give no definite answer; he resorted to the time-honored story of never having considered his daughter's marriage, "she being now but in her seventeenth year, which I think upon the whole, rather too early to engage in the married state." But he politely had no objection to this particular suitor, "and will even ingeniously own to you that I seem to observe in yr manner of writing certain marks of

[45] February 27, 1764; *ibid.*, II, 105.
[46] October 11, 1761 [sic]; *ibid.*, I, 99.
[47] To Charles Carroll of Annapolis, May 15, 1763; Carroll Papers, I, 93.

candour & worth that rather incline me to wish I might not find any." [48] On this slender encouragement Charles Carroll dropped his law studies again — there was really no comparison between law and Louisa — and hurried to Bath. "My Physician had advised me to drink the waters, and I think I find myself benefited by them," he explained elaborately to his father: "for this some time I have felt a gradual decay of strength and wasting of flesh attended with unusual low spirits: my nerves are week and my whole frame very delicate," and so on. [49] His father wrote back dryly: "Your complaints give me pain; I hope they, in a great measure, proceed from ye Anxiety your passion for Miss Baker gives you. I wish you a happy issue to it. . . ." [50]

In spite of the beneficial effects of the waters of Bath, however, young Mr. Carroll did not hesitate to forego them when Mr. Baker, whom he had overtaken there and found to be "a man of sense and honour," [51] obliged with an invitation to spend some days with the Baker family at Grove Place, their country seat. Miss Louisa, of course, remained in her Parisian convent, but he had the doubtful pleasure of meeting her mother, Mr. Baker's second wife. The two heartily hated each other at sight. "The mother of the young lady is living," her house-guest wrote with appreciable regret, "she is no favourite of mine, nor I of hers. if the daughter's temper resembles the mother's I shall leave England next May or June. . . ." [52] Even when he was in love, Charles Carroll always had a clear and concise way of putting things.

The prospect of mother-in-law trouble was not the only disadvantage which soon became apparent. Louisa was not, as Mr. Crookshanks had told him at first, the only daughter and sole heiress of a wealthy father. John Baker had several other

---

[48] December 15, 1763; *ibid.*, II, 104A.
[49] January 27, 1764; *ibid.*, II, 104.
[50] February 12, 1764; Field, *Unpublished Letters*, p. 84.
[51] To Charles Carroll of Annapolis, January 27, 1764; Carroll Papers, II, 104.
[52] *Ibid.*

children by his first wife. And his fortune, far from being the prodigious amount that had been rumored, was — in the polite language of the day — "very inconsiderable." Mr. Baker explained that his affairs were "at present" very much involved, and "from this circumstance and from several other hints I plainly understood I was not to expect any ready money with his daughter at least no considerable sum." [53] This was a blow; but both Carrolls, so often accused of stinginess, stood up under it manfully. Charles Carroll of Annapolis merely expressed the hope that Louisa's "merit may in a great measure make up for wt her fortune may fall short of"; [54] and his son wrote philosophically: "I have greatly exceeded this last year my allowance of £300 by my journey to Holland & France" — not to speak of Bath and Grove Place — "but I expect to be amply repaid the expence of that expedition in the possession of a sensible, agreeable, & virtuous woman. . . ." [55]

In the end, though, he had to write off these extra-curricular expenses to experience. For he did not win Louisa. Nobody knows exactly why. Perhaps it was the fact that he lived in barbarous Maryland; perhaps, that Louisa was not as attracted to the serious young student — handicapped by that unbecoming wig! — as he was to her. More likely the trouble was her termagant of a mother. And one writer hints mysteriously at "her meddlesome sister." [56] At any rate, in April Mr. Baker said "No." He did not actually use the word; he merely told young Mr. Carroll that if he would come back three or four or even five years later "(for that would be time enough)" they would see then about his marrying Miss Louisa. It did not take a great deal of perspicacity for the disappointed suitor to "plainly see, by ye above speech & by his manner, that he was not very desirous of its taking place." Charles replied formally that, under these conditions, he was

[53] To Charles Carroll of Annapolis, January 27, 1764; Carroll Papers, II, 104.
[54] To Charles Carroll of Carrollton, February 28, 1764; ibid., II, 106.
[55] To Charles Carroll of Annapolis, March 21, 1761; ibid., II, 108.
[56] Paul M. Hollister, Famous Colonial Houses (1921), p. 46.

no longer interested, and he made as graceful an exit as the circumstances permitted.[57]

All that weight lost for nothing! — for he had been losing weight steadily ever since last October.[58] Yet he had gained in wisdom. He had proved to his own satisfaction that women were more trouble than they were worth. It was a lesson he never forgot, for he never let himself go about anybody again.

Somehow, during the last arduous months, he had managed to finish his study of the law; and now that Louisa was lost to him there was no occasion for his remaining in Europe. He planned to sail on the *Randolph* "the middle of September at farthest." He still had his pride, and so he tried to pretend that it was of his own accord that he was returning to Maryland without a wife; but it was apparent that the grapes tasted very sour as he wrote: ". . . the young lady had been bread up with very high notions not at all answerable to her fortune; a domestick wife not so fond of show and parade, who is not above the business of her family, will best suit me: the mother is a vain empty woman who knows but the daughter may take after her? I do not chuse to run the risk. . . . this will be my last from London." [59]

[57] Charles Carroll of Carrollton to Charles Carroll of Annapolis, April 19, 1764; Carroll Papers, II, 110.
[58] Charles Carroll of Carrollton to Charles Carroll of Annapolis, January 27, 1764; Carroll Papers, II, 104.
[59] To Charles Carroll of Annapolis, July 26, 1764; Carroll Papers, II, 113.

CHAPTER IV

Annapolis in the Province
of Maryland

1765–1773

USUALLY THE *Maryland Gazette* scorned social items (rich marriages and the deaths of politicians only excepted), but in the issue of February 14, 1765, the editor found important enough to record: "Tuesday last arrived at his Father's House in Town, Charles Carroll Jun'r. Esq. (lately from London by way of Virginia) after about sixteen years absence from his Native Country at his Studies and on his Travels."

Old Charles Carroll was tremendously proud of the son he was introducing to Annapolis. The young man was definitely presentable. Though small and very slight in stature, he was well made, with fine hands and regular features. He had entirely outgrown his adolescent habit of "stooping & pokeing out" his head,[1] and moved with the smooth grace of the expert swordsman. His conversation bore the stamp of foreign elegance and it is to be hoped that his clothes did too. His father had been extremely anxious about them. "I understand you dress plainly," he had written when Charles' return to Annapolis seemed imminent; "I commend you for it, but I think you should have Clothes suitable to occasions, and upon your first appearance among us some show may not be improper. You may contrive to be supplied with Waistcoats of Silk for genteel Summer-Suits, Velvets, etc. from France at ye best

---

[1] Charles Carroll of Annapolis to Charles Carroll of Carrollton, August 30, 1758; Carroll Papers, I, 36.

hand and in ye newest Taste; after your first appearance you may be as plain as you please." [2] So it was probably a modishly attired young gentleman who moved among the guests in the big house on Spa Creek, where candles blazed as they had not blazed since Elizabeth Carroll's death, and who, in spite of his outspoken preference for "study and Retirement," appeared with his father at routs and assemblies and cardparties. Mr. Tasker, who had promised him a ball on the occasion of his return to Maryland, no doubt made good his word; [3] and no doubt other family friends were not far behind. Gentlemen complimented Mr. Carroll on his son's horsemanship, his grasp of the political situation in England, and his quotable knowledge of the classics. Ladies praised his ability to answer questions about Vauxhall and Ranelegh and the doings of the Royal Family. Very young ladies put their heads together and found his manners polished, his person agreeable, and his taste in work'd ruffles above reproach. His religion was, of course, against him — but, my dears, all that money!

Young Mr. Carroll, for his part, found an Annapolis which made him blush to remember the letters he had written from abroad, calling Maryland a "barbarous Country" and Marylanders "an uncultivated insolent rabble." [4] Unimpressive as to size, Annapolis could nevertheless amaze sophisticated travelers. It had become a London in miniature. It was no more uncivilized than London was. If there were appalling social conditions outside the Governor's set, this was a side of life with which Charles Carroll did not come in contact, any more than he had come in contact with the similar appalling conditions in London. People called it the gayest city in North America. Its streets were lined with the charming brick mansions of the great and the would-be great. Its statehouse, overlooking blue water from the top of the town's highest

[2] September 2, 1762; Field, *Unpublished Letters*, p. 72.
[3] Charles Carroll of Carrollton to Elizabeth Brooke Carroll, August 12, 1760; *ibid.*, p. 50.
[4] E.g., to Charles Carroll of Annapolis, August 14, 1759; Carroll Papers, I, 42.

hill, was one of the "neatest Edifices" in America. Its harbor teemed with trade; the shops along Church and West Streets had shelves piled high with just such "European and East-India Goods" as the fashionable London merchants showed. Its assembly-rooms were famous throughout the colonies, its coffee-houses among the best. It had for years supported a theater. Half a dozen gentlemen's clubs flourished, so like their English examples that guests felt quite at home. The Jockey Club had been founded even before the English Jockey Club, and gentry from all over America flocked to the spring and fall race-meetings at Annapolis. Extravagance was quite as rife, gossip as scandalous, and wines as much valued for bouquet as in London or in Paris either. Young Charles Carroll had to admit that he had never seen higher stakes at European card tables, or European ladies who boasted more fashionably absurd hoops and coiffures.

He had disliked many of these sophisticated frivolities in London and disliked them no less on this side of the water. But he liked Annapolis. Sixteen years out of the province, he had returned to his birthplace more than half resolved that, if his father still wished it, they would sell the rest of their Maryland lands and try their fortunes in a climate more healthy for Roman Catholics. The elder Carroll, broken by his wife's death and considering his own life mostly behind him, disheartened by his son's lack of enthusiasm for the project, had left the decision up to him. Charles's point of view had not changed. He still thought it was a shame to run away from the situation in Maryland; it was not his way of trying to correct an abuse. But the loss of Louisa still colored his outlook on things in general. He felt now that it did not greatly matter, and if it would please his father. . . . Yet within a few months this noble sentiment had entirely slipped his mind. He was as ardently a Marylander as if he had never left the province. Abandoning the supercilious, outsider's attitude he had had in Europe, he learned to speak familiarly and possessively of "our Weather," "our Races," and even "our oppressive Laws." He tried to conceal this growing partiality under the flimsy disguise of *on dit*: "Many who have travelled through the colonies give ye preference to Maryland, both in point of climate, ye fertility of the soil, and ye sociability of its inhabitants." [5] And far from deciding to remove himself out of Maryland, he began to write (half in jest, but only half) to the friends of his student-days abroad, "I advise you to sell your estate in England, and to purchase lands in this province. . . ." [6]

According to a promise made during the affair of Louisa, Charles Carroll of Annapolis made over to his son Carrollton Manor, a large tract of land in Frederick County. He also put the entire estate at his disposal, lands and slaves and money alike; but this manor was peculiarly the younger Carroll's own, and from it he took the title — Charles Carroll of Carrollton — which he needed at once to distinguish him from the flock of Charles Carrolls in and around Annapolis. Thus he signed his letters almost from the day of his arrival in Maryland, adding to one such signature, ". . . by which appellation, if you favour me with an answer, direct to me your letter." [7]

From now on we too shall have to speak of him as Charles Carroll of Carrollton, and we shall find it increasingly hard, on account of that title's sonorous syllables, to speak of him as a human being.

Naturally enough, the new landed proprietor did not betake himself to Carrollton Manor and set up an establishment in lonely grandeur. He lived instead with his father, whose own favorite residence, next to the town house in Annapolis where he always spent the provincial capital's self-important little "season," was the impressive manor house which the Attorney-General had named Doughoregan, or House of Kings. Only occasionally they stayed a few days or weeks at one of the other country places. (Charles Carroll never did become particularly fond of Carrollton, perhaps because he had expected to bring Louisa there.) But wherever they were, the two Car-

[5] To —— Bradshaw, November 21, 1765; Field, *Unpublished Letters*, p. 97.   [6] *Ibid.*
[7] To Edmund Jennings, November 3, 1765; Field, *Unpublished Letters*, p. 100.

rolls never had to concern themselves with domestic matters, for "Cousin Rachel Darnall" lived with them and kept their house.

Mrs. Darnall had become a member of the Carroll household in circumstances interesting to consider along with the many stories of the stinginess and selfishness of Charles Carroll of Annapolis. She was his cousin and his wife's niece; she had come to take care of Elizabeth Carroll during her last illness and had remained to assume full management of the establishment. It has usually been inferred — as was the charitable intention of even those historians who knew better — that Mrs. Darnall was one of those widowed relatives for whom a niche had to be created, sooner or later, in every Southern family. On the contrary, she had a husband living. Henry Darnall the Younger was also a relation of the Carrolls and one of those black sheep that will occur among the connections of most of us. From childhood of an "indolent easy character," [8] Darnall had in 1754 chosen the easy way to rise in the world. By abjuring the Roman Catholic religion in which he had been reared but against which, as Governor Sharpe admitted, it was the popular "fashion to be clamorous," [9] he made himself eligible for public life. It was no part of his plan that he should sacrifice his career to his principles, as his cousin Carroll of Annapolis had done. Darnall had his eye on membership in the governor's council, no less. In the meantime he accepted the important posts of Attorney-General and Naval Officer of Patuxent. His brother John Darnall, who must have apostasized too in order to become clerk of Frederick County, and Charles Carroll of Annapolis, to whom blood was thicker than water, went on his bond for the latter.[10]

It was one of the few mistakes in financial judgment old Mr. Carroll ever made. Probably no one had been so impolite as to hint to him that his cousin would have been better placed

[8] Charles Carroll of Carrollton to Charles Carroll of Annapolis, October 13, 1761; *Maryland Historical Magazine*, XI, 179.
[9] Horatio Sharpe to Cecilius Calvert, March 8, 1756; *Archives*, VI, 356.
[10] Horatio Sharpe to Frederick Calvert, 6th Lord Baltimore, May 5, 1761; *ibid.*, IX, 511–12.

"in office where the receptn of Cash is not requisite." [11] Anyway, between the years 1755 and 1761 the Naval Officer of
Patuxent quietly embezzled about sixteen hundred pounds
sterling. Found out, and facing the probability "that if he
should be carried to Prison he must expect to remain there as
long as he lives," Henry Darnall quietly "quitted his House &
plantation" and a little later slipped aboard a ship for England.[12] Still later he was reported "gone over to the continent
to live in retirement in what place tis not known. . . ." [13]
There was a tremendous scandal and Darnall's two bondsmen
forfeited according to law one thousand pounds sterling.[14]

At the time all this happened Mrs. Darnall was still in Annapolis, straightening out the confusion caused in the Carroll
household by its mistress's death. Under the suddenly changed
circumstances Charles Carroll of Annapolis promptly invited
her and her little girl to stay and make their home permanently
with him.

Mrs. Darnall was an amiable, kind-hearted, pleasure-loving
lady who had been very nice about writing to young Charles
while he was away at school. Though she was not one of the
relatives whom he remembered from his early childhood in
Maryland, he was fully prepared to love her for the sake of
her devoted attention to his mother, and did. He did not remember either, of course, her daughter Molly, now a delicate
girl nearly sixteen. She was extremely pretty and well-mannered and Charles Carroll of Annapolis, suspecting with some
reason that Molly had brains, had seen to it that she received
an education far beyond the instruction in raised embroidery
and harpsichord-playing considered adequate for females. If
he had not, with Louisa, lost all his interest in young ladies,
Charles might have found her charming. As it was, he gave
his serious consideration to American politics.

[11] Cecilius Calvert to Horatio Sharpe, May 20, 1755; *Archives*, XXXI, 480.
[12] Horatio Sharpe to Frederick Calvert, 6th Lord Baltimore, May 5, 1761;
ibid., IX, 511.
[13] Charles Carroll of Carrollton to Charles Carroll of Annapolis, October
13, 1761; *Maryland Historical Magazine*, XI, 179.
[14] Stephen Bordley (Attorney-General of Maryland) to Horatio Sharpe,
April 29, 1761; *Archives*, XXXII, 12.

He had returned home in a year when politics were especially important, the year of the Stamp Act. Since 1764, when the unpopular measure had first been proposed, the coffee-houses had talked of little else; now that it had actually become a law, all America was in an uproar.

The Stamp Act was part of a taxation program devised by Prime Minister George Grenville's government, who had a sizable financial problem on their hands. Great Britain had emerged from the recent war with France covered with glory and weighted with debt. Though she had proved herself the most important power on earth, she needed about one hundred and fifty million pounds — pounds, not dollars — to pay off her funded debt and the annual interest charges thereon.

Now nearly half this debt had been incurred in the defense of the American colonies against the threat of French domination. It seemed to the British ministry that this was a good reason why the people of those colonies should help provide the money to pay it off. The ministry also thought that in any case the British empire in general should share the general British debt.

As one of the means to this end, Grenville's government had proposed that the Stamp Act be extended to America. This act, which had been in force in England for a number of years, provided that taxed and stamped paper be used for all legal documents, newspapers, pamphlets, almanacs, and playing-cards. The rate was not high, and the articles on which the tax was levied were seldom required by the generality of people. Only the upper classes, remember, could read newspapers or wanted to. Most of the population found their recreation in bull-baitings and wrestling-matches rather than card-playing. They had little property to will or sell; they settled their arguments not in court but with their fists; and they frequently dispensed with the empty form of marriage licenses. So while lawyers, landed proprietors, importers, and other such Englishmen had disliked the tax on paper, most people considered it as inoffensive as any tax could be. Generally speaking, it was paid by the people who could best afford to pay it.

It was Grenville's hopeful expectation that the Stamp Act would be found equally inoffensive in the American colonies. He had, however, failed to reckon sufficiently with the fact that there was another way of looking at the Stamp Act and that the Americans would inevitably take it.

America promptly saw the Stamp Act as a flagrant example of internal taxation. Colonial assemblies met and passed nearly identical resolutions to the effect that they had the "only and sole exclusive right and power" to tax the colonial people. There were some pointed and rather indiscreet comments on the assumption and even the tyranny of the British ministry. Down in Virginia one of the members of assembly made a speech that was quoted from Carolina to Connecticut. "Caesar had his Brutus," said Patrick Henry, "Charles the First his Cromwell, and George the Third" — he finished what he had to say in spite of the cries of "Treason! Treason!" and the pounding of the Speaker's gavel — "may profit by their example. If this be treason — make the most of it." [15]

Treason or not, there were certainly treasonable acts to follow. As the stamped paper began to arrive in America and the stamp collectors appointed by the Crown began to open offices to carry on their business, mob violence broke out all up and down the Atlantic coast. In Pennsylvania, Massachusetts, and North Carolina the stamp collectors had to resign to save their own necks. In New York and Massachusetts mobs tore down the dwelling-houses of officials and destroyed their personal property. In Connecticut the stamp collector was hanged in effigy, significantly companioned by an effigy of the devil.

The stamp collector for Maryland was Zachariah Hood, an Annapolis merchant. Though not on the social level of the Carrolls, he was nevertheless a solid and respected citizen until he threw in his fortunes with what his neighbors naïvely

[15] No authentic account of this famous speech has survived. Although the clerk faithfully recorded just what Mr. Henry said, the members of assembly decided next day, in the cold light of sober second thought, that it had better be expunged from the journal. Nor had anybody noted it down privately, so far as we know. The various subsequently remembered versions — of which this is the most common — differ a little in words but not at all in substance.

called "the forces of evil." Then he shed his respectability overnight. As soon as certain Annapolitans heard of his appointment they made an effigy of Hood and, placing it in an ignominious one-horse cart, drove it through the streets to the hill where various instruments of colonial justice stood awaiting malefactors. There the effigy, holding several sheets representing stamped paper before its face, was in turn whipped, pilloried, hanged, and burned.[16]

Mr. Hood was also hanged in effigy in other parts of Maryland. It was in Annapolis, however, that he attempted to land on his arrival from England. Evidently he had not heard what a prominent person he was, for he made no effort to conceal his arrival. A large crowd met him at the City Dock and forcibly prevented his landing, so he had to retreat and sneak ashore later at a less conspicuous point. Also, the mob found out that he was preparing to store the stamped paper in one of the houses in town, and they promptly tore the house to pieces.[17] Mr. Hood was not prepared to risk his hide for king, country, and the lucrative office of stamp collector, and eagerly offered to resign; but Governor Sharpe refused to accept his resignation. It was manifestly dangerous for him to stay in Annapolis, so he "retired some weeks before the Stamp Act was to take place to New York." [18] He went so hastily that he rode his horse to death.[19]

The mobs who had pretended to hang Mr. Hood and who had actually torn down his house were not, of course, representative of the best class of Annapolitans. They were mostly made up of young boys and of the village hoodlums, as were the mobs in Massachusetts and the other colonies. But there was another riot soon afterward in one of the fashionable coffee-houses. Charles Carroll of Carrollton may even have been present, though this is pure surmise. At any rate the other gentlemen involved were his friends. Fire-eating young Mat-

---

[16] *Maryland Gazette*, August 29, 1765.
[17] *Maryland Gazette*, September 5, 1765.
[18] Horatio Sharpe to Christopher Lowndes, February 10, 1766; Proprietary Papers 1704–1775 (unpublished Maryland archives), Black Book IX, part 1, 84.
[19] *Maryland Gazette*, October 3, 1765.

thias Hammond got into a fight with one of the British officers
from the sloop *Hornet*, which happened to be in Annapolis
harbor, and was badly worsted. The British victory was tact-
less to say the least, considering the fact that the Britishers
were surrounded and far outnumbered by Maryland gentlemen outspokenly opposed to the Stamp Act. To make matters
worse, Mr. Hammond quietly took his leave; whereupon his
friends raised a fearful disturbance. Even in the absence of
the *corpus delicti*, they concluded that he had been murdered
by the British. They enthusiastically started a free-for-all
fight, but fortunately there were some moderates in the coffee-
house and the whole thing came to nothing.[20] The incident
was significant only in that it showed how feeling about the
Stamp Act was spreading to all classes of Marylanders.

We are in no doubt as to how Charles Carroll of Carrollton
felt about the tax. Though he took no active part in denouncing it publicly — Roman Catholics, his father had warned
him, had no business airing their views on any public matter,
for the officials were too likely to decide to make an example
of somebody — he was busy writing letters about it to his
friends in England. In none of these did he take into consideration the fact that he might be treading on delicate ground. For
the first time, though not the last, he was standing up for his
political convictions no matter what other people might think.

To William Graves, the master in chancery with whom he
had traveled on the Continent, Charles Carroll wrote: "in these
times of necessity and oppression it is a duty every man of
fortune owes his country to set an example of frugality and industry to ye common people: 'Necessity,' says ye proverb, 'is
ye mother of invention.' I may add, of industry too: . . . our
inability, while loaded with oppressive taxes to purchase your
manufactures, will oblige us to manufacture for ourselves: the
worst of evils this, that can possibly befall England, the loss of
liberty excepted: that indeed seems already lost, or near ex-
piring. Must we not think so, when ye guardians of the sub-

[20] The official account: Horatio Sharpe to Cecilius Calvert, September 10,
1765; *Archives*, III, 226-7.

jects' rights are the first to infringe them? That they have been infringed by ye late acts and, more particularly, by ye Stamp Act is the general opinion of these colonies: not all ye eloquence of Mansfield can persuade us that Englishmen by leaving their country to settle in these parts, thereby lose the privileges of Englishmen and the benefit of ye Common Law. By that Law, ye most favourable to liberty, we claim the invaluable privilege, that distinguishing Characteristick of ye English constitution, of being taxed by our own representatives; to say (and this has been said and insisted on too) that we are virtually represented is only adding to ye oppression ye cruel mockery of our understandings. . . . Whatever threats are thrown out or force employed to make ye Americans as compliant as ye Parliament, they will never depart from the essential right of internal taxation without which our property would be at ye mercy of every rapacious minister. England restrains our trade, she appoints our Governors, lays duties on our exports and imports: and ye exertion of this power or right, as a necessary consequence of our dependence on ye mother country, has all along been admitted and acquiesed in by ye colonies. . . . The preamble of ye Stamp Act is as alarming as ye Act itself; the sole reason given for passing it is because such and such duties had been granted to his Majesty ye preceeding Sessions; thus they may go on ad infinitum; allowing this unbounded power in a set of men at so great a distance, so little acquainted with our circumstances, and not immediately affected with ye taxes laid upon us, what security remains for our property? what fence against arbitrary enactions? are we to trust to ye moderation of a British Parliament? have we reason to rely solely on that? Men who have been so profuse and lavish with their constituents' money — will they be sparing of ours and better managers for strangers? The Stamp Act has taken away in part ye Trial by Juries: has curtailed ye liberty of ye Press: petitions, altho' the subject has an undoubted right to petition, were rejected with scorn on ye frivolous pretence — no petitions would be *read* when ye house had once gone upon a money Bill — do not these proceedings carry with them the strongest marks of despotism? You, I know, from your love of liberty, detest them as much as we do. The Stamp master at Boston has been obliged to throw up his office: ours, I imagine, will follow his example or may repent it. The house building at Boston for ye stamps, and the house in this place hired for ye same use, have been levelled with ye ground: this spirit of opposition to Stamps, and stamp men, and stamp laws is diffused thro'out ye colonies from ye Cape of Florida to ye land of Labrador." [21]

This letter is typical of the ones he wrote to his friends Bradshaw, Bird, Jennings, and Barrington. It shows him already a well-rounded politician, though he himself would have promptly denied it. We can see from this one letter how his own thought incorporated all three of the points of view which had fused in America to oppose the Stamp Act.

The first of these was, of course, opposition to the tax as a matter of principle. In every colony there were idealists who hated the Stamp Act purely because it seemed to them unjust and tyrannous, an unconstitutional assumption of authority on the part of the British king and his ministers. They remembered Magna Carta. They quoted English common law and also the charters of their respective colonies. (In the Maryland Charter, 1632, "The King Covenants by the 20th Section not to impose any impositions customs or other taxations upon any goods or Merchandizes within the Ports or Harbours of this Province.") [22] They thought and spoke in capitals: The Rights of Englishmen; The Heritage of Freedom; The Blessings of Liberty. They were honest and earnest and absolutely sincere. Their names appear in deservedly big type in our history books. But though they convinced themselves and were able to convince other intellectual idealists in England as well as in America — like Pitt and Edmund Burke — they were never able to win a large following. By themselves they would never have amounted to much. It took something more con-

[21] September 15, 1765; Field, *Unpublished Letters*, pp. 88–91. He gives Mr. Graves' first name, mistakenly, as Henry.

[22] Charles Carroll of Annapolis to William Graves, May 29, 1775; Carroll Papers, III, 284A.

crete than theoretical rights to lead thirteen colonies into a revolution.

Another group of people translated the Stamp Act into terms of money instead of infringed liberty, and amounted to a great deal more. These were the people upon whose businesses the tax would actually impose more or less financial hardship — the lawyers, the merchants, and the owners and editors of newspapers. With one eye on posterity, they spoke, like the idealists, in capitals. Unlike the idealists, they were not sincere in doing so, for most of them cared very little for the beautiful abstractions of liberty. They were interested in money, and they rebelled at the idea of being taxed from two sources instead of one; the colonial assemblies, they considered, were bad enough without adding to them the Crown. The lawyers were afraid that a tax on legal documents would take the joy out of the great eighteenth-century recreation of going to court about little or nothing. The editors, much poorer than the lawyers as a class, dreaded a tax which would hit them two ways, since it affected advertisements as well as newspaper. The merchants resented any move to regulate the customs — by the use of stamped paper or otherwise — for many of them had been successfully smuggling their goods in for years. One historian declares that nine-tenths of the American merchants were smugglers, and he includes among the gentlemen mixed up in the smuggling trade such luminaries as Alexander Hamilton, Jonathan Trumbull, and John Hancock.

The third group — the most important group, because it was many times larger than the other two combined — was made up of people to whom the Stamp Act itself meant little or nothing, but to whom it furnished an excuse for rebellion. They were mostly poor people, the underdogs in an economic system which could not have existed without them. They might quite justifiably have complained about bad housing and low wages and disfranchisement — their poverty kept them from voting or holding public office — but they had never known anything better, and in normal times accepted with remarkably little fuss the condition of life to which it had pleased God to call them. Underneath, however, there was always a smoldering resentment toward constituted authority. Clever politicians could very easily stir it up. So in Stamp Act days the idealists remained idealistic and aloof, and the merchants and lawyers and editors, who had their own reasons for not wanting the law enforced, never bothered with such messy jobs as tarring and feathering officials and such back-breaking jobs as tearing the officials' houses to bits. The common people, with enthusiasm worthy a cause nearer home, did it for them.

Within this third group, legitimately in it yet differing vastly from the undernourished malcontents who had never been taught how to use their heads, was an interesting minority nowhere better represented than in Maryland. It was made up of well-educated and sometimes wealthy people who, thoughtfully and intelligently, hated living under English rule. Most of them, legally British subjects, did not consider themselves Englishmen at all. Some of them were loyal followers of the grandson of the last Stuart king, whom his enemies called the Young Pretender. They had fought under his standard at Culloden and had lost the field; as political prisoners they had been loaded into ships bound for America, to serve out their term at the mercy of whoever chose to buy them. These people were fiercely Scotch. Others were as fiercely Irish. These had the typically Irish feeling that they owed no loyalty whatever to the country that had conquered theirs. They resented not only their national subjugation; they resented equally the persecutions which had been put on them as a conquered people. Some of these persecutions had even followed them to America, prominently the religious disabilities placed upon them as Catholics.

The Carroll family, of course, serves as an excellent example. All the Carrolls felt very strongly about being Irish. The Attorney-General, the only one who could claim the Sod as his birthplace, was extremely anxious that his children should never forget their heritage. When his boys were at school at

St. Omer he wrote instructing them to sign their theses "Mary-lando-Hibernus." [23] His son, Charles Carroll of Annapolis, was many years later still conscious of "ye Duty all Irish men owe to ye Glory and Honour of their Country." [24] His grandson, as a young student planning a tour of Europe, deliberately left Ireland out of his itinerary: "The present situation of that Isleland, will only renew the memory of past wrongs." [25]

He had been thoroughly educated in the family tradition, had Charles Carroll of Carrollton. His opinion of the English government was, even more than he himself realized, as hered-itary as his high-bridged nose. He was a born fighter, a born crusader, a born rebel — in a word, he was an Irishman. Hatred of political England had been bred into him. He had hated it consciously ever since his father, that day eight years before in Paris, had summed up the family history and the family situation. Ever since then he had wanted passionately to be, some day, free of the oppression which English rule had meant to his people. He saw the Stamp Act controversy, clear-eyed, as an opening wedge.

Yet it would not be fair to picture Charles Carroll of Car-rollton entirely as the descendant of an unfortunate Irish fam-ily, as a malleable young man whose thought was easily shaped by the opinionated father he adored. He had a mind of his own, and used it. No gentleman in America, not even the ones who were up to their necks in politics, had a clearer idea of the essence and implications of the Stamp Act than Charles Carroll had; and not even Patrick Henry could flame out against tyranny more effectively than Charles Carroll could. His sympathies were whole-heartedly with the first class, the idealists who believed that taxation without representation was all wrong.

He was practical and hard-headed too, as well as idealistic. He could sympathize with the people who felt the financial disadvantages of the Stamp Act. He himself, as the manager

[23] To Charles Carroll of Annapolis and Daniel Carroll, July 7, 1719; Field, *Unpublished Letters*, p. 232.
[24] To Charles Carroll of Carrollton, July 1761; *ibid.*, p. 61.
[25] To Charles Carroll of Annapolis, March 28, 1761; Carroll Papers,. I, 62.

of a large estate, would in a measure feel the pressure of a tax
on indentures and other legal documents; and more especially
he feared the Stamp Act as precedent to other acts which
would take away "the essential right of internal taxation without which our property would be at ye mercy of every rapacious minister." [26] He sympathized also with the necessity for
bringing the masses of people into line if the Stamp Act were
to be effectively opposed, and he was not too idealistic to mind
letting the end justify the means. "The clamour of the People
out of doors proceeds from their ignorance, prejudice and passion," he wrote succinctly to Daniel Barrington; "it is very
difficult to get the better of these by reasoning: we have a
much more persuasive and shorter argument and better fitted
to their capacities than reasons drawn from ye principles of
government and from our own in particular, an argument
rather levelled at their pockets than understandings which
may indeed greatly contribute by emptying of those to open
these. . . ." [27]

No doubt of it, he was a born politician. But a politician
out of a job. Carroll's use of the words "we" and "our" was
the wistful assumption of having some part in the politics of
his native country. He really should have said "they" and
"their," for public affairs were taking their course entirely
without him. He might sit at his desk and write letter after
letter to his English friends, but his circumstances forced him
to remain in the background of events. He was personally
unambitious but he was beginning to wish that he were in a
position to take a part in the doings against the Stamp Act.
And he could not even vote. He felt the philosophies of his
student days wavering. "Among all the disadvantages a Rom:
Catho: labours under there is still this advantage," he had
thought a year or two before: "he may be honourable, honest,
independent. . . . Socrates the wisest & most virtuous of the
Heathens declined all offices of State from a persuasion that a

[26] To William Graves, September 15, 1765; Field, *Unpublished Letters*,
pp. 89–90.
[27] March 17, 1766; *ibid.*, p. 110.

man cou'd not long be great & virtuous." [28] For the first time he began really to understand his father's bitterness about the state of affairs in Maryland.

There were other zealous patriots in America, however, and the Stamp Act did not lack opposition. Newspapers in all of the colonies were unanimous in their support of what people were beginning to call the Patriot Cause. Private citizens and even officials who held public office spoke and wrote against the unpopular tax. Prominent among the latter was Daniel Dulany of Annapolis, who in 1765 published a pamphlet called *Considerations on the Propriety of Imposing Taxes in the British Colonies, for the Purpose of raising a Revenue, by Act of Parliament.* It was an extremely able exposition and was widely read among the upper classes. Carroll of Carrollton recommended it to his friends in England; Pitt used its arguments as the basis of his speech in favor of repeal. It was the most important single influence which led Maryland to send delegates to the Stamp Act Congress to which Massachusetts had invited the other colonies.

The British ministry still did not entirely understand why the Stamp Act had stirred up so much excitement in America, but since it had they decided to repeal it, and did so in March 1766. At the same time, however, they published the so-called Declaratory Act, asserting their right to "bind the colonies in any case whatsoever." This declaration was paid little attention to in the joy over the victory implied by the repeal of the Stamp Act. Most people thought it simple defiance on the part of the British government, an attempt to save face which meant nothing at all. Those gentlemen who had objected to the Stamp Act chiefly as a dangerous precedent — Charles Carroll was one of them — did not like it. But for the moment everything was serene on the surface.

Now that the Stamp Act no longer occupied Maryland minds to the exclusion of everything else, people began to notice that young Mr. Carroll, of Carrollton, was taking long horseback rides which apparently had nothing to do with the

[28] To Charles Carroll of Annapolis, June 14, 1763; Carroll Papers, I, 95.

management of his father's estate, for they always ended at the house of Miss Rachel Cooke. Before many weeks had passed, the two had become formally engaged, and the wedding was fixed for July. Annapolitan tea-parties had long since agreed that it was high time the none-too-robust heir to the Carroll fortunes was taking steps to insure the succession; and most of them, personal twinges aside, thought Miss Rachel a very proper young lady to receive his addresses. They were cousins, but the eighteenth century did not consider that an objection. Maryland gentry, and more particularly Roman Catholic gentry, were likely to be more or less related. Her dowry, though far smaller than the Carroll estate, would be "respectable"; she was of a "proper age," twenty-two or -three; she was pretty and even-tempered, virtuous, "accomplished," and sensible. The prospective bridegroom described her characteristically: "A greater commendation I cannot make of the young lady than by pronouncing her no ways inferior to Louisa, and that the sweetness of her temper and other amiable qualities have contributed to efface an impression which similar qualities had made on a heart too susceptible perhaps, of tender feelings, and on a mind not sufficiently strengthened by philosophy to resist those and the united power of good sense and beauty." [29]

So Louisa was still the criterion, even after nearly three years and across three thousand miles of water. We wonder if Rachel Cooke knew about her; and we must suspect Charles Carroll of having told her himself, with more honesty than tact. He was never one to eke the praise of new loves by lying about the old. In fact he never did learn to lie like a gentleman when the occasion warranted it. It is extremely probable that he told Rachel to her face that she was "no ways inferior to Louisa," but refused to stretch the point to admit that she was definitely superior. In any case, she must not have found very exciting this lover who, as soon as he was safely engaged to her, could not help seeking of an English friend the information he most wanted. But he had his pride and came to the

[29] To Christopher Bird, September 17, 1766; Rowland, *Life*, I, 79.

point only after a long, carefully indifferent, and perfectly transparent introduction: "Well then, since the subject has somehow unaccountably led me on to the young lady, I may mention her name. How is Louisa? There was once more music in that name than in the sweetest lines of Pope; but now I can pronounce it as indifferently as Nancy, Betsy, or any other common name. If I ask a few questions I hope you will not think I am not quite as indifferent as I pretend to be. But I protest it is mere curiosity, or mere good will, that prompts me to inquire after her. Is she still single? Does she intend to alter her state or to remain single? If she thinks of matrimony my only wish is that she may meet with a man deserving of her." [30]

In love with one woman, on the point of marrying another. But such things happened every day. One owed a duty to one's family. So although his passion for Louisa was still an uncomfortable part of him, he threw himself into plans for his marriage to Rachel Cooke, to whom he was sincerely devoted. Gifts for the bride were ordered from Europe, and a fashionable new "curricle" bought for the wedding journey. The ladies of the Carroll family, including young Molly Darnall, ordered fine silk dresses to wear at the important ceremony. But in the midst of the preparations the bridegroom fell ill. He had always been "of a puny constitution," pale and thin, and constantly subject to chills and fevers; his friends feared "his falling into consumption." [31] This time he was ill for nearly two weeks. Though he was up and about in July, when the wedding was to have taken place, he felt unwell during all the rest of the summer. But, "If I continue thus recruiting," he wrote August 26th, "I hope to be married early in November." [32]

So family and friends forebore to mention the old superstition that postponements were unlucky, and a wedding date was fixed again, this time November fifth. "It happens to be

[30] To Esther Bird (?) Browne, October 6, 1766; Rowland, *Life*, I, 80.

[31] William Graves to Charles Carroll of Annapolis, January 14, 1770; Carroll Papers, II, 124 B-C.

[32] To ———— Bradshaw; Rowland, *Life*, I, 79.

gunpowder plot," Carroll wrote cheerfully to his friend Jennings, " — but no wonder that a bloody minded Papist should chuse for feasting and merriment a day which had like (if you believe ye story) to have proved so fatal to a Protestant King and Parliament." [33]

He had now entirely recovered and renewed plans for the wedding went on apace. A dispensation was granted "to Mr. Charles Carroll of Carrollton to marry his Cousin Miss Rachel Cooke," [34] and on November first Governor Sharpe issued the marriage license, endorsed "To the Reverend Mr Brogden" — of the Church of England — "or any other Minister legally Qualified." [35] With the license in his pocket, young Carroll was in high spirits as he danced at the wedding of his friend Jack Brice, promising to follow his example just two days later. But again illness interfered. Almost at the last moment Rachel Cooke was suddenly stricken and the marriage had to be postponed for a second time. Her sickness was not at first considered mortal — "the doctor either knew not or dissembled her danger" — but three weeks later, while Carroll was making one of his frequent visits to the house, Rachel Cooke died.[36]

So the fine imported wedding gown was folded carefully away and the disappointed bridegroom locked in a secret drawer of his writing-desk the lady's miniature and a lock of her dark hair. To his less intimate friends he was not expansive about his bereavement, but to Christopher Bird in England he wrote: "I really know not how it is, but either from lowness of spirits, or from a puny, weakly frame, perhaps from both, as reciprocally the cause and effect, I am grown quite indifferent to everything in this world, even to life itself. I assure you — I speak without affectation, and with due submission to the will of God — I care not how soon a period is put to this dull tameness of existence here, but I am

[33] To Edmund Jennings, October 14, 1766; Field, *Unpublished Letters*, p. 134.

[34] October 14, 1766; Field, *Unpublished Letters*, p. 135.

[35] *Ibid.*

[36] To Christopher Bird, March 8, 1767; Rowland, *Life*, i, 82.

sensible, to merit immortal happiness, we must patiently submit, I was going to say cheerfully, but I have not virtue
enough to do that — to the crosses and trials of this life, nay
we must drink up the very dregs of it. I am now come to the
dregs of mine. . . ." [37]

If young Mr. Carroll now sought retirement nobody blamed
him. The death of Rachel Cooke, stricken so tragically just
before her wedding day, set him aside as a romantic figure and
insured him the sympathy even of those people who thought
Roman Catholics had no right to any luck at all.

During this trying period the friendship between father
and son, always strong, became so firmly cemented that it was
never to be equaled by other attachments. Together the two
lived quietly in Annapolis or at Doughoregan Manor, super-
vising the affairs of the farm, reading together from their
precious books, arguing together over points in the political articles now regularly printed in the *Maryland Gazette*. Gradu-
ally, of course, Charles Carroll of Carrollton felt a lightening
of the weight of his "dull tameness of existence" and on August 13, 1767, we find him writing characteristically to a friend
in England:

"Dear Jennings:
"Perhaps before you receive this I shall be married. I have
been so successful as to gain the affections of a young lady
endowed with every quality to make me happy in the married
state. Virtue, good sense, good temper. These too receive no
small lustre from her person, which the partiality of a lover
does not represent to me more agreeable than what it really
is. She really is a sweet-tempered, charming, neat girl — a
little too young for me I confess, but especially as I am of
weak and puny constitution — in a poor state of health but
in hopes of better. 'Hope springs eternal in the human
breast.' " [38]

[37] To Christopher Bird, March 8, 1767; Rowland, *Life*, I, 82–3.
[38] Rowland, *Life*, I, 84.

The young lady so happily endowed was, as believers in the power of propinquity will not be surprised to learn, his young cousin Molly Darnall. The wedding was planned for September or October.

Again, he was not in love with his fiancée. But again the practical eighteenth-century mind pointed out that man was not made to mourn — at least not forever. Charles Carroll of Carrollton was thirty-one years old, an age at which most colonial gentlemen were already the fathers of several sons apiece; his confirmed ill health made his hold upon the Carroll fortune too tenuous to be left unstrengthened. From the dynastic point of view Molly Darnall was an ideal selection. She was well born — there was a black sheep or so among the Darnalls, but good family is good family in Maryland, where people take the position that a clan which cannot stand a few disgraces was not very solid socially to start out with — she was pretty and possessed of all the admired female virtues. Besides these, she had been carefully educated and was developing (of all things!) a flair for politics. She had no fortune whatever, but her fiancé said magnificently: "I prefer her thus unprovided to all the women I have ever seen — even to Louisa —" [39] No portrait of Molly has survived, but this is portrait enough.[40] She must have been delightful! In short, the marriage was so suitable, so apparently made in heaven, that Charles Carroll *père* realized that people would suspect him of having made it on earth. "You must also know she was entirely His owne Choice," he appended to pages in praise of his new daughter-in-law. "He had not the most distant Hint from me yt Miss Darnall would make a good Wife." [41]

The marriage, originally fixed for the fall of 1767, was postponed for legal reasons but finally took place June 5, 1768, at the Carroll house in Annapolis.

[39] To William Graves, January 16, 1768; Rowland, *Life*, I, 87.

[40] The year after his marriage, Charles Carroll sent portraits of himself and his wife to Edmund Jennings in England. They seem to have arrived there safely but have not been heard of since.

[41] To William Graves, December 23, 1768; Carroll Papers, II, 120 A & B.

It might be supposed that the marriage of his son to his housekeeper's daughter would have preserved the family circle as it had been for the past three years, but instead it had the opposite effect. Charles Carroll of Annapolis, who had strong opinions on most subjects, firmly believed that no young married couple ought to live with their relatives-in-law; and he stood by his principles even in this surely exceptional case. The groom's father, who had practically brought up the bride (she called him "Papa" just as his son did) and the bride's mother, who had been a second mother to the groom, accordingly "Retired to a very Pleasant Healthy Seat in ye Country" (Doughoregan Manor), leaving the town house to Mr. and Mrs. Carroll of Carrollton.[42]

Molly liked society, and even at nineteen was thoroughly conversant with the complexities of social Annapolis, which though not much bigger than a village was overwhelmingly conscious of being "the genteelest town in North America." Her gaiety and talent for getting along with people effectively offset the formality which hid her husband's bashfulness in company; and because she was a female and therefore not expected to know about Issues (but she did) some of her best friends were people whose official position might have kept her husband from intimacy with them had she not acted as his sponsor. One of Molly's favorite companions, for example, was Mary Ogle Ridout, daughter of a former governor and wife of the secretary who, people said, was the power behind Governor Sharpe's administration. She blithely ignored the circumstances that "Papa" had quarreled openly with both gentlemen. And when Sharpe was succeeded by Robert Eden, Molly and Caroline Eden promptly became bosom friends. Molly had no idea of suffering socially for the Catholic Cause. That was apparent to everybody; only a few people realized that Molly was clearing obstacles out of her husband's path every time they appeared together in company. It was mostly because of Molly that the young Charles Carrolls were invited everywhere; it was certainly

[42] To William Graves, December 23, 1768; Carroll Papers, II, 120 A & B.

because of Molly that they went. She never did convert him to playing cards, even in dire social emergency, but he still loved to dance and the Annapolitan assemblies were famous all over America for their brilliancy. Mr. and Mrs. Carroll of Carrollton were seen regularly at the races, the functions at Government House, and the theater. They went to routs and drums and tea-parties and they filled their own house with company — company for dinner, for tea, for supper, spend-the-day company, spend-the-week company, stay-as-long-as-you-can company. Their hospitality was famous. They were popular and socially prominent and Molly, at least, had a wonderful time.

The climax to their success was Carroll's invitation to join the celebrated Homony Club of Annapolis. This was a real feather in the family cap. With all his wit and learning and personal magnetism, the elder Carroll had never been asked to become a member of any of the Homony Club's predecessors — such as the South River and Tuesday clubs — which had flourished in his earlier day. It was an inflexible rule that neither politics nor religion was to be discussed, and Charles Carroll of Annapolis was known to have some trouble holding his tongue in such matters. Nor could he always control his temper. Membership committees reluctantly realized that they could not expect him to spend any given evening smoking peacefully with a set of officials who had spent their working-day passing oppressive anti-Catholic laws. The invitation to his self-contained, uniformly courteous son was the tribute to a born diplomat.

Some kind-hearted historians, conscious of the greatness of the Homony's members, have tried to dignify the club by speaking of it as a "literary society." It did produce some literature, of which this from the quill of the poet laureate is a fair sample:

> Lo swifter than wind
> All cares left behind
> Mr Jenning approach
> Though it rains without coach
>   . . . .

What he has said is very right
I've cum so fast I'm out of Breath quite.
T J and L D
Are Men of Gumption you see.[43]

If this be literature make the most of it. Actually, the Homony Club was designed purely for foolishness and relaxation. It was patterned after the famous English clubs of the early eighteenth century, and more immediately after the Tuesday Club of Annapolis, and combined a little poetry, a little song, and a little mock majesty with a good deal of horseplay and hard liquor. Reading the minutes with twentieth-century eyes, we may fail to realize its attractions; but we must remember we are not great. Certainly the Homony Club's foolishness appealed to the genuinely great minds of some of its members.

Among the gentlemen who thus met together in homony (full credit for the pun must be given to the club's secretary) and who were Charles Carroll's best friends in Annapolis were Samuel Chase and William Paca, who a few years later would sign the Declaration with him; Governor Robert Eden, the attractive young drunk who knew Horace by heart;[44] William Eddis, his more serious but no less erudite secretary; Jonathan Boucher, the brilliant rector of the local Church of England; and Lloyd Dulany and Richard Sprigg, joint presidents of the Maryland Jockey Club. There were prominent lawyers — John Brice, John Hall, Thomas Jennings — and wealthy merchants — Anthony Stewart, Charles Wallace, Robert Couden. And there were also (surprisingly, if one is not familiar with the code of Annapolis' social clubs which made personal merit the only qualification for membership) certain young men of little wealth or social background, like the saddler and tooth-puller Charles Willson Peale who was beginning to paint portraits in his smelly little shop on Church Street.[45]

[43] Gilmor Papers, III, division 1. T J and L D stand for Thomas Jennings and Lloyd Dulany.
[44] *Correspondence of the Reverend Jonathan Boucher (1759–1802)*, p. 161.
[45] In 1766 several Annapolis gentlemen financed Peale's trip to England,

It must not be supposed that because Charles Carroll of Carrollton had fitted himself into the social life of Annapolis he was doing nothing, these few years after the repeal of the Stamp Act, but go to tea-drinkings and balls and club meetings. He worked hard. Though he could not, of course, practice law, and most people would have told you that he was one of the idle rich, he had his hands full with the management of the huge Carroll estate, which his father had entirely turned over to him. Charles Carroll of Annapolis was now reaping the benefits of those hard years when he had kept his homesick son at his European studies, determined that he should receive a finished education. He pottered happily around Doughoregan Manor, reading, raising a few exotic crops, bottling a little fine wine. He was old and he was enjoying it. He no longer worried about compound interest or his shares in the Baltimore Iron Works; whenever he wanted money for anything he simply asked his son for it. The younger Carroll controlled an annual income which was a staggering sum for those days, kept all the account books of the loans and mortgages in which most of the family fortune was invested. The "Italian method of book-keeping," which he had studied in London, now stood him in good stead; so did his training in surveying. He superintended the management of his plantations, sent his tobacco to market, and saw to the welfare of his many slaves.

Molly was busy too. Marriage in the days of the colonies was a full-time job. Just as Charles Carroll of Annapolis had turned over his duties and problems to his son, thinking that responsibility was good for young people, so Rachel Darnall

---

and enabled him to study there under Benjamin West. Charles Carroll of Carrollton has always had credit for being one of these. Certainly he could have been, for though Peale left Annapolis after the Stamp Act riots had ruined his business, he later returned, and came back from England to stay in 1769. It is possible, however, that Charles Carroll of Carrollton's name is being confused with that of Charles Carroll the Barrister. In the latter's letter-book (p. 316), he writes to a London friend to introduce "Charles Wilson Peale a young man of this Town has a Turn for Limning and some other Branches of Painting." It was this Charles Carroll who later advanced Peale money, on various occasions, "as his circumstances are but low."

had turned over to Molly her basket of keys. In addition to running her town house in Annapolis, she was supposed to supervise those phases of plantation life which called for feminine control — making clothes for the slaves and indented servants, preserving fruits and vegetables to see the huge plantation families through the winer, dealing out shoes and vermifuge and Christmas presents, teaching the young, visiting the sick, and providing plenty of flannel for the new black babies.

She was busy too with babies of her own. The next generation of Carrolls were beginning to arrive with true colonial regularity. Little Elizabeth was the first, born in the year after the marriage. She did not live long; they accepted her death with the fatalism of the age. After her, in 1770, came Mary, also called Molly, Polly, and finally Mary again. She grew up to be her father's favorite child, though he did not begin even to like her until she was about two years old. He was one of those men who loathed all squalling, soggy infants, but especially his own. Charles Carroll of Annapolis frequently sent from the Manor "My love & Blessing to you all & tell Molly to give littell Molly a kiss for me I know you will not do it." [46] In 1772 there was still another girl, whom her father named Louisa Rachel. Louisa for Miss Louisa Baker, Rachel for Miss Rachel Cooke. He had certainly found the "good natured Complaisant Complying" wife his own father had wished for him. Not every woman would have agreed to give her baby a name which so neatly summarized her husband's previous love-life. For that matter, not many husbands would have expected it. Charles Carroll expected it of Molly as a matter of course.

The incident was typical of their early married life. On the surface, the Carrolls presented a serene front to the world. The code of their class prevented criticism of each other in public. Even their closest friends would probably have told you that it was an ideally happy marriage, and certainly it was not a definitely unhappy one. Charles and Molly Carroll had

[46] March 28, 1771; Carroll Papers, II, 153.

much in common; they were used to living in the same house with a minimum of friction. They genuinely admired and liked each other, and on Molly's side there was more than a touch of passionate hero-worship, long before anyone else saw any justification for it. But Charles Carroll never forgave Molly for not being Louisa Baker, and Molly, not unnaturally, resented it. She hated the constant if tacit comparisons to this paragon. Louisa, she was sure, would never have been so inconsiderate as to bear three girl-babies in a row. Louisa would never have been guilty of the light-mindedness which her husband found so serious a fault in her — and which seeming light-mindedness, incidentally, was helping him lay the foundation of a career.[47] Louisa would never have had to play second fiddle to her father-in-law. Louisa, though her Parisian education had been within convent walls, would have been trusted to order her own clothes, instead of being expected to rely on the taste of the aunt of one of her husband's school friends — a good Christian woman, Molly had no doubt, but certainly middle-aged and probably dowdy.[48] Louisa's babies would never have aroused so little enthusiasm. Louisa — but there was no end to Louisa.

In his own way, Charles Carroll too coped with the green-eyed monster. He was jealous politically. His opinion of organized politics had not improved and he was still entirely without personal ambition; he had not changed but the world around him was changing. In ordinary times he might have lived out his life quietly enough without envy of the public activity that was denied him, but the times were far from being ordinary.

The Declaratory Act of 1766, passed at the time of the repeal of the tax on stamped paper, had had its fruition in the Townshend Acts of 1767. The British ministry, now under the guidance of a new and able chancellor of the exchequer,

[47] Charles Carroll of Annapolis to Charles Carroll of Carrollton, May 4, 1770; Carroll Papers, II, 129.
[48] Charles Carroll of Carrollton to Esther Bird (?) Browne, October 20, 1768; Field, *Unpublished Letters*, pp. 152-4.

Charles Townshend, was making another attempt to impose a tax upon the American colonies. This time the tax was placed on paint, paper, glass, and tea which were imported from England.

Unlike the Stamp Act, this measure could not be objected to on the ground that the British ministry had no right to impose it. It was not an internal tax but an external one. But even so the ministry had anticipated protests, and had tried to soften it by guaranteeing that the money which it proposed to raise would not be used anywhere except in America. That is, while the tax would take money from the American colonies, it would do so for the purpose of giving it right back to them.

Again, the British ministry deceived itself. For again it became clear that the American colonists had no idea of accepting taxation, internal or external, at any valuation but their own.

The old arguments against the Stamp Act were brought out and dusted off. Most of them were as good as new; if some of them were not quite as applicable to a case of external taxation as they had been when the right of internal taxation was the question, the common people would not know the difference. But some arguments had legitimately improved with age — the one about the imposition of financial hardship, for example. The articles taxable under the Townshend Acts were in far more general use than the stamped paper of 1765 had been. Glass had become the usual material for windowpanes in the houses of poor as well as rich; paints were as widely used; and practically everybody in America — remember that they were Englishmen, with the tastes as well as the rights of Englishmen — drank tea morning, noon, and night. Also the argument that England was trying to discourage American manufacture could be more effectively presented in 1767 than in 1765. "Ye mistaken policy of England . . . will force us to be industrious," Charles Carroll of Carrollton had written in the year of the Stamp Act: "our inability, while loaded with oppressive taxes to purchase your manufactures, will oblige us to manufacture for ourselves: the worst of evils this, that can possibly befall England, the loss of liberty excepted. . . ." [49]

Two years later, this was what he thought of the Townshend Acts: "Without any pretensions to prophecy I foretell it will give great disgust, and such impositions on goods of ye manufacture of Great Britain or exported from thence will certainly lessen the consumption of them, and will have this further bad effect — ye increased value of English manufactures will force ye colonists to manufacture for themselves. Though I expect to hear soon of some act to restrain us from manufacturing altogether: there is already an act prohibiting slitting mills in America. Why not make an act to prohibit us from making shoes, stockings, coarse linens and woollens? In short an act might be so penned as to oblige us to purchase all those articles from England at what price the English shopkeeper chuses to put on them; or in case of our inability to pay for them, to go naked. This would be a very wise act and productive of the following salutary effect: . . . .

"If ye greatest part of the Americans were constrained to go naked, as they certainly would be by such an act as above mentioned, it is more probable ye many diseases incident to this climate would soon put a stop to population; ye severity of ye weather would pinch to death thousands of poor naked Americans who had heretofore been used to cloathing. England would then have nothing to fear from our numbers, whatever she might from our resentment of such usage. You know ye old proverb — nothing so dangerous as to provoke a person able to revenge ye provocation. If England forces her colonies to rebellion, she must take ye proper steps to make that rebellion ineffectual by reducing their strength, and ye most effectual way of doing this is by putting a stop to ye increase of our people; but whether this will answer ye end of colonization, I submit to ye wisdom of higher powers." [50]

Sarcasm, yes; but some of it in deadly earnest. Certain im-

[49] To William Graves, September 15, 1765; Field, *Unpublished Letters*, p. 89.
[50] To William Graves, August 27, 1767; Field, *Unpublished Letters*, pp. 148-9.

plications stand out. Already, in 1767, he has made up his mind that there will be rebellion against Great Britain. Armed rebellion. And with the foregone conclusion of victory.

That mind of his was many years ahead of its time. Most of the influential patriot leaders still believed, and wanted to believe, that reconciliation with the mother country would come. Charles Carroll of Carrollton did not believe it and did not want to believe it. Already, in 1767, he was looking eagerly forward to liberty in America. It would have been unwise for him to advertise the fact. He did not do so. He waited, watching the progress of affairs.

In Maryland manufacture had indeed received an impetus from the passage of the Stamp Act. Especially in the making of woolen and linen materials its progress was "Surprising & Astonishing." [51] A stocking manufactory in Annapolis had set the patriotic keynote by making "a large Quantity of Thread Stockings, with this Device in Place of the Clock, AMERICA." [52] Annapolitans who had hitherto imported their hosiery from London appeared in public with this gaudy legend proudly adorning their legs. It became popular for "Gentlemen of the first Rank and Fortune, to appear Clad in Home-made Cloths," [53] and one of these was Charles Carroll of Annapolis, of course. He still had more patriotism than tact, though he was still adjuring his self-contained, diplomatic son to be circumspect about all public commitments. When the Stamp Act was repealed, he gladly laid aside the homely garments and manufactured no others for himself or his household; but when the Townshend Acts came into being his was one of those manufactories which were "reassumed not with a noisy & Ostentatious Parade, But wth a Sullen Resentment & determined Resolution never more to abandon them. . . . I have this year," Charles Carroll of Annapolis wrote in 1768, "Built a Commodious House for as many

---

[51] Charles Carroll of Annapolis to William Graves, December 23, 1768; Carroll Papers, II, 120 A & B.
[52] *Maryland Gazette*, August 16, 1764.
[53] *Ibid.*, March 27, 1766.

manufacturers as will be able to Cloath between three & four Hundred Slaves. . . ." [54]

Hand in hand with the revival of colonial manufactures, in protest against the passage of the Townshend Acts, came the Non-Importation Agreements. They were rapidly adopted all up and down the eastern seaboard. In June 1769 Maryland fell into line when an enthusiastic meeting of citizens was held in Annapolis and a large number signed "articles of non-importation of British superfluities, and for promoting frugality, economy, and the use of American manufactures." [55] Just to be sure that the agreements would be carried out, committees were appointed for the various Maryland counties. The committee for Anne Arundel — the county in which Annapolis was located — soon had occasion to exercise their authority, for in February 1770, the brig *Good Intent* attempted to land in Annapolis a cargo of goods which had been shipped contrary to the association. A public meeting was called and a special committee appointed to inquire into the merits of the case. As the result of their findings, the captain of the *Good Intent* was politely but firmly refused permission to land his goods, and though there were no demonstrations and he had the outspoken support of the Governor he somehow decided that it would be better if he made no protest. The *Good Intent* sailed meekly back to England and the Maryland patriots savored the taste of first blood.[56]

Massachusetts was not as orderly as Maryland in the enforcement of its non-importation agreements. In fact, there was so much rioting at the waterfront, with destruction of British property and tarring and feathering of British customs officials, that two regiments of British troops were sent from Halifax to preserve order in Boston. Their presence in town did not make the Bostonians feel at all kindly toward the

[54] Charles Carroll of Annapolis to William Graves, December 23, 1768; Carroll Papers, II, 120 A & B.

[55] David Ridgely, *Annals of Annapolis* (1841), p. 142.

[56] *The Proceedings of the Committee Appointed to examine into the Importation of Goods per the Brigantine Good Intent, Capt. Errington from London, in February 1770* (1770).

British. They went out of their way to call the soldiers names and to get into street fights with them on every occasion. Finally, on March 5, 1770, a Boston mob began to throw stones at a squad of soldiers in front of the custom-house, and the soldiers replied with gunfire. Six Bostonians were killed and several others were wounded. The affair got into the papers as the "Horrid Massacre in Boston."

Repercussions of the massacre were felt in every colony. Lurid accounts of eyewitnesses, all varying widely, and the engravings circulated from the shop of Mr. Paul Revere kept the people in a turmoil of excitement. In the midst of all the hullabaloo, the British ministry decided to repeal the Townshend duties. All, that is, except the tax on tea. King George insisted that that be retained.

Again the great masses of people were jubilant over having made the British ministry recant, and attached little importance to the fact that the tea duty was still in force. And again the wiser patriots found it a bad sign.

In Maryland, however, people were too much occupied with local politics to brood greatly on the possible consequences of national ones. The province was divided in the worst quarrel between Governor and Assembly which had occurred in twenty years. Though the question was a purely provincial matter, it aroused particular interest because it was in implication similar to the question of whether or not the British government had a right to tax its American colonies.

The subject of controversy was the regulation of officers' fees and the stipends of the clergy of the established Church. To understand its bitterness it is necessary to understand something of the growing resentment against the proprietary government in Maryland.

The brave Utopian beginnings of the province, under George and Cecilius Calvert, respectively the first and second Barons Baltimore, were only memory. By 1770 Maryland was as intolerant as any of the thirteen colonies and its politics were quite as rotten. For this rottenness Marylanders entirely blamed the Baltimore family, latter generations of whom

had made themselves unpopular by showing too plainly that
they were less interested in Maryland's welfare than in its
revenues. As far as governing virtues were concerned the
family had petered out. It was a far cry from the idealistic,
able, fair-minded Cecilius — who must have turned over in his
grave to know his descendants converted to the damn-your-
souls-make-tobacco theory of government — to Frederick, the
sixth and last Lord Baltimore. Frederick was a downright
degenerate.

The idea of paying revenues to a non-royal Lord Proprietary had never been popular, even in the days when the
proprietary had been a person deserving of loyalty. But the
main thing that Marylanders objected to was the Baltimore
lust for power. Not satisfied with appointing the governor,
the governor's council, and most of the important officials of
the province, successive Lords Baltimore had plainly shown
their resentment of the House of Burgesses, or Lower House
of Assembly. This was the representative body elected by
the people — though it was not very representative, for after
disqualifying Catholics, females, slaves, indentured servants,
and all those freemen whose worldly wealth did not come up
to a certain standard, only a fraction of the population was
left to vote. Nor did it always reflect the will of those people
who did have the franchise. Elections were far too commonly
"managed." Members of the Lower House were often inclined to support the governor's policies because such members were often suitably rewarded with opportunities to rise
in the world. And even when the incorruptibles had a majority in the Lower House, Lord Baltimore's governor still held
the winning card. He had the power not only to convoke
but to prorogue the Assembly. Few of the recent governors
had failed to take advantage of this power; whenever the
sessions of the Lower House did not go to suit them they
simply sent the people's representatives home. (Maryland, we
must remember, was a palatinate and had been chartered in
the reign of that King of England who had prorogued his
Parliament and ruled without one for eleven years.)

Another grievance against the Baltimore family was their nepotism. Every eldest son inherited the failing as surely as if it had been blue eyes or a big nose; and there had been occasions when the Governor's Council, sitting around the official table, looked like a family dinner party. Some of these nepotistic appointees turned out surprisingly well, but more of them did not. Merit was certainly a secondary consideration in the choice of office-holders, and by 1770 Maryland was generally pretty sick of being managed by gentlemen who had either been born Calverts, married Calverts, or flattered or blackmailed Calverts into appointing them to high position.

Governor Robert Eden, who arrived in 1769, was one of those who had married Calverts. His wife was the sixth Lord Baltimore's sister. He managed to make himself personally popular, being "a handsome, lively and sensible man . . . with . . . such a warmth and affectionateness of heart, that it was impossible not to love him . . . he had great quickness of parts, and a large experience of the world. . . ." [57] Even his faults were the accepted gentlemanly faults of his day and age: drinking too much, gambling too much, failing to pay his bills. "He is a hearty, rattling, wild young Dog of an officer," the Reverend Mr. Boucher, one of his brethren in the Homony Club, wrote; "with, however, but one very bad symptom, which is, that He has a sett of the arrantest Rascals around Him, for his Court, I have ever met with. I hope These were palm'd upon Him by the Idiot Lord, his Bro'r in Law, and not of his own chusing. He is too a Bit of a Scholar — has Horace all by Heart, of whom, indeed, He is a faithful Disciple. In short, as was said of poor Charles, were He any Thing but a Governor, He w'd be a very clever Fellow. . . ." [58]

The last sentence summed up Governor Eden's position in

---

[57] Jonathan Boucher, *Reminiscences of a Maryland Loyalist 1738–1789* (1925), p. 68.

[58] *Correspondence of the Reverend Jonathan Boucher*, p. 161. Mr. Boucher, of course, is using "clever" in the colloquial sense to mean pleasant or agreeable. It is not generally thus used in the South, any more, but visitors are still sometimes puzzled to hear: "No, he doesn't have any sense at all, but then he's *very* clever."

Maryland very accurately. However personally acceptable he was to Marylanders he was still the official mouthpiece of "the Idiot Lord" and the scapegoat for the many grievances which had piled up against the Baltimores through the years.

Everything he did politically was unpopular. Not long after he arrived in Annapolis he had to prorogue the Assembly to keep it from protesting officially against the Townshend Acts. This was a sample of the arbitrary use of that power which Maryland most resented in the hands of Lord Baltimore's representatives. There was unusual high feeling. Assemblies had been dissolved before, many of them; but the people of Maryland had never been in quite this frame of mind. It was extremely unfortunate for Governor Eden that the question of regulating fees should have come up at just this time.

The salaries of the various officials of government were fixed by Act of Assembly, and set forth in a table of fees — so much for the Commissary-General, so much for the Naval Officer of Patuxent, and so on. The stipends of the clergy were similarly fixed. Clergymen did not profit any too handsomely (though in a number of individual cases they got more than they deserved) but the officers' fees were quite high. Too high, the Lower House thought, especially considering the fact that many of the offices were sinecures. So, when the old law was about to expire in 1770, and the Assembly was called upon to provide suitable legislation to take its place, the Lower House promptly framed a new law in which the officers' fees were much reduced.

They knew the Council would not approve, and expected trouble. They got it. Leading the fight against the proposed law were council-members Daniel Dulany, Secretary of Maryland, and Walter Dulany, Commissary-General. The Lower House saw it as a suspicious circumstance that these gentlemen personally benefited by the fact that the existing table of fees was high; they pointed out that they themselves were acting with perfect disinterest for the welfare of the province, citing the example of Mr. Samuel Chase, who though the son of a clergyman had voted to reduce the stipends of the clergy. But the Council refused to yield an inch, and the matter was argued back and forth with increasing bitterness. Finally Governor Eden, seeing that the Lower House and the Council were deadlocked, resorted to the time-honored solution of prorogation. His reasoning was excellent. With the Assembly dissolved, the Governor had his usual power to deal with between-session emergencies. The expiration of the old table of fees, and the necessity for a new one, constituted an emergency. On November 26, 1770, Governor Eden therefore issued a proclamation in which he arbitrarily fixed the officers' fees at the old high rate.

This high-handed procedure turned against the proprietary's government many people who had hitherto warmly supported it. They had heard too much about tyranny in the national sense not to recognize it when they encountered it locally. Besides, the recent trouble with the mother country had made Marylanders tax-conscious, and supporters of the proposed revised table of fees did not hesitate to point out that these fees were almost exactly like taxes. As long as the representatives of the people fixed them, very well. As soon as the Governor stepped in and fixed them to suit himself, it was another flagrant case of internal taxation, of tyranny, and of the usurpation of the rights of Marylanders.

There were no physical demonstrations. Maryland was not ready to act. But there was a great deal of rebellious talk and governmental and patriotic parties drifted farther and farther apart. The subject was never out of mind; two years later there was still as much indignation, on both sides, as if the proclamation had just been issued yesterday.

The bitterness overflowed on January 7, 1773, into the columns of the *Maryland Gazette*. An unsigned dialogue between "First Citizen" and "Second Citizen" set forth the issues of the quarrel between Governor and Assembly. "Second Citizen," an adherent of the Governor, presented very ably the arguments of his party; but "First Citizen," the supporter of the patriot cause, was allowed to do little but ask the proper question at the proper moment, in order that "Second Citizen" might effectively bring out his points.

The dialogue was widely read and its probable authorship, of course, much discussed in and around Annapolis. Most people had no difficulty in arriving at the correct conclusion. Gentlemen who had legal educations and Latin dictionaries were accustomed to writing political articles for the paper, usually over a pseudonym; and readers of the *Gazette* had through practice become quite acute at identifying them. In this case there was little doubt in most minds that the piece had been written by Daniel Dulany (called "the Younger"), the famous Annapolitan lawyer. A former commissary-general of the province, he was at the time of this writing still Secretary of Maryland and a member of the Governor's Council.

Unlike many of his contemporaries who held high public office, Dulany was noted for his learning and ability. The son of an Irish indented servant who had in Maryland become a man of wealth and influence, the younger Dulany had been educated at Eton and Cambridge and had studied law in the Middle Temple in London. He had inherited a fortune from his father and he had married wisely and well — Rebecca, the daughter of President-of-the-Council Benjamin Tasker. He was famous for his knowledge of law; his brethren at the bar usually forebore to argue with Mr. Dulany because it was practically a foregone conclusion that he would be right and they wrong. He was famous too for some of his previous writings; the *Considerations* and *The Right to the Tonnage* [59] had been praised by the best minds in England as well as in America, and Mr. Pitt had flourished a copy of the former pamphlet under Parliamentary noses while he denounced the Stamp Act. Even Charles Carroll of Annapolis, who did not personally care for Mr. Dulany, could not deny his abilities: "He is a

[59] *Considerations on the Propriety of Imposing Taxes in the British Colonies, for the Purpose of raising a Revenue, by Act of Parliament* (1765); *The Right to the Tonnage, the Duty of Twelve Pence per Hogshead on all exported Tobacco, and the Fines and Forfeitures in the Province of Maryland* (1766).

Man of Great Parts, of Generall Knowledge indisputably ye best Lawer on this Continent, a very entertaining Companion when he Pleases But wth this weakness yt his Veracity is Questioned, He is very Vain, Proud, & Designing & so much of a Politician as not to be ever Scrupulous in ye Measures he takes to answer his Ends." [60]

Charles Carroll of Carrollton had "met the great Dulany" in London, in 1762, and had relayed his impressions to his father: "Dulany has an easy fluent and persuasive tongue: is bold in asserting positive in his assertations, ready to contradict, impatient of contradictions, imperious, decisive & dogmatical." [61] He tacitly agreed that Dulany would be a bad man to pick a quarrel with.

Now, ten years later, backed by an impressive reputation for invincibility, Mr. Dulany in the role of newspaper correspondent seemed apt to have not only the first but the last word. Gentlemen shied away from the honor of answering his arguments in the public prints. Had the supporter of the Governor's cause been anyone else at all there would have been a number of legal lights glad to shiver a lance for the patriot argument. William Paca, Brice Worthington, Samuel Chase, George Plater, and Thomas Johnson were only a few of those who could have handled the subject ably. But, since the opponent was the great Dulany, not one of them could have handled it adequately. Dulany could have made a fool of any one of them, and they knew it.

So nearly a month passed without anyone's having come forward to answer the author of the dialogue. The members of the bar were increasingly unwilling to bell the cat, and it seemed settled that the argument would go by default to the Governor's party. Governor and Council had put on smug little smiles and Mr. Dulany walked the Annapolis mud with the stately tread of the one who has come down from Olympus for the week-end. He was having the time of his life.

[60] To Charles Carroll of Carrollton, April 17, 1761; Carroll Papers, I, 64.
[61] To Charles Carroll of Annapolis, November 11, 1762; Carroll Papers, I, 85.

CHAPTER V

The First Citizen

1773–1776

O N FEBRUARY 4, 1773, the *Maryland Gazette* gave space to a second dialogue between "First Citizen" and "Second Citizen." Like last month's, it was unsigned; but it was plain enough that, although it took the same form, it had not been written by the same person. This article emphasized the point of view of the "First Citizen," who protested that the original dialogue had been incorrectly reported, and therefore submitted his own version.

"The editor of the dialogue between two Citizens, it seems, is the same person, *who overheard and committed to writing the conversation*," he wrote. "I was willing to suppose the editor had his relation at *second hand*, for I could not otherwise account for the lame, mutilated, and imperfect part of the conversation attributed to me, without ascribing the publication to downright malice, and wilful misrepresentation. . . .

"The sentiments of the first Citizen are so miserably mangled and disfigured, that he scarce can trace the smallest likeness between those, which really fell from him in the course of that conversation, and what has been put in his mouth.

". . . . Since much depends on the manner of relating facts, the first Citizen thinks he ought to be permitted to relate them in his own way."

That, stripped of its conventional eighteenth-century verbiage, was calling a spade a spade.

With this introduction, the article proceeded to present the arguments of the patriot party. This time the "First Citizen" did most of the talking and the "Second Citizen" took the unaccustomed role of stooge. Even the adherents of the governor's party admitted that the subject was well handled. The unknown author was, unbelievably, a man with a brain and a knowledge of law which quite equaled the great Dulany's. Government officials were more than a little worried, and Mr. Dulany, for his part, was furious. It had been a good many years since anybody had dared to call him a liar. Now "First Citizen" had done it in no uncertain terms, and with the greatest assurance in the world. Dulany could not for the moment think who this upstanding patriot could be, and it maddened him because it was obvious that his opponent knew him. Though pretending that he neither knew nor cared who the "editor of the dialogue" might be, he had made several pointed allusions and had even quoted — to his own advantage — from the *Considerations* which had made Dulany so popular in '65 and which now seemed coming back to haunt him. One by one Dulany thought of and discarded the men who were even remotely capable of writing as the "First Citizen." Ultimately and inevitably, he was forced to the conclusion that the culprit was that impudent ingrate of a disfranchised Catholic, Charles Carroll of Carrollton.

On February 18th the *Gazette* published Dulany's second contribution on the question of the regulation of fees. This time he abandoned the dialogue form — wisely enough, for the argument between First Citizen and Second Citizen was getting too violent to be kept within the bounds of a conversation. It was, plainly, going to be a fight with no holds barred. Dulany signed this letter "Antilon." [1] When Carroll answered it in the *Gazette* of March 11th, he too abandoned the dialogue form and signed to his article the obvious penname "First Citizen."

[1] Elihu S. Riley, the Maryland historian who published the *Correspondence of "First Citizen" — Charles Carroll of Carrollton, and "Antilon" — Daniel Dulany Jr., 1773, With a History of Governor Eden's Administration in Maryland 1769-1776* (1902), quotes Richard J. Duvall of the Naval Academy Library as saying that "Antillon" (not "Antilon") is a nearly obsolete

The letters were arousing excited comment all over Maryland but especially in Annapolis, where both the writers lived and which town, as the provincial capital, was especially interested in the politics involved. This question of the regulation of officers' fees seemed more important than either the Stamp Act or the Townshend Acts had been, for the Lord Proprietary, and not the British king or ministry, had always been the factor to be reckoned with under Maryland's unusual system of government. In any case the principle of taxation was the same. Every Marylander capable of understanding the arguments in the case was following the debates with avidity.

They were read also by numbers of people who entirely missed the fine points of the quoted law and who skipped the copious Latin quotations, but who found the Dulany-Carroll controversy as absorbing as the latest scandal. There was no doubt that the personal element was giving a fillip to the affair. In those days politics went in for personalities less daintily than they do today. It was not considered unduly surprising when, after a hard-fought contest in one of the Maryland counties, one of the candidates bit off the other candidate's nose; and if there was any scandal or libel law in existence it was a dead letter. The great Dulany was famous not only as a master of law but as a master of invective, and in the Antilon–First Citizen letters he did not disappoint his public. The public was even more delighted to find that Mr. Carroll of Carrollton had been concealing behind his mild and unassuming good manners the ability to hit equally hard.

Everybody in Annapolis knew that there was bad blood between the Carroll and Dulany families. The cause may not be exactly determined at this distance; but it originated in a quarrel between Daniel Dulany the Elder and Charles Carroll of Annapolis. Very probably it concerned religion and religious disabilities. The two men arrived in Annapolis only a year apart; they lived as neighbors for more than thirty years,

---

Spanish word meaning a stinging, drawing plaster — obviously, to draw out poison.

but they were never friends. Dulany, an Irish emigrant who somewhere along the line had got to be a member of the Church of England, was enjoying a brilliant political career. Carroll's religion destroyed all his chances. Dulany doubtless sneered at Carroll for being a Roman Catholic; Carroll certainly sneered at Dulany for being an indented servant. It is pure surmise, though certainly not unjustifiable, to wonder whether Carroll or his father the Attorney-General, in touch with relatives in Ireland, had not known the circumstances of Dulany's being bound as a servant to come to America, and that they were not the nice story-bookish ones assigned by tradition — which says that Dulany was a high-spirited young man who left home because he could not get along with his stepmother.[2] It seems entirely out of character for Charles Carroll of Annapolis to taunt a man with the fact of his servitude if there were nothing else against him. There were plenty of honorable gentlemen in Annapolis who had "served out their time," and at least one of them, Mr. George Neilson, was Carroll's intimate friend.

Whatever the cause, the animosity held over to the next generation of Dulanys and Carrolls. Daniel Dulany the Younger took occasion to speak slightingly of Charles Carroll of Annapolis, when the latter's young son was introduced to him in London; and Charles Carroll of Carrollton never forgave him the rudeness.[3] In Annapolis, in 1769, the great lawyer's half-brother, Lloyd, challenged Carroll of Carrollton to a duel — provoked, the Carrolls said, by Daniel him-

[2] Charles Carroll of Carrollton to Charles Carroll of Annapolis, October 1, 1769; Carroll Papers, II, 121–2&3.
[3] Charles Carroll of Carrollton to Charles Carroll of Annapolis, January 5, 1762; Carroll Papers, I, 77. It is apparently getting ahead of the story to quote here from one of the rebuttals printed in the *Maryland Gazette* several weeks after Antilon and the First Citizen had both stopped writing. But this satire in verse, called "A new edition of the letter of thanks, address'd to the representatives of the city of Annapolis to the *First Citizen*, with notes," shows another reason why Dulany and Charles Carroll of Carrollton were at odds. I have already mentioned the facts that Carroll had planned to marry Molly Darnall in the autumn of 1767, and that "for legal reasons" the wedding had to be postponed until summer of the following year. Though five or six years had passed the incident was — obviously — still recalled. The

self, who "is engaged too deep to retreat with honor — He thought to have slipped his neck out of the collar by engaging his brother Lloyd in the quarrel." [4] It was certainly a family affair on both sides; Lloyd's sizzling challenge mentioned "that Monster of Vice & profligacy, your father." [5] Charles Carroll of Carrollton was opposed to the practice of duelling but he wrote back that he expected to "ride out as usual to my quarter near town. . . . Tomorrow morning . . . at 6 o'clock, & I shall then be prepared to give you a proper reception if you come in my way, as I shall be provided with pistols. . . ." [6] And two days later he recorded (casually, in the postscript of a letter to his father): "I have heard no more from Mr Lloyd — I think the scurrilous rascal should be exposed to public shame by a suit at law — I can not conceive what deed of yours he alludes to, when he hints at perjury — it is some thing he has taken up upon trust from that oracle of truth his Brother Daniel. . . ." [7]

The Antilon–First Citizen letters, then, interested Annapolis because of the duel that had never taken place. They were interesting also because a disfranchised Catholic was arguing out a point of justice with a powerful government official. Such a thing could not have happened before the Stamp Act and the Townshend Acts had presaged British tyranny; everybody, and not just the Dulanys, would have considered it gross im-

---

published satire puts these words into the mouth of Charles Carroll of Carrollton:

> "When your letter I read, my heart leap'd for joy,
> That I an occasion so apt might employ
> My rancour, and *venom innate* to let fly
> At a man I abhor — and, I'll whisper you why.
> I could not be married — (you've heard of the fact)
> Before I had got 'an *enabling* act.'
> For, a man, you'll allow, would cut a poor figure
> (Tho' big as myself, or, perhaps, somewhat bigger)
> Who, to any fair virgin his honour shou'd plight,
> Without being ENABLED to do — what is right.
> In this he oppos'd me. . . ."

[4] Charles Carroll of Carrollton to Charles Carroll of Annapolis, undated; Carroll Papers, II, 121–6.

[5] September 29, 1769; *ibid.*, II, 121–1 [sic].

[6] *Ibid.*

[7] *Ibid.*, II, 121–2&3.

pertinence for a Roman Catholic to speak out on a public matter. Now, amazingly, they were applauding what the Roman Catholic said.

Of course there was nobody half so interested as old Charles Carroll of Annapolis, who, out at Doughoregan Manor, was not getting either the newspapers or the gossip as promptly as he wished. Though the roads were almost impassable with the early spring mud, he managed to come to town extremely often; between times he seized the thinnest excuses to send a slave in on an errand. "I send downe a Boy as Mrs. Darnall tells me she can send you some Butter," he wrote to his son, who kept several perfectly good cows in town: "Let ye Boy return early on Sunday, by him informe me How Countenances appeared at ye Rout [Mrs. Upton Scott's], what is sayed of ye 1st Citizen & how it is Relished, I shall be much disappointed if it does not meet with a Generall Cordiall reception." [8]

He was not disappointed. Subscriptions to the *Maryland Gazette* poured in upon the surprised and delighted Widow Green, who with her son was struggling to carry on her husband's printing business. On Thursdays, when the paper came out, their "Office was a long time Crouded" and "ye Publick Houses were yt night as quiet as private Ones" — everybody, presumably, was devouring the First Citizen letters.[9] The First Citizen himself had become famous overnight. Whenever he appeared in public "ye Whisper immediately Ran there is ye 1st Citizen," [10] and everybody turned to stare — admiringly, for his cause was a popular one, but with the naïve curiosity of people viewing a freak at the county fair. Most of them would have had trouble analyzing their sentiments. Many strong members of the Governor's party supported the proclamation because it was to their personal financial advantage, but some of them admitted to themselves that it was unjust, and later changed their al-

[8] March 12, 1773; Carroll Papers, III, 212.
[9] Charles Carroll of Annapolis to Charles Carroll of Carrollton, March 17, 1773; Carroll Papers, III, 213A.
[10] *Ibid.*

legiance. Some of his associates, too, heartily disliked the haughty Mr. Dulany and enjoyed seeing him struggle — against a man fifteen years younger than he, and with absolutely no experience in the practice of law! — to maintain the supremacy which had made him so insufferable. Even the Toriest Tories, who believed firmly that the governor was exactly right and that First Citizen was an impudent and seditious rebel, admired Carroll's writings while they disagreed with him. Thus Jonathan Boucher, the rector of St. Anne's, who while Antilon had been engaging First Citizen on the subject of officers' fees had been writing against Chase and Paca on the question of clergymen's salaries, admitted that Charles Carroll of Carrollton was "an author wth whome it was an Honor to Contend." [11] Daniel of St. Thomas Jenifer, also in the opposite camp, wrote to old Charles Carroll of Annapolis: "Your son is a most flaming Patriot, and a red hot Politician: He and I have frequent skirmishes in the Field of Politics, each retiring Victor, and of consequence always ready to renew the Attack. . . ." [12]

On the other hand, large numbers of people who inclined toward the patriotic brief were prejudiced against its champion for his Catholicism; they had so long and so thoroughly been convinced that no one who believed in the doctrine of transubstantiation could have normal good sense that they halfway discredited the arguments of the popular party because it was a Roman Catholic who was advancing them.

It was Antilon himself who brought these stragglers into line, forcing them against their will to sympathize with Charles Carroll of Carrollton and hence with the patriot cause. He had been holding back his best weapon against the First Citizen — his unpopular religion — and in the third letter which he wrote to the *Maryland Gazette* (April 8, 1773) he struck out with it. "After all," wrote the great Dulany, "who is this man that calls himself a citizen, makes his address to the

[11] Charles Carroll of Annapolis to Charles Carroll of Carrollton, May 20, 1773; *ibid.*, III, 226.
[12] March 28, 1773; *ibid.*, III, 216.

inhabitants of Maryland, has charged the members of one of
the legislative branches with insolence, because in their inter-
course with another branch of the legislature they proposed
stated salaries, and has *himself* proposed a *different* provision
for officers; contradicted the most public and explicit declarations of the Governor; represented *all* the Council but *one* to
be mere fools, that he may represent *him* to be a political
parricide; denounced infamy, exile and death; expressed a
regard for the *established* Church of England? Who is he?
He has no share in the legislature, as a member of any branch;
he is incapable of being a member; he is disabled from giving
a vote in the choice of representatives, by the laws and constitution of the country, *on account of his principles*, which
are *distrusted* by those laws. He is disabled, by an express
resolve, from interfering in the election of members, on the
same account. He is not a Protestant."

Mr. Dulany may have been the most famous lawyer in
America, but he was a bad judge of public feeling. The con-
ceit that encased his excellent mind was practically bomb-
proof. It had not been penetrated by the immense interest
the public had shown in the articles of the First Citizen; Dulany
did not know, therefore, that the old taunt of his opponent's
Catholicism was not the *coup de grâce* it might have been a
few months earlier. Public opinion was undergoing a most
surprising change. Charles Carroll of Carrollton had won the
people's respect legitimately. He had championed their cause
at a time when no other adequate champion had been willing
to come forward. He was beating the great Dulany, point for
point, in a manner that left no doubt as to his ability and good
sense. Yet — he was a Roman Catholic. It was amazing. Or
was it amazing, after all? Could they, all these smug good
Church-of-Englanders, have been making a mistake all these
years? Could it be that a man's religion was his own business,
and not an affair of state? That a man could be good and
useful and patriotic and fearless even though he differed from
them in his interpretation of the Sacrament? Many people

who had previously consigned Catholics to outer darkness, quite as a matter of course and convention, began to use their heads. The First Citizen's letters had fully convinced them that there was something wrong with a government which imposed on colonists an arbitrary table of officers' fees. Now the excellence of those letters made them wonder if there were not something even more wrong with a government which excluded from voting or from the holding of public office this man who had convinced them of his ability and worth. They liked him — Roman Catholic though he was. They resented in his behalf Dulany's vicious attack, seeing it quite accurately as the last resort of a legitimately defeated opponent. And they gloried in the First Citizen's fearless reply to Antilon's threats against his person: "To what purpose was the threat thrown out of enforcing the penal statutes [against Catholics] by proclamation? Why am I told that my conduct is very inconsistent with the situation of one who owes even the *toleration* he enjoys to the favor of government? If by instilling prejudices into the Governor, and by every mean and wicked artifice, you can rouse the popular resentment against certain religionists, and thus bring on a persecution of them, it will then be known whether the toleration I enjoy be due to the favor of government or not. . . ." [13]

So Dulany's choicest weapon had proved a boomerang, and he and the other members of the court party were edified by the spectacle of the Maryland public not only wildly acclaiming an "accurs'd Roman Catholick" but even finding sympathy for the discouragement he had struggled against. It was a thing to make Governor and Council shake their heads and wonder what in the world Marylanders were coming to.

Charles Carroll of Carrollton knew very well.

There was another letter from Antilon in the *Gazette* of June 3rd, which First Citizen duly answered on July 1st. But the victory had been already won. Most people agreed with the opinion that Antilon "would not Have filled so much of

[13] *Maryland Gazette*, May 6, 1773.

His Piece with Scurility if He could have substituted Reason insted of it." [14] The honors of the argument were unquestionably with the patriot party.

During the months when the famous articles were appearing in the papers, the behavior of the First Citizen had been warmly commended. Unlike Antilon, who in the latter stages of the controversy professed an illness which many people believed far from serious, Mr. Carroll of Carrollton had gone everywhere as usual, even to the Governor's house. Molly, that excellent young politician, had managed to keep on good terms with the Edens even though the Governor looked "very cool" upon his ex-brother of the Homony Club.[15] This admirable organization, unable to live up to its name, had "broken up only when the troubles began and put an end to everything that was pleasant and proper." [16] Its ex-members were leaders of the opposing political parties — Eden, Eddis, Boucher, and Stewart on the side of the existing government; Carroll, Paca, Chase, Jennings, and Johnson on that of the patriots. Mr. Paca, in the heat of a quarrel over the regulation of clergymen's salaries, challenged the Reverend Mr. Boucher to a duel.

The First Citizen letters determined the outcome of the May election of 1773, held just a few days after Carroll had replied to Dulany's attack upon his religion. It was a landslide for the patriot party. Every county sent to the Assembly representatives who could be counted on to oppose Governor Eden's policies. Even in Annapolis, which as the seat of government and hence the home of all the government officials and their adherents was a Toryish town, the patriot party won a real triumph. "William Paca and Matthias Hammond were chosen by a very great majority of freemen, indeed, without any opposition," reported the *Maryland Gazette*.[17]

[14] Charles Carroll of Annapolis to Charles Carroll of Carrollton, April 13, 1773; Carroll Papers, III, 221.
[15] Charles Carroll of Annapolis to Charles Carroll of Carrollton, April 8, 1773; Carroll Papers, III, 220.
[16] Boucher, *Reminiscences*, p. 67.
[17] May 20, 1773.

"Much was expected, as Mr Anthony Stewart had long declared himself a candidate for this city, even before a vacancy
by the resignation of Mr Hall, whose friends in the county
insisted on his taking a poll there. Mr Stewart's private character justly recommended him to the esteem of his fellow
citizens; but as he was originally proposed to turn out Mr Hall
or Mr Paca, who stood high in the esteem of the people, and
as a strong suspicion was entertained of his political principles
and Court connexions, Mr Hammond was put up in opposition to him, and on the morning of the election so great was
the majority of voters for Mr Hammond, that Mr Stewart
thought it prudent to decline."

After this triumph it seemed to the patriot party that a
celebration was in order. As soon as the polls closed in Annapolis, a large procession of citizens marched out to the
gibbet and hung from it a little coffin in which had been decently enclosed a certain obsolete proclamation. The ceremonies were accomplished very solemnly to the accompani-
ment of the firing of minute guns. Finally someone touched
off a bonfire and they cremated the coffin, which bore this
epitaph:

> The Instructions to the Registers of the
> Land Office
> born 24th November 1770
> Also
> The Proclamation
> born 26th November 1770
> The Children of Folly and Oppression
> Departed this Life
> On —— Day of May 1773
> And were buried
> by
> The Freemen of Anne-Arundel County [18]

This fun was of course entirely unofficial, but the first official action of the new representatives from Annapolis was
quite as irregular and considerably more daring. In the same

[18] *Maryland Gazette*, May 27, 1773.

issue of the *Gazette* which announced their election, William Paca and Matthias Hammond signed an open letter to the First Citizen, Charles Carroll of Carrollton:

"Your manly and spirited opposition to the arbitrary attempt of government to establish the fees of office by proclamation, justly entitles you to the exalted character of a distinguished advocate for the rights of your country. The proclamation needed only to be thoroughly understood to be generally detested, and you have had the happiness to please, to instruct, to convince your countrymen. It is the public voice, sir, that the establishment of fees by the sole authority of prerogative is an act of usurpation, an act of tyranny, which in a land of freedom cannot, must not, be endured.

"The free and independent citizens of Annapolis, the metropolis of Maryland, who have lately honored us with the public character of representatives, impressed with a just sense of the signal service which you have done your country, instructed us on the day of our election to return you our hearty thanks. Public gratitude, sir, for public services, is the patriot's dues; and we are proud to observe the generous feelings of our fellow-citizens towards an advocate for liberty. With pleasure we comply with the instructions of our constituents, and in their name we publically thank you for the spirited exertion of your abilities."

This letter was typical of the tributes which soon followed from the representatives of the various Maryland counties. Thanks to the First Citizen so cluttered the pages of the *Gazette* that members of the governor's party quite lost their taste for reading newspapers.

On July 2, 1773, the Lower House unanimously declared the governor's proclamation illegal. Then they adjourned and in a body marched through the streets of the capital — with most of the townspeople following after — to the Carroll House on Spa Creek, where they thanked the First Citizen in person. He accepted their speeches as gracefully as if he had been a public character all his life. In fact, he was so calm and self-contained that he rather disappointed his audience.

THE BURNING OF THE PEGGY STEWART
By Charles Yardley Turner
(the panel showing Charles Carroll of Carrollton)

Many of these people were seeing Charles Carroll of Carrollton for the first time as a person, not just as a Roman Catholic. Even his friends, the gentlemen with whom he had smoked in the Homony Club and drunk in the coffee-houses and laid bets at the race-grounds, were unfamiliar with the workings of his mind. He had had to wear his mask of caution even with them. To his fellow townspeople in general he was almost completely unknown. Everybody knew him by sight, of course — a short, small-boned man whose excessive thinness and frailty of body made people wonder how he had ever reached his present age, which was thirty-five. He had keen bright-blue eyes, an aquiline nose, and a notably firm mouth. His reddish hair was powdered and dressed simply, tied back with a narrow ribbon. His clothes were often black and always as plain as fashionable clothes might be, but he was fastidious about his linen and lace. He had beautiful manners and a quiet dignity that was as much a part of him as his ears or his nose. He also had a protective sort of dignity, which he put on partly because he had never quite got over being shy in company and partly because it barred out intimacies which might have been dangerous in his peculiar circumstances. Most people thought him reserved; people who owed him money said that he was hard and cold. But old ladies liked him, and men of all ages found him easy to drink with. Notably, these men always called him "Carroll," never "Charles" or "Charley." He was good company, a good conversationalist with a nice wit, and a better listener. He could get along with anybody, for though he had the Carroll hair-trigger temper he kept it under such magnificent control that one of the English friends who knew him best made the mistake of crediting him with "the evenest & best temper I ever met with." [19] He liked the good things of life, was a connoisseur of wines, and had an eye for a pretty girl. In a community where horseflesh was a fetish he was notable for his "good hands," and he considered his daily ride only less indispen-

[19] William Graves to Charles Carroll of Annapolis, January 14, 1770; Carroll Papers, II, 124 B-C.

sable than his daily session with his books. He was too studi-
ous, everybody agreed to that. He liked to shut himself in his
library and stay there for hours, with only his favorite bitch
for company, reading not only the newspapers and the current
books, but the same worn old Latin and French authors that
he had discovered at St. Omer and by this time nearly had by
heart. He kept too much to himself, and as a result of it he
was more than normally self-centered. He loved money, too.
Even allowing for the family feeling that it was necessary to
pile it up if the Carrolls were not to be swept away in a
Protestant world, he did gaze unduly long upon a shilling
before he spent it. He had a number of redeeming extrav-
agances, though; for instance, he held that "Money cannot be
laid out better . . . than in the purchase of valuable books," [20]
and when his children (those same children he had ignored in
their squirming, slobbering infancy) began to grow up, he
spoiled them badly by giving them too much money to spend.
With his servants he was strictly just but not at all lenient; he
was full of nervous energy himself, filling every day with
"perpetual occupation" in "business, exercise & study," [21] and
he simply could not understand why any able-bodied person
should want to sit and stare into space. In his business dealings he was, again, strictly just and as strictly uncompromising — even his devoted biographer would have hated to bor-
row money from him. There is no doubt at all that he had a
number of unpleasant little traits; but on the other hand there
is no doubt of his essential greatness of soul. Marylanders
glimpsed it for the first time that day when the legislature
came to thank him for his services to a province which had
never treated him with anything but intolerance and injustice. Some of these legislators, who now talked so glibly of
the rights of men and the land of freedom, remembered un-
comfortably their own attitude toward the Catholic Mr.
Carroll of Carrollton, in the days before the First Citizen let-

[20] To William Graves, August 14, 1772; *Maryland Historical Magazine*,
XXXII, 215.
[21] *Ibid.*, p. 218.

ters; but there was not the slightest hint of sarcasm, or of remembered bitterness, or of the consciousness of personal
triumph, in the even voice which responded with such grave
politeness to the flowery periods.

Everybody who was present that day was conscious of im-
pending change. Everybody knew that the First Citizen,
Catholic or not, was going to have some part in the future
government of Maryland. Most of them were vague as to how
the existing laws — under which Carroll was still disfranchised — were going to be changed; but at least a few of them
must have realized that the American Revolution, in Maryland, was already well under way.

News came from Boston — always to be depended upon, in
these exciting years, as a source of news. This time it was the
famous Boston Tea Party.

Tea was the only commodity mentioned in the late un-
lamented Townshend Acts on which the impost duty had
been retained. Patriots in the various colonies were still bound
by the non-importation agreements which they had signed
several years before, so by common consent the business of
importing tea became recognized as a nefarious one. According to law it might not be imported by the British colonies
from any country except England; and the colonies had no
idea of paying the English threepence tax. The most high-
minded patriots favored doing without tea altogether; but
others enjoyed killing two birds with one stone by not only
boycotting the British but smuggling into America tea bought
from the Dutch or other competitors of the British. Needless
to say it was the latter idea which took hold, and tea smuggling became a recognized and profitable business.

The British ministry knew perfectly well what was going
on but did not quite know how to stop it. So when the officials of the East India Company proposed a plan which, they
hoped, would save themselves from bankruptcy, the government gave unqualified approval. The plan was built around a
new low price for British tea. The company proposed to ship
the tea direct to warehouses of its own which it would set up

in America, and from these distribute it to the American merchants. This would be far less expensive than the old procedure of bringing the tea from China to London and selling it there to London merchants, who in turn sold it to the American agents or importers, who in their turn sold it to the merchants in America — with profits all along the line, of course. It would therefore be financially possible for the company to underbid the prices on the non-British tea which was being smuggled into America.

Again there was violent protest from the thirteen colonies. And again motives were very much mixed.

Disinterested patriots thought that, no matter how cheap the tea was, it was too expensive as long as it had that threepence tax on it. They objected to buying it as a matter of principle.

Other patriots had something at stake besides a principle. Many of the most prominent were merchants who had made a fortune out of tea-smuggling — drawn to the business because it was not only profitable but, from a certain point of view patriotic — and the East India Company's proposed plan would put them quite out of business.

Still other Americans, who were not overmuch concerned with the pure theory of taxation without representation and who were not in the tea-smuggling business, were brought into line by clever propaganda. It was represented to them that the East India Company's intention was to run the American tea merchants out of business by offering tea at sensationally low prices and then, when they had the field to themselves, to put the price up again. It was also represented that the company would not stop short with the tea business, but would establish other warehouses and ship other goods to America and, the first thing anybody knew, would run every merchant in America out of business and force Americans to buy British goods at British prices.

They certainly would have done this if they had had any business sense at all. But probably the Americans need not have worried, for it soon developed that the East India Company was not overburdened with sense of any kind. They proceeded to ship an experimental cargo of cheap tea to Boston — Boston of all places.

When the vessel with the tea dropped anchor in Boston harbor, several hundred indignant and energetic Bostonians dressed up as Indians and dumped the whole cargo into the water. Customs officials had their strong suspicions as to who some of these noble redskins were. However, they could not prove anything on anybody and, rather than let the incident go unremarked, the British ministry decided to penalize the whole town of Boston. The tea party had taken place on December 16, 1773; in March 1774 the Bostonians were served notice that, unless by June first they made good the price of the tea destroyed, the capital would be moved to Salem, Marblehead would replace Boston as a port of entry, and Boston harbor would be indefinitely closed. This was the famous Boston Port Bill.

When the news reached Annapolis, in May 1774, there was wild excitement. A great crowd of townspeople promptly convened; and it was noted with pleasure by the patriots and with grave apprehension by the governor's party that the crowd included not only the hoodlums of the Stamp Act days but some of the most prominent and irreproachable gentlemen in the province. One of them was Maryland's First Citizen, Charles Carroll of Carrollton.

This meeting passed the resolution which was being adopted all up and down the string of seaboard colonies — "to stop all importation from, and exportation to, Great Britain" until the repeal of the Boston Port Bill. It also adopted, though by no means unanimously, the less worthy resolution "that the gentlemen of the law of this province bring no suit for the recovery of any debt due from any inhabitant of this province, to any inhabitant of Great Britain, until the said act be repealed." Then like the other colonies it resolved to boycott "that colony or province, which shall refuse or decline to come into similar resolutions with a majority of the colonies." [22] And a committee of correspondence was appointed

[22] Elihu S. Riley, *The Ancient City. A History of Annapolis, in Maryland. 1649–1887.* (1887), p. 165.

for Annapolis; its members were John Hall, Thomas Johnson Jr., William Paca, Matthias Hammond, and Charles Carroll of Carrollton.

It was his first post in public life.

The first of June, the day on which the Boston Port Bill went into effect, was observed throughout the colonies as a day of fasting and prayer. Many of the patriots, looking back on the repeal of the Stamp Act and of most of the Townshend duties, had not really expected to see it enforced. Now it was obvious that the British ministry had at long last resolved to take a firm stand. Very well, then, the Americans would take a firm stand too. All of the colonies except Georgia chose delegates to a Continental Congress which met in Philadelphia September 5, 1774.

When Marylanders considered the problem of representation their first thought for a delegate was, of course, of the First Citizen, Charles Carroll of Carrollton. Though there were a dozen men who could ably and creditably speak for Maryland there was no doubt in anyone's mind that Carroll was head and shoulders above them all. To the credit of his fellow Marylanders, they had accepted him fully at last, Catholicism and all. They admired that religion no more than they ever had, but they did admire this man who followed it; so they decided to take the bitter with the sweet and to hold it against him no more seriously than they would have held the more approved superstitions about broken mirrors and black cats. Having once arrived at this decision, they were not to be shaken from the conviction that there was no one, Protestant or Catholic, whom they would be as proud to send as a representative to Philadelphia.

But Carroll was wiser than they. Though there is every reason to believe that he was asked to be a delegate to the Congress, he refused. He knew that the First Citizen letters had established him in Maryland minds as an able and disinterested patriot, one who could be trusted to keep his religion in its proper relation to other matters; but he also knew that his stand in a provincial controversy had done little for his reputation in the other colonies. The districts north and south of Maryland retained their prejudice against him and others of his religion. He hoped yet to win them over, to convince them too that a man's religion was his own business and his own privilege. But this was not the moment. The First Continental Congress, meeting just after the passage of the Quebec Act, convened at a time when Catholics were held in more than ordinary opprobrium. Carroll felt that he could not serve his province to the fullest extent of his capacities at such a time, since certain other members of Congress would inevitably view his presence with distrust. And, as things turned out, he was exactly right; for the Congress, indignant over the Quebec Act by which the head of the Anglican Church had extended the Canadians' boundaries and sanctioned their Roman Catholic religion, proceeded to pronounce that faith inimical to liberty and a danger to the state.

But Charles Carroll of Carrollton was too valuable a man to be left behind when the Maryland representatives set out for Philadelphia. An unofficial member, he accompanied the delegation. He advised them on every point and they told him everything they knew. "When I see you I shall be able to give you a full account of their [the Congress's] deliberations," he wrote to his father, in the same letter in which he said: "The debates are kept secret, and the deputies are under a tie of honor not to reveal what passes." [23]

Carroll did not seem to mind the ambiguous position in which he had placed himself. He was convinced that it was for the best; besides, poor man, he had been in an ambiguous position most of his life and a little longer did not seem to matter. He was satisfied to serve his province without honor or recognition; satisfied to stay in the background and do the work while others got the credit. He was pathetically grateful merely for the chance to serve. He was that rarest of all human accidents, a born politician who was completely free from personal political ambition; far from seeking a career, he did not even want one.

[23] September 12, 1774; Carroll Papers, III, 261.

This circumstance distressed his friends, who were fore-sighted enough to predict a potentially great career for him. They hated to see it nipped in the bud by the religion to which his father and grandfather had so stubbornly clung at the price of their own careers; and some of them ventured to suggest that, since the Roman Catholic Church was only one of several acceptable means of entry into the Kingdom of Heaven, Charles Carroll might be well advised to try one of the others. One which was not outcast by the kingdoms of this earth.

Unlike his father, who would have lost his temper and thrown things had such an apostasy been suggested in his presence, the younger Carroll received these suggestions in good part. He recognized and appreciated the motives of his friends. But he wrote to one of them, William Graves:

"Well, I see, you want to make a convert of me, not out of religious zeal. But all modes of Religion being in yr estimation indifferent to our Creator, I may as well embrace that which my countrymen have embraced." That is, the Church of England, to which most Marylanders belonged. "What if they have embraced an absurd one? Yes, certainly, because ye one I have been brought up in is still more absurd. Granted, for argument's sake; What, then, do you advise me to quit a false religion & adopt one equally false, & this merely to humour the prejudices of fools, or to be on a footing with knaves? I have too much sincerity and too much pride to do either, even if my filial love did not restrain me — for I can truly say, *Nequeo lachrymas perferre parentis.* I am a warm friend to toleration; I execrate ye intolerating spirit of ye Church of Rome, and of other Churches, for she is not singular in that. Designing & selfish men invented religious tests to exclude from posts of profit & trust their weaker or more conscientious fellow-subjects, thus to secure to themselves all ye emoluments of Government: Wharton's saying was a true as well as a witty one: The oaths to Government were so framed as to damn one part of ye nation, & to shame the other.

"If my countrymen judge me incapable of serving them in a public station for believing ye moon to be made of green cheese, in this respect their conduct, if not wicked, is not less absurd than my belief, and I will serve them in a private capacity notwithstanding — nay, I have done it, as Eden or Dulany himself would acknowledge, could they forgive a man who had contributed to check their attacks on ye constitution of his country." [24]

Mr. Graves made no further suggestions. What could you do with a man like that?

Much of the time of the First Continental Congress was taken up by the efforts of the moderates to formulate a plan by which the colonies might be honorably reconciled with the mother country. The leader of the conservative wing was able Joseph Galloway of Pennsylvania, and he came very close to getting his scheme voted on favorably. There were a great many moderates in the first Congress; only a few of the delegates wanted independence, and one of these, John Adams, said that on this account he "was avoided like a man infected with the Leprosy. I walked the streets of Philadelphia in solitude, borne down by the weight of care and unpopularity." [25] He should have looked up Mr. Carroll of Carrollton, who would have been glad to walk with him. Carroll had never wavered from his belief that separation from England was both inevitable and desirable. "I still think," he wrote plainly on September 12th, "this controversy will at last be decided by arms." [26] Nevertheless he dreaded the consequences of war. "I am dejected at ye gloomy prospect before us — & dread the event," he admitted in a letter written from Philadelphia. "We have as much to fear from victory as a defeat. — In a civil war there is, & ought to be, no neutrality — indeed were I permitted to remain neuter I would disdain the offer — I will either endeavour to defend the liberties of my country, or die with them: this I am convinced is ye sentiment of every true & generous American." [27]

[24] August 15, 1774; *Maryland Historical Magazine*, XXXII, 222–3.
[25] W. E. Woodward, *George Washington; The Image and the Man* (1926), p. 251.
[26] To Charles Carroll of Annapolis; Carroll Papers, III, 261.
[27] To Charles Carroll of Annapolis, September 7, 1774; *ibid.*, III, 258.

The First Continental Congress produced a Declaration of Rights which was sent to the British ministry. Neither the ministry nor his Majesty paid a great deal of attention to it. It also produced the Continental Association, a new set of resolutions which boycotted not only importations from Great Britain but exportations thereto. Finally it made the very bad diplomatic blunder which probably cost the American colonies the support of Canada. All forty-nine of the members of Congress were, according to Carroll, "sensible & Spirited men . . . not one weak man among them — several of great abilities," [28] but they were inexperienced in national politics and their work showed it. Many years later Thomas Jefferson wrote to ask John Adams about some detail of the proceedings of this first Continental Congress and Adams wrote back: "I really know not who was the compositor of any one of the petitions or addresses you enumerate. Nay, farther, I am certain I never did know. I was so shallow a politician, that I was not aware of the importance of those compositions. They all appeared to me, in the circumstances of the country, like children's play at marbles or push-pin, or, rather, like misses in their teens, emulating each other in their pearls, their bracelets, their diamond pins and Brussels lace.

"In the Congress of 1774, there was not one member, except Patrick Henry, who appeared to me sensible of the precipice, or, rather the pinnacle, on which we stood, and had candor and courage enough to acknowledge it. America is in total ignorance, or under infinite deception, concerning that assembly. . . ." [29]

The Congress adjourned late in October 1774, agreeing to meet again the following May; but some of the Maryland delegates, "together with Mr. Carroll of Carrollton," had already hurried back to Annapolis. There was great excitement in the Maryland capital; Annapolis, in fact, was having a tea party of its own. On October 14th the brig *Peggy Stewart*

[28] To Charles Carroll of Annapolis, September 12, 1774; Carroll Papers, III, 261.
[29] November 12, 1813; *The Works of John Adams* (1850–6), x, 78.

had arrived there with a cargo of fifty-odd indentured servants and *more than a ton of English tea*. The italics are the Marylanders'. They considered the defiant importation of tea, in the face of the non-importation agreements, the existence of a local committee of correspondence, and the temper of the times, an impudence, an affront, and a piece of daring rascality. And they were definitely not going to put up with it.

Public animosity fixed itself on Mr. Anthony Stewart, the owner of the brig. We have already met him as the gentleman whose "private character justly recommended him to the esteem of his fellow-citizens" [30] — but not enough to keep him from being defeated by the outspoken patriot Matthias Hammond. Mr. Stewart had been suspected then of being a tool of the governor's party; he had later been one of those who signed a protest against the resolution to have no Maryland lawyer bring suit on behalf of an English client against an American. Nevertheless he had remained popular enough until the affair of the *Peggy*. He was a respected and prosperous merchant and a personal friend of Charles Carroll of Carrollton, both of them having been members of the Homony Club in the untroubled good old days before the First Citizen letters.

By entering his ship and cargo at the customs house and by paying the duty on the tea, Mr. Stewart had, however, brought down upon his head the wrath of the committee of correspondence, who promptly met and decided to make an example. A meeting of citizens was called for the same day, and the deputy-collector of the port of Annapolis, the owner and the captain of the *Peggy*, and James and Joseph Williams, local merchants for whom the tea had been imported in Mr. Stewart's brig, were curtly ordered to attend. In the absence of Charles Carroll of Carrollton, Matthias Hammond acted as leader of the committee.

The Williams brothers, scared to death, promptly produced the excuse that they had ordered the tea in May, before the non-importation agreements had been signed at Annapolis, and that they had regretted it ever since. In fact, they had

[30] *Maryland Gazette*, May 27, 1773.

been "in great hopes that the tea would not have been shipped." [31] Now that it had "unluckily come to hand" nobody was more desolated than they. They were more than willing to join Mr. Stewart in signing the abject apology which Mr. Hammond kindly prepared for them. Stewart, however, did not get off so easily, for he did not have even so good a story. It was a glaring fact that he had voluntarily paid the duty on the tea; and though as a last resort he attempted to convince his neighbors that he had not done so because he wanted the tea landed in Annapolis — indeed, there had been nothing farther from his mind! — but because he felt sorry for the crew and the indentured servants, who had not set foot on ground for nearly three months, Annapolitans failed to be convinced by Mr. Stewart in the role of humanitarian. And they laughed aloud when Captain Jackson, the master of the *Peggy*, related that he had not even known he had any tea on board his vessel. He implied that it was a question whether human hands had loaded it in England while his back was turned or whether a roc had dropped it into the hold while the brig was in mid-ocean.[32]

A majority of the citizens' meeting would have been willing to let Mr. Stewart off with confiscating his tea and making him read his apology aloud, but the vociferous minority, many of whom came from the outlying counties, threatened to hurry home and return with reinforcements who would "proceed to the utmost extremities." [33] Tarring and feathering was the mildest punishment that was suggested, and the unhappy importer saw that he had better take steps to save his own skin and that he had better take them fast. Tradition says that he consulted his old friend, Charles Carroll of Carrollton, who had just got back to Annapolis and was characteristically back in the saddle. Anyway, Mr. Stewart decided by the nineteenth

---

[31] William Eddis, *Letters from America, Historical and Descriptive; Comprising Occurrences from 1769 to 1777, Inclusive* (1792), pp. 180–2. Eddis' account of the whole affair seems to me the best of the several extant. The issues of the *Gazette* for October 20th and 27th and November 3rd (1774) are detailed but patently biased.
[32] Eddis, p. 177.
[33] Eddis, p. 183.

that he would forestall the "frantic zealots among the multitude" by setting fire himself to the *Peggy*.[34] He accordingly
went on board, ordered the vessel run aground, and applied
the torch in the presence of a large and enthusiastic audience.
If the painting in the Maryland State House is true history,
Mr. Stewart carried off his humiliation with an air which won
him considerable respect.

The affair of the *Peggy Stewart* for some reason appears in
very small type — if at all — in the pages of American history.
Maryland historians, who record it in very large type indeed,
are indignantly at a loss to understand why. Though it did
not occur as early as the more celebrated Boston Tea Party,
they feel that the Annapolis affair showed the more fearless
American spirit. Nobody bothered to dress up like an Indian,
or in any way tried to conceal his part in the business and thus
avoid possible punishment. And though Mr. Stewart undoubtedly acted under at least moral compulsion, they were still
doing things decently and in order in Maryland.

It took more than a tea-burning to disturb Annapolis' social
life. A few evenings after the *Peggy* had sunk off Windmill
Point Mr. Lloyd Dulany gave a party, and Mr. Carroll of
Carrollton was one of his guests. They were still politically
far apart, and neither had forgotten the reasons why they had
almost fought a duel in '69; but the society of a small town like
Annapolis had to depend on a sort of gentlemen's agreement
that such quarrels would not be carried too far. According to
the story — which cannot be authenticated but which sounds
authentic anyway — a new silver punch-bowl graced Mr. Dulany's table, and in reply to many admiring questions he admitted that it had come over in the *Peggy Stewart*. He went
on to explain, rather elaborately, that it had been sent to him
by a friend in England, entrusted to the care of Captain Jackson personally, and that it was in no way a part of the brig's
cargo. The captain had placed it in the cabin with his own
private property, and had delivered it himself. Otherwise it
would have been filled with salt water that minute, instead of

[34] *Ibid.*, p. 182.

with well-spiked punch. In the little silence that followed
this explanation, the company looked to Mr. Carroll of Carrollton for an answer, and Mr. Carroll smiled and said the
right thing as usual: "We accept your explanation, provided
the bowl is used to draw always this same kind of tea." [35]

Governor Eden was not at the party; in fact he had missed
all recent excitement, for not long after the First Citizen letters
had turned Maryland upside down he had thought it advisable
to go to England on "official business." When he returned,
the month after the Peggy Stewart Tea Party, the patriots
were still in the dark as to what the official business might be
and they were on tenterhooks to know just what had passed
between Eden and his brother-in-law Lord Baltimore. "You
have not sayed one Word to me about ye Governor Since His
Arrivall," old Charles Carroll of Annapolis complained to his
son, "Has He not been Drunk? When so He is very Leaky
& Communicative." [36] Eden, however, took no one into his
confidence either drunk or sober. He let nobody know how
he felt about returning to a province which, during his months
of absence, had learned how to do without a proprietary governor and which now gave him politely to understand that it
was accepting him back only as a figurehead. He still lived in
the official governor's mansion, he still got low bows and
plenty of lip-service, and he still went through the form of his
duties as governor. But real government had slipped out of his
hands. By July 1775 this was so much an established fact that
even the Tories admitted it. "Government is now almost
totally annihilated," Eden's secretary William Eddis wrote
home to England, "and power transferred to the multitude.
Speech is become dangerous; letters are intercepted; confidence
betrayed; and every measure evidently tends to the most fatal
extremities: the sword is drawn, and, without some providen-
tial change of measures, the blood of thousands will be shed
in this unnatural contest. . . . The inhabitants of this province are incorporated under military regulations; . . . in

[35] Riley, *The Ancient City*, pp. 309–10.
[36] November 16, 1774; Carroll Papers, III, 277.

Annapolis there are two complete companies; . . . almost every hat is decorated with a cockade; and the churlish drum and fife are the only music of the times. . . ." [37]

The real governors of Maryland were the members of the various patriotic committees, of which the Committee of Safety was the most important. No one man was supposed to be in charge of provincial affairs, but Charles Carroll of Carrollton was outstandingly more active than anybody else. He was the busiest man in Maryland. It seemed that people thought the First Citizen (he was still spoken of by that title as often as by his real name) had been kept in the background too long as it was; now they could not appoint him on enough committees. In November, at a meeting of the voters of Annapolis and Anne Arundel County, he had been placed on the committee "to represent and act for this county and city, to carry into execution the association agreed on by the American Continental Congress" and on the committee of correspondence." [38] He was also chosen a delegate to the provincial convention which would meet at Annapolis a few days hence. In June he acted as chairman of the committee of observation, in the case of the *Adventure*; in July, he was one of nine gentlemen named on a committee to "consider the ways and means to put this province into the best state of defence." [39] In August he was appointed to the Committee of Safety. In September he was again placed on the Committee of Observation, on the Committee of Correspondence, and on a committee to license suits. He was also expected to represent his county and city in such provincial conventions as might be held; and, after the first one in November 1774, they were held every month or two.

Many of the gentlemen who served on Maryland committees, like many of the delegates to the First Continental Congress, still believed that this state of affairs was temporary. The colonies had been badly spoiled by having the British

[37] Eddis, *Letters from America*, pp. 215-7.
[38] *Maryland Gazette*, November 10, 1774.
[39] *Archives*, XI, 5.

ministry knuckle under to them in 1766 and again in 1770. They felt it was only a matter of time until the mother country would again yield to pressure and take away the tax on tea and repeal such objectionable coercive acts as the Boston Port Bill. Until that happened, the patriot committees would fill the breach. Later, when good feeling had been restored by the colonies' having got what they wanted, the committees would disband and the patriots would be good loyal subjects of King George again.

Some of his closest associates thought Charles Carroll of Carrollton a dangerous radical because he never wanted to be a British subject again, and said so. They considered him a visionary because he was always thinking toward impossibilities in the future — a new country, a new liberty, a new people. Toward Maryland, at long last, *cum libertate.*

Old Charles Carroll of Annapolis was so proud of his son that Mr. Dulany in his palmiest days had not been more insufferable. (Dulany, by the way, was a country gentleman these days, avoiding Annapolis like the smallpox. An advertisement in the newspapers, supposedly Mr. Samuel Chase's idea of wit, asked the public to apprehend him as a "Runaway.") [40] The younger Carroll considered his numerous public posts as part duty and part privilege, all worry and hard work; now that he knew more about committee-meetings, he found that he did not enjoy them very much. But his father was happier than he had ever been in his life. He was enjoying vicariously the career which he had always wanted for himself.

Everything was coming at once. In the spring of 1775 the long-wished-for heir was born, Charles Carroll the Fourth. After three little girls this was something of an event. "Mrs Carroll has brought me 3 daughters, of wh. only one is now living, a fine child about 3 years old & of sweet & lively temper," Charles Carroll of Carrollton had written to an English friend, in August of the year before. "She is now big with a son & heir — at least so the old Gentleman wishes. I believe

[40] Charles Carroll of Annapolis to Charles Carroll of Carrollton, October 2, 1775; Carroll Papers, IV, 309.

he will lose all patience should it turn to a girl." [41] But though the son had duly arrived there were still troubles. Molly was far from well and could not nurse her baby.[42] She had never been strong and after the birth of this child she was seldom free from pain. At twenty-five she was suffering chronically from "female complaint," which, resulting usually from having too many babies too close together, was as prevalent among eighteenth-century ladies as gout among eighteenth-century gentlemen. Molly had given birth to four children in six years and had had at least one miscarriage; she was perceptibly weaker after each blessed event. She hated being sick. She faithfully tried all the remedies her friends suggested, and even the "philters" concocted by old negresses who dabbled in voodoo; finally, about the time her boy was born, she discovered that laudanum really helped the pain and from that time on she took too much of it for her own good. This circumstance distressed her devoted father-in-law, who filled his letters with concern for Molly and imprecations against "ye poison Laudanum." [43] Molly tried to stop but she never could. Eventually laudanum completed the wrecking of her health — laudanum and her unwillingness to take sensible care of herself.[44] She was never one to stay at home and miss the gaiety of Annapolis society, even though she was physically miserable; and she realized, too, the advisability of keeping up with all her friends of the pre-liberty days, Ridouts and Taskers and Ogles and Dulanys who were as pro-Tory as her husband was pro-Whig. She even managed to keep on friendly terms at Government House.

The northern colonies simply could not understand the attitude that the opposing parties in Maryland were taking toward each other. The Carrolls were by all odds the most important couple in the patriot camp — and imagine their going right on

[41] To William Graves, August 15, 1774; *Maryland Historical Magazine*, XXXII, 221.
[42] Charles Carroll of Annapolis to Charles Carroll of Carrollton, April 10, 1775; Carroll Papers, III, 288.
[43] E.g., to Charles Carroll of Carrollton, April 22, 1779; *ibid.*, VI, 516.
[44] Charles Carroll of Annapolis to Charles Carroll of Carrollton, December 1, 1775; *ibid.*, IV, 317.

seeing the governor and his lady socially! Such a thing could never have happened in Massachusetts, for instance, where they took their patriotism neat.

Up in Massachusetts everything was wild excitement over the battles of Concord and Lexington. Marylanders sympathized hotly, but it was not until the Second Continental Congress, which convened at Philadelphia in May 1775, appointed as commander-in-chief of the revolutionary forces George Washington of Virginia that they fully realized that this was a war involving all the colonists and not merely the embattled farmers in the northern districts. Marylanders knew George Washington well. He was in the habit of coming to the spring and fall race-meetings at Annapolis and a few years earlier he had been forever making hopeful extra trips there to see if his lazy young stepson, Jacky Custis, were doing any better under the tuition of the Reverend Mr. Boucher. While he was in town he often "Lodgd at the Governor's" [45] and "Dined at Mr. Carroll of Carrollton." [46]

The Governor was probably not much pleased to hear of his old friend's appointment — Eden was a soldier himself and had too great respect for Washington as such — but the Carrolls were delighted. "I am pleased with Washington's appointment to be Generalissimo," father wrote to son, "there may be as brave & as good officers to the northward," — this with snobbish sectional doubt — "but we know Him to be a Cool prudent Man. . . ." [47]

Charles Carroll of Carrollton, again, had not been a delegate to the Continental Congress. But again he made the trip to Philadelphia in an unofficial advisory capacity. He did not stay long; Molly's condition and his own pressing duties as a member of the various patriotic committees in Maryland made his presence in Annapolis necessary. But he was kept fully conversant with the affairs of the Continental Congress, quite as if he were actually a member, and he made the acquaintance

[45] *The Diaries of George Washington 1748–1799*, edited by John C. Fitzpatrick (1925), April 15, 1773, II, 107.
[46] *Ibid.*, October 10, 1772; II, 83.
[47] June 24, 1775; Carroll Papers, IV, 297.

of a number of the delegates from the other colonies, who promptly set down in their diaries or their letters home that Mr. Carroll of Carrollton was well educated, courteous, and sensible, even though he was a Roman Catholic.

Outside of Maryland that religion of his was still being held against him. The thought habits of a lifetime are not easily broken, as Carroll himself readily understood. He did not entirely blame these gentlemen, so soon to dedicate their lives, their fortunes, and their sacred honor to the cause of liberty, for doubting that he had as much right to his religion as they had to theirs. But he would have been more than human — and he was not — if he had not rather enjoyed the Congress's politic change of front. Before so many months had passed, these same prejudiced but well-meaning gentlemen were glad enough that America had produced an inexplicable man who was patriotic and intelligent and well-educated and still a member of the Church of Rome. They needed him for a very delicate mission of national importance, a mission on which his religion would not be a handicap but a decided asset.

The First Continental Congress had — the Second Congress knew it now — expressed themselves far too emphatically on the subject of the Quebec Act. They had not stopped at describing it as "an act for extending the province of Quebec so as to border on the western frontier of these colonies, establishing an arbitrary government therein, and discouraging the settlement of British subjects in that wide extended country; thus, by the influence of civil principles and ancient prejudices, to dispose the inhabitants to act with hostility against the free Protestant colonies, whenever a wicked Ministry shall choose so to direct them," but had found themselves unable to "suppress our astonishment that a British Parliament should ever consent to establish in that country a religion that has deluged your island in blood, and dispersed impiety, bigotry, persecution, murder and rebellion through every part of the world." [48]

It was no time to call the Catholic Church names, no matter

[48] Address to the People of Great Britain; *Journals of the Continental Congress*, I, 81-9.

what the merits of the case. The American colonies could not afford to insult Canada, from which they needed not only friendship but substantial military support, and the Canadians were French and Catholic. Eventually the Congress realized that they had made a mistake, and on the last day of the session they were not ashamed to address the people of Canada thus:

"We are all too well acquainted with the liberality of sentiment distinguishing your nation, to imagine, that difference of religion will prejudice you against a hearty amity with us. You know, that the transcendent nature of freedom elevates those, who unite in her cause, above all such low-minded infirmities. The Swiss Cantons furnish a memorable proof of this truth. Their union is composed of Roman Catholic and Protestant States, living in the utmost concord and peace with one another, and thereby enabled, ever since they bravely vindicated their freedom, to defy and defeat every tyrant that has invaded them." [49]

It was beautifully expressed and full of beautiful thoughts. The contempt for "such low-minded infirmities" as religious prejudice was particularly commendable. Unfortunately, it was not very convincing. The Canadians remembered earlier and less considered expressions of the Congress and refused an invitation to send delegates to Philadelphia.

The American colonies could not afford to spare either the troops or the money for a military expedition into Canada, but now that the first amateurish attempts at diplomacy had failed General Washington succeeded in convincing Congress that it was the only thing to try. He shared the prevalent American belief that Canadian help was absolutely necessary to the success of the rebellion against England, and felt sure that an armed force sent not to oppress but to liberate and incidentally conciliate the Canadians would immediately encourage them to rebel too against the mother country. All America joined him in thinking that Canada really longed to rebel, but simply lacked the moral courage. Washington and America were later proved to have been mistaken — but this

[49] *Journals of the Continental Congress*, I, 115–7.

was only September 1775. For a while the Canadian campaign went well enough: General Richard Montgomery captured Montreal and there was great hope that General Benedict Arnold would be as successful at Quebec. Instead, Arnold was defeated and severely wounded and Montgomery, one of the most brilliantly capable American officers, was killed. Not only had the attack upon Quebec failed; there was little prospect of facility to make another attempt.

Congress thought this bulletin disquieting, as were other reports that found their way back to Philadelphia, reports of smallpox and hunger and desertion in the army, of General Arnold's trouble with General David Wooster, and of General Wooster's tactlessness with the Canadians. But Congress had no idea of the extent to which the American cause had become unpopular in Canada, thanks to the lack of American money and manners; they had no idea of the extent to which the American army itself had become a problem. In the first place, it was in miserable physical condition. Arnold's command had arrived before the walls of Quebec after undergoing the most appalling hardships. The men were not dressed or equipped to withstand the unaccustomed rigor of the Canadian winter. Their provisions had given out, and they had been forced to eat roots and boiled old leather breeches and a pet dog belonging to one of the officers. Men had dropped dead from sheer weariness. There had been a virulent outbreak of the dreaded smallpox. All these conditions had been bearable while they had been buoyed by the hope of victory, but after the defeat at Quebec the soldiers saw the Canadian situation in its true colors. They began to desert the army in appalling numbers, and their own commanders could not greatly blame them. They had not been paid for many weeks, and there was no way of even feeding them without pillaging from the Canadians. The well-fed Congress, back in Philadelphia, had instructed their officers not to alienate the Canadians, but failure to do so, and at the same time keep an American army in Canada, seemed under the circumstances an impossible paradox.

Congress, still hopefully determined to conclude a Canadian

alliance by one means or another, decided to try diplomacy again. "We have at last hit upon a plan which promises fair for success," John Adams wrote in February 1776.

"Dr Franklin and Mr Chase of Maryland and Mr Charles Carroll of Carrollton are chosen a Committee to go to Canada. . . ." [50]

[50] To James Warren, February 18, 1776; *Letters of Members of the Continental Congress*, edited by Edmund Cody Burnett (1921–31), I, 352.

CHAPTER VI

"This Civil Conflict. . . ."

1776–1778

THE THIRD MEMBER of the committee was practically unknown. Dr. Benjamin Franklin was, of course, already famous on many counts, and Mr. Chase of Maryland was rapidly making a name for himself in national affairs. But the members of Congress were kept busy writing letters to explain who Mr. Carroll of Carrollton was and why they had chosen him anyway.

"Carroll's Name and Character are equally unknown to you," John Adams wrote to a friend from Massachusetts. "I was introduced to him about Eighteen Months ago in this City and was much pleased with his Conversation. He has a Fortune as I am well informed which is computed to be worth Two hundred Thousand Pounds Sterling. He is a Native of Maryland, and his Father is still living. He had a liberal Education in France and is well acquainted with the french Nation. He speaks their Language as easily as ours; and what is perhaps of more Consequence than all the rest, he was educated in the Roman Catholic Religion and still continues to worship his Maker according to the Rites of that Church. In the Cause of American Liberty his Zeal Fortitude and Perseverance have been so conspicuous that he is said to be marked out for peculiar Vengeance by the Friends of Administration; But he continues to hazard his all, his immense Fortune, the largest in America, and his Life. This Gentleman's Character, if I foresee aright, will hereafter make a greater Figure in America. . . ."[1]

Such letters made the situation plain indeed. Congress optimistically hoped that the Canadians would mistake Mr. Carroll of Carrollton for a typical American, and thus arrive at the conclusion that the Americans were very *simpatico* people indeed. Whatever his other qualifications for public service might incidentally be, the mere presence of a Roman Catholic, as the official envoy of the American Congress, should do much to wipe out memory of the offense given in '74; and the Congress hoped that Mr. Carroll would do a little recruiting, also, in his fluent French. They expected that on account of his congenial religion he would have more influence on the Canadians than both the experienced Doctor Franklin and the enterprising Mr. Chase combined; but to make matters really sure they asked — urged — him to prevail on "Mr. John Carroll, a Roman Catholic Priest, and a Jesuit, a Gentleman of learning and Abilities," to accompany the commission.[2] Remember Jacky Carroll, of Bohemia Manor and the College of St. Omer? Father Carroll's function would be to "administer Baptism to the Canadian Children and bestow Absolution upon Such as have been refused it by the toryfied Priests in Canada. The Anathema's of the Church so terrible to the Canadians having had a disagreeable Effect upon them . . . ."[3]

Naturally, the idea of going to Canada did not appeal to John Carroll. He was not as used to left-handed compliments and ambiguous positions as his cousin by this time had become; besides, he had "observed that when the ministers of

[1] To James Warren, February 18, 1776; Burnett, *Letters of Members of the Continental Congress*, I, 354.

[2] *Ibid.*

[3] *Ibid.* I have said "Father Carroll" here because it may be less confusing to the twentieth-century reader; but in actual point of etiquette John Adams was right and I am wrong. In his period Roman Catholic priests were commonly called "Mr." The Mr. Crookshanks who introduced Charles Carroll to Louisa was a member of the Society of Jesus, and in the Carroll correspondence there are mentions of Mr. Ashton, Mr. Lewis, Mr. Chanche, and so on.

religion, leave the duties of their profession to take a busy part in political matters, they generally fall into contempt, and sometimes even bring discredit to the cause in whose service they are engaged." [4] But he was ardently interested in freedom too, and Charles Carroll of Carrollton talked him over.

Carroll left Annapolis the first part of March, expecting to set out from Philadelphia almost as soon as he got there; but Congress paused to make a number of changes in the commissioners' instructions, and it was nearly a month later when the four gentlemen set off for Canada. The wasted time, however, had not been entirely wasted from Charles Carroll's point of view. Though it was not in him deliberately to approach his problem from the social angle, as Molly had made him do with such success in Annapolis, he was too polite to refuse his invitations when everybody in Philadelphia knew that he was not at all busy, but was simply waiting for Congress to give the commissioners their papers. And Philadelphia society found that Mr. Carroll of Carrollton definitely improved upon acquaintance. By the time he left town there were quite large numbers of people who had come to the conclusion that it did not really matter whether he were a Catholic or not.

In accordance with the custom he had followed during his student days abroad, Carroll kept for his father's benefit a journal of the trip to Canada.[5] It is the only one of his journals which seems to have survived, and therefore specially interesting. Covering the period from April 2nd, when he sailed from New York up the Hudson, to June 10th, when he made the last entry back in Philadelphia, it is something of a literary effort. Weather conditions, geological formations, the exertions of the crew, and especially the beauties of nature were all disposed of in voluminous detail. At Thunder Hill Bay, an accident to the mainsail forced the boat to anchor and the

[4] Peter Guilday, *The Life and Times of John Carroll* (1922), p. 97.
[5] Brantz Mayer, *Journal of Charles Carroll of Carrollton, During his Visit to Canada in 1776, As One of the Commissioners from Congress; with a Memoir and Notes* (1876).

diarist had opportunity to explore the country thereabouts, which, he recorded, had "a wild and romantic appearance." With Samuel Chase, he "landed to examine a beautiful fall of water," but due to the divided attention of Mr. Chase, who was not primarily a nature-lover, this expedition had to be cut short. That gentleman was so "very apprehensive of the leg of mutton being boiled too much" that he hurried Carroll back on board before he had half recorded the scene to his literary satisfaction.

The commissioners found each other's company even better than the scenery. Chase and the two Carrolls were already more or less intimate, and Doctor Franklin, although a stranger, proved the ideal traveling companion. Charles Carroll had met him only a few weeks before and had liked him at sight; further acquaintance prompted him to write home to his father: "Docr Franklin is a most engaging & entertaining companion of a sweet even & lively temper full of facetious stories & always applied with judgment & introduced apropos — he is a man of extensive reading, deep thought & curious in all his enquiries: his political knowledge is not inferior to his literary & philosophical. In short I am quite charmed with him: even his age makes all these happy endowments more interesting, uncommon, & captivating. . . ." [6] Franklin was at this time seventy, and in wretched health; he had only just returned to America from England and nothing was farther from his personal desire than another diplomatic mission. Like Carroll, however, he found it always a pleasure and a privilege to sacrifice his personal desires in the cause of liberty.

Weather conditions permitting, the little ship made excellent time. On April 6th she covered ninety-six miles, bringing the commissioners nearly to Albany. There, Carroll recorded, "GENERAL SCHUYLER, . . . understanding we were coming up, came from his house, about a mile out of town, to receive us and invite us to dine with him; he behaved with great civility; lives in pretty style; has two daughters (Betsy and Peggy),

[6] March 29, 1776; Carroll Papers, IV, 330.

lively, agreeable, black-eyed girls." [7] Betsy was later Mrs. Alexander Hamilton.

General Schuyler and his family (there was also a Mrs. Schuyler whose impression on Carroll he did not find worth recording) and General John Thomas now joined the party, which proceeded by wagon to Saratoga, thirty-two miles away. The trip took a whole day, bad weather and bad ferry service making it far less pleasant than the sail up the Hudson. Carroll, however, was busy establishing with General Schuyler the friendly relations which were to last until the latter's death. "At six miles from Albany," he related, "I quitted the wagon and got on horse-back to accompany the generals to view the falls of the Mohawk's river, called the Cohooes." This time nobody hurried him and he provided his father with a full report of the situation: "The perpendicular fall is seventy-four feet, and the breadth of the river at this place, as measured by General Schuyler, is one thousand feet. The fall is considerably above one hundred feet, taken from the first ripple or still water above the perpendicular fall. The river was swollen with the melting of the snows and rains, and rolled over the frightful precipice an impetuous torrent. The foam, the irregularities in the fall broken by projecting rocks, and the deafening noise, presented a sublime but terrifying spectacle. At fifty yards from the place the water dropped from the trees, as it does after a plentiful shower, they being as wet with the ascending vapor as they commonly are after a smart rain of some continuance." [8]

The persistence of winter weather, a six-inch snow and the failure of the ice to break, delayed the commissioners several days at Saratoga. But the Schuylers' hospitality enabled their guests to take the delay philosophically. Carroll in particular, in his letters home, stressed the "agreeable company: G. Schuyler has two fine girls: they are lively & sensible, & appear to be blessed with sweet tempers. . . ." [9] And when on

[7] *Journal*, pp. 53–4.
[8] *Journal*, p. 55.
[9] To Charles Carroll of Annapolis, April 8, 1776; Carroll Papers, IV, 333.

the sixteenth the party was finally able to set off from Saratoga, he "parted with regret from the amiable family of General Schuyler; the ease and affability with which we were
treated, and the lively behavior of the young ladies, made
Saratoga a most pleasing séjour, the remembrance of which
will long remain with me." [10] Molly, at home with the babies,
no doubt found this repetition wearisome.

But Doctor Franklin, sick as he was, was still lively enough
to make up for the Schuyler girls. Carroll was to remember
much later his "flow of spirits." [11] It was needed, for the most
pleasant part of the journey was now behind the commissioners. Up to this time the four gentlemen might have been
taking a tour for amusement. They had done nothing much
but exclaim over the scenery, interest themselves in the local
customs, and get acquainted with the charming people they
met. But now, after the gay hospitalities of Saratoga, everything was suddenly changed. Real hardships were beginning.
And Charles Carroll, for one, was beginning his military
education.

This expedition was to prove of the greatest importance to
him. Aside from the fact that it is a little notable as the first
American diplomatic mission to a foreign country, it made
no real impression on history. It had never had a chance of
success. But it did make a useful public servant out of a man
who might have gone through the war an impatient idealist.
Charles Carroll had done quite a lot of phrase-making in the
early stages of the Revolution. "Stop *writing* Parliament and
give it bayonets!" is one of the grandiloquent exclamations
with which history has credited him. Like many another
patriot, he had not bothered to find out, before doing all he
could to talk his country into a war, whether such a war
would be a success or a suicide. Charles Carroll knew exactly
nothing about military affairs. He would never have made a
soldier, even if his health had permitted it. He had in fact
been more than a little bored with all the talk about troops

[10] *Journal*, p. 58.
[11] To Benjamin Franklin, August 12, 1777; Rowland, *Life*, I, 208.

and boats and rations that he had heard in Philadelphia. These things were outside his ken; they seemed almost unreal compared with such familiarities as civil rights and the necessity for liberty. He might easily have served through the war, as many of his capable contemporaries did, without ever realizing facts. The history of the American Revolution is the history of a well-meaning civilian Congress working at cross-purposes with an army whose problems it did not understand. If there had not been in Congress a few men who saw both sides of the question the result would have been tragedy. Carroll was to be one of these men. Thanks to the expedition to Canada, which thrust on him an insight into military problems he would never have been tempted to seek at first hand, he was never one of those politicians who, as Washington commented with understandable bitterness, found it easy "to draw remonstrances in a comfortable room by a good fireside. . . ." [12]

There were no more hospitable patroon mansions along the way. The commissioners were "accomodated with beds" at the "good large inn" at ruined Ford Edward, where Colonel Sinclair's regiment were already quartered; they stopped again at "Mr Wing's tavern . . . in the township of Queensbury, and Charlotte county." As they penetrated farther north, the weather grew more severe, the bays and rivers were choked with ice, and Carroll, a connoisseur of Maryland mud, recorded that he had "never travelled through worse roads." ("Through" is the word he used, not on or over.) At Fort George the commissioners were joined again by General Schuyler, and proceeded with him by boat into Montcalm Bay, where they landed for a brief refreshment — namely, "drinking tea on shore." [13] Probably a very enjoyable party, for all these gentlemen had been used to tea all their lives and appreciated the opportunity to break their patriotic fast. They hoped, though, that Canada would soon decide to do without English tea.

[12] To the President of Congress, December 23, 1777; Jared Sparks, *The Writings of George Washington*, v (1835), 200.   [13] *Journal*, p. 65.

The boats on which the commissioners traveled — thirty-footers which had been built to carry soldiers across Lake George and Lake Champlain — had been thoughtfully fitted with awnings for the occasion; even so, the four civilians were uncomfortable enough as the boats struggled through the rough waters, "entangled in the ice." [14] General Schuyler's boat, in which Chase and Carroll traveled part of the way across Lake George, had to be hauled "over a piece or neck of land thirty feet broad." Later, passing into Lake Champlain from the river connecting it with Lake George, the boats had to be placed on carriages and transported about a mile and a half overland before navigable water could again be reached. But the commissioners, determinedly cheerful, had no complaints to make. Even Doctor Franklin, physically miserable and privately convinced that he would never live to see Montreal, professed to be in the best of spirits; and Charles Carroll, suffering from the "chills and fevers" that always beset him on much slighter provocation, regretted no hardship except that the "season was not sufficiently advanced to admit of catching fish, a circumstance we had reason to regret, as they are so highly prized by the connoisseurs of good eating, and as one of our company is so excellent a judge in this science." And Molly would have been horrified to find her delicate husband, the care of whose weak chest she considered her most important mission in life, deliberately going out of his way to taste the hardships which made up a soldier's everyday life. Though the commissioners had brought comfortable beds all the way from Philadelphia, and though there was plenty of room to make up all four of them under the awning which "could effectually secure us from the wind and rain," Carroll recorded on the twenty-fifth of April: "Mr Chase and I slept this night on shore under a tent made of bushes."

General Schuyler was kept quite busy answering the questions of Mr. Carroll of Carrollton, who seemed determined to fill in the space of a few weeks the military gaps in his educa-

[14] *Journal*, p. 66.

tion. He was an apt and interested pupil. He began to fill his
journal with military minutiae, instead of with burblings about
the scenery; and before long he was able to comment intelligently. He made it his business to inspect, with Schuyler, the
forts along the way. Most of them he found in wretched
shape — Fort George "in as ruinous a condition as Fort Edward," and only "the small remains of Fort William Henry,"
which Montcalm had taken in the previous war. Crown Point
was "in ruins; it was once a considerable fortress, and the
English must have expended a large sum in constructing the
fort and erecting the barracks, which are also in ruins. . . ."
"Ticonderoga fort is in a ruinous condition; it was once a
considerable fortification. The ramparts are faced with stone.
I saw a few pieces of cannon mounted on one bastion, more
for show, I apprehend, than service. In the present state of
affairs this fort is of no other use than as an entrepot or magazine for stores. . . ." Out of his new knowledge of things
military, he also expressed the opinion that Ticonderoga had
been built in a place "not judicially chosen for the location of
a fort."

Though discouraged by what he saw, Carroll was still very
hopeful of the success of the commissioners in Canada. With
Washington, he felt sure that the aid of Canada was nearly
necessary. His enthusiasm for the mission had transcended,
too, the cold in his chest; it was undimmed when, six days
after Ticonderoga, on the afternoon of the twenty-ninth of
April, the gentlemen arrived safely in Montreal.

Tired out from their journey, on the last part of which the
roads had been particularly miserable, the commissioners were
"received by GENERAL ARNOLD, on our landing, in the most
polite and friendly manner; conducted to headquarters, where
a genteel company of ladies and gentlemen had assembled to
welcome our arrival. As we went from the landing place to
the general's house, the cannon of the citadel fired in compliment to us as the commissioners of congress. We supped at
the general's, and after supper were conducted, by the general
and other gentlemen, to our lodgings, — the house of Mr.

Thomas Walker, — the best built, and perhaps the best furnished in this town." [15]

Carroll was much pleased with General Benedict Arnold. Not only did he think highly of that gentleman's social presence and the society in which he moved, but he was impressed by his obvious efficiency as a soldier. "If this war continues, and Arnold should not be taken off pretty early," he wrote home the day after his arrival in Montreal, "he will turn out a great man; he has great vivacity, perseverence, resources, & intrepidity, and a cool judgment. . . ." [16] Carroll's own judgment was, as usual, shrewd; but as things turned out Arnold, by being "taken off pretty early" in not quite the way Carroll had meant, achieved only greatness of a certain kind.

In Montreal Carroll received from home a packet of the first letters he had had since leaving Philadelphia. Most of them were from his father. He had hoped to hear from Molly — "she has little to do and therefore may write long letters" [17] — but he was, as usual where Molly was concerned, too undiscerning to connect her silence with the liveliness of the black-eyed Schuyler girls.

The commissioners had not been in Montreal twenty-four hours before they realized that they had come on a wild-goose chase. Matters had gone too far to be easily corrected. And, which was more to the point, the commissioners had been sent to Canada with their hands effectually tied. They had received from Congress such extensive powers that Carroll, for one, felt the "almost unbounded trust . . . very burthensome"; [18] they had been given full jurisdiction over the military affairs in Canada, with authority to settle disputes and administer discipline within the army, negotiate with the Indians, and sit and vote in the councils of war. But along with these powers Congress had failed to supply them with any more money

---

[15] *Journal*, pp. 92–3.
[16] To Charles Carroll of Annapolis, April 30, 1776; Carroll Papers, IV, 340.
[17] *Ibid*.
[18] To Charles Carroll of Annapolis, March 21, 1776; Carroll Papers, IV, 326.

DOUGHOREGAN MANOR
HOWARD COUNTY, MARYLAND

than they needed for their own expenses. And it became almost immediately apparent that the whole Canadian situation hinged on money. The first letter of the commissioners to Congress struck the keynote:

"It is impossible to give you a just idea of the lowness of the Continental credit here, from the want of hard money, and the prejudice it is to our affairs. . . . The general apprehension that we shall be driven out of the Province as soon as the King's troops can arrive, concurs with the frequent breaches of promise the inhabitants have experienced, in determining them to trust our people no further. . . . Therefore, till the arrival of money, it seems improper to propose the Federal union of this Province with the others, as the few friends we have here will scarce venture to exert themselves in promoting it, till they see our credit recovered, and a sufficient army arrived to secure the possession of the country." [19]

Money was needed not only to impress the Canadians and to pay the debts already contracted — for the latter purpose the commissioners asked Congress for twenty thousand pounds in specie — but to purchase necessities for the troops: "The want of money frequently constrains the commanders to have recourse to violence in providing the army with carriages, and other conveniences, which indispose and irritate the minds of the people." This was very probably an understatement. "We have reason to conclude that the change of sentiments, which we understand has taken place in this colony, is owing to the above-mentioned cause, and to other arbitrary proceedings." [20]

In short, the necessity for money was so vital, so essentially a first hurdle, that the commissioners found they could do nothing at all. They themselves were discredited in the eyes of the Canadian people, since they had been expected to bring money with them; when they arrived without a cent, the Canadians arrived without difficulty at the obvious conclu-

[19] Peter Force, *American Archives*, v, 1166.
[20] Benjamin Franklin, Samuel Chase, and Charles Carroll of Carrollton to John Hancock, President of Congress, May 6, 1776; *American Archives*, v, 1214.

sion that Congress had provided their commissioners with no money because there was no money to provide. No wonder they wanted Canada to join them in their war! The diplomacy of Franklin, the eloquence of Chase, the French education and Catholic religion of the two Carrolls were of no avail until "hard money" healed the breach between the Americans and the Canadians. Nothing else would satisfy. Even the Indians, no longer simple savages to be put off with beads and beaver hats, promised neutrality and accepted a little gift only on condition that "when the hatchet is delivered up" a much larger present would be forthcoming.[21] The commissioners had no notion where this larger present was coming from.

Father Carroll had a duty apart from the military duties of the official commissioners, and he did it doggedly, knowing now that there was no use to try. The leaders of his church were barely polite to him. In Canada, they told him, church property had always been respected until the Americans came. Church services had not been interfered with. Priests had been treated courteously. Naturally, the Canadian Catholics had not been favorably impressed with that representative of General Washington, General David Wooster, who had closed the churches on Christmas Eve, and had said pleasantly to a committee that called upon him afterwards: "I regard you all as enemies and rascals."[22] Nothing that Father Carroll could say did any good. In fact there was little that he conscientiously could say.

None of the commissioners was enjoying the stay in Montreal. To Congress they reported themselves "in a critical and most irksome situation, pestered hourly with demands, great and small, that they cannot answer, in a place where our cause has a majority of enemies, the garrison weak, and a greater would, without money, increase our difficulties."[23] This embarrassment must have been far more annoying to

[21] *Ibid.*
[22] Edward Dean Sullivan, *Benedict Arnold: Military Racketeer* (1932), p. 125.
[23] May 8, 1776; Force, *American Archives*, v, 1237.

Carroll, who had never lacked sufficient money in his life, than, for example, to Mr. Chase.

Still the commissioners would not despair. If Congress would only send them the money, if the God of Battles would send a little success to back it up, it might yet "be possible to regain the affections of the people, to attach them firmly to our cause, and induce them to accept a free Government, perhaps to enter into the Union." [24]

This letter was written the eighth of May. It was not until two days later that the commissioners learned that General Thomas, commanding the inadequate garrison at Quebec, had been surprised by British warships coming up the river. Landing a force of a thousand men and six cannon, the enemy proceeded to overwhelm two hundred and fifty Americans, the outposts of the garrison, capture all the cannon and small arms, and take possession of the camp and the two hundred inactives who were left behind when the retreat turned into a rout. Coupled with the intelligence that Congress professed itself unable to send any money, it was a fatal blow to the American cause in Canada. "We are afraid," the commissioners were forced to report to Philadelphia, "it will not be in our power to render our country any further services in this Colony." [25]

Doctor Franklin thought he might as well go home. The poor old man had been suffering from the cold weather, the gout, and the weight of his seventy years all along the journey. Even by the time the commissioners reached Saratoga he had concluded that the Canadian expedition would be his last in the service of his country; and, feeling himself a dying man, composed certain letters "by way of farewell." But the Schuyler hospitality had restored his flagging optimism if not his health, and he had recovered sufficiently to compose songs for the company to sing,[26] and to resume the trip in his familiar capacity as the life of the party. He was pitifully unwell,

[24] *Ibid.*
[25] To Philip Schuyler, May 10, 1776; *American Archives*, VI, 451.
[26] Enclosed in a letter from Charles Carroll of Carrollton to Mary Darnall Carroll, April 15, 1776; Carroll Papers, IV, 335.

however, during all of his stay in Canada, and suffered intensely from the cold. Doctor Franklin would have been the last person to turn back until it was sure that the mission was a failure; but once this was established the other two commissioners encouraged him to make all haste home to Philadelphia. There were still matters to attend to, but Chase and Carroll could handle them, and Father John Carroll, whose presence was certainly no longer required, offered to accompany the invalid. A real friendship, one that would last to the end of their lives, had been established between the wise old deist and the two Catholic Carrolls; hearty, extroverted Mr. Chase had frequently been bored by the three-cornered discussions with which the others had brightened their journey.

The commission broke up the eleventh of May, and Carroll resumed his entries in the unofficial journal he was keeping for his father. And, now that there was no longer any particular reason for diplomatic secrecy, his letters home became more informative. "The principal part of our Commission is frustrated by this sudden turn in our affairs," he wrote, reporting the British victory, "and tho' our stay can be of no great service yet as in the present circumstances our departure would discourage our troops & friends in the country we have resolved to remain here till further advices from below. . . ." [27] Chase and Carroll had also to inquire more fully into the situation of the army. The three commissioners had recommended that General Wooster be removed from his high command, and hoped that this would correct a large part of the abuses. General Thomas's command, which had retreated to Deschambault after the disastrous encounter with the British, was urged to make a stand at the mouth of the Sorel River near Montreal. Carroll himself went to La Prairie to inquire into the practicability of the idea; "went to St. John's to examine into the state of the garrison, and of the batteaux"; went to Chambly where a council of war would shortly be held. Everywhere he found the situation of the American cause

[27] To Charles Carroll of Annapolis, May 10, 1776; Carroll Papers, IV, 342.

distressing. "We are unable to express our apprehensions of the distress our Army must soon be reduced to from the want of provisions, and the small-pox," Chase and Carroll wrote to General Schuyler. "If further reinforcements are sent without pork to victual the whole Army, our soldiers must perish or feed on each other. Even plunder, the last resource of strong necessity, will not relieve their wants." [28] And the journal records: "We got early this morning [May 23rd] to Chamblay, where we found all things in much confusion, extreme disorder and negligence, our credit sunk, and no money to retrieve it with. We were obliged to pay three silver dollars for the carriage of three barrels of gunpowder from Little Chamblay River to Longueil, the officer who commanded the guard not having a single shilling." [29]

Wearied and disgusted with the situation in which they found themselves, and still unable from want of money to relieve it, the commissioners looked eagerly forward to the time when they might conscientiously return to Maryland. "I long most ardently to be at home and am quite sick of the confused state of things in this province," Carroll wrote to his father; [30] and again, "I have never suffered so much uneasiness in my life as during my stay here: we are incessantly occupied & obliged to act in twenty different characters. . . ." [31] But finally, on May 30th, he was able to record in his journal: "The council of war was held this day, and determined to maintain possession of the country between the St. Lawrence and the Sorel, if possible; — in the meantime to dispose matters so as to make an orderly retreat out of Canada."

Home the two commissioners started without appreciable delay; we must suspect them of having had their portemanteaux already packed. The more advanced season made the weather pleasanter for traveling; there was no ice this time to delay them, and in little more than a week after they had

---

[28] May 11, 1776; Force, *American Archives*, VI, 481.
[29] *Journal*, p. 99.
[30] May 16, 1776; Carroll Papers, IV, 343.
[31] To Charles Carroll of Annapolis, May 17, 1776; *ibid.*, IV, 344.

set out from Chambly Carroll made the last entries in his journal:

"9th. Arrived at New York at one o'clock, P. M.; waited on General Washington at Motier's; — saw Generals Gates and Putnam, and my old acquaintance and friend, Mr. Moylan. About six o'clock in the evening got into General Washington's barge, in company with Lord Stirling, and was rowed round by Staten Island and the Kilns, within two miles of Elizabeth-town, where we got by ten at night.

"10th. Set off from Elizabeth-town half-past five. Got to Bristol at eight o'clock, P. M.: — at nine, embarked in our boats, and were rowed down the Delaware to Philadelphia, where we arrived at two o'clock in the night."

The Journal of Congress records that on the eleventh of June "Mr. Chase and Mr. Carroll of Carrollton, two of the Commissioners being arrived from Canada, attended and gave an account of their proceedings and the state of the army in that country." The next day Congress received from the commissioners a formal report in writing. This document seems not to have survived, but no doubt it said much what Charles Carroll had said in a letter written from Montreal: "War must decide who are to be masters of Canada, George the 3d or the united Colonies: our commission was to settle a governt, or rather to induce the Canadians to settle one for themselves: this is no longer practicable they must receive a governt from their masters, they are not fit to choose one for themselves. . . ." [32]

If the commissioners were the bearers of nothing but bad news to the Congress, the Congress had a piece of good news for them. Carroll felt like cheering when he heard that Richard Henry Lee of Virginia had within the last few days introduced a resolution that "the United Colonies are, and of right ought to be, free and independent States, and that all political connection between them and the State of Great Britain is, and ought to be, totally dissolved." [33] This resolution was not

[32] To Charles Carroll of Annapolis, May 17, 1776; Carroll Papers, IV, 344.
[33] June 7, 1776.

yet to be voted upon, but Carroll found that the "desire of Independence is gaining ground rapidly." [34]

This was in the neighborhood of Philadelphia. News from Annapolis was not so encouraging.

With Chase and Carroll in Canada — both of them influential leaders of the more radical element which felt that it was too late to talk of reconciliation with the mother country — it had not been too difficult for the conservative wing to control the convention which had met in Annapolis May the eighth. This convention accordingly instructed its delegates to Congress: "That as this Convention is firmly persuaded that a reunion with Great Britain on constitutional principles would most effectually secure the rights and liberties, and increase the strength and promote the happiness of the whole empire, objects which this province hath ever had in view, the said deputies are bound and directed to govern themselves by the instructions in its session of December last, in the same manner as if the said instructions were particularly repeated." [35]

Chase and Carroll were disgusted. Carroll in particular had been increasingly sure, during the Canadian trip, of the need for separation. English dealings with the Indians had been, he felt, the last straw: "What do you think of the british Governt that can stoop to hire such allies?" he wrote from Montreal. "Shall we not bid an eternal adieu to that detestable Governt? — I execrate it from my soul. . . ." [36]

But there was still hope that the damage might be undone. Action in Congress on the motion to declare the colonies free had been delayed to July fourth; and, in the meantime, on June twenty-first, there would be a new Maryland convention. Maryland conservatives had fervently hoped that Chase and Carroll would both be delayed past that time, either in

[34] To Charles Carroll of Annapolis, June 11, 1776; Carroll Papers, IV, 348.
[35] Rowland, *Life*, I, 177, quoting the convention journal.
[36] To Charles Carroll of Annapolis, May 28, 1776; Carroll Papers, IV, 346. About the time Carroll was writing this letter, the Congress of his own country was authorizing General Schuyler to engage the services of two thousand Indians.

Canada or at least in Philadelphia. But on the twenty-first, when the convention met according to schedule in Annapolis, there sat Samuel Chase, looking so terribly pleased with himself that his red face beamed like a diabolical sunrise. On the twenty-fourth Charles Carroll of Carrollton also took his seat. It is significant that, four days later, the convention "Resolved, that the instructions given to the Convention of December last (and renewed by the Convention in May) to the delegates of this Colony in Congress be recalled, and the restrictions therein contained removed; that the deputies of this Colony attending in Congress, or a majority of them, or any three or more of them, be authorized and empowered to concur with the other united Colonies, or a majority of them in declaring the United Colonies free and independent States, provided the sole and exclusive right of regulating the internal government and police [sic] of this Colony be reserved to the people thereof." [37]

"Principally instrumental in obtaining the passage of this resolution," says McSherry flatly, "was Charles Carroll of Carrollton." [38] Though the evidence is purely circumstantial, the records show us no reason to quarrel with his assertion.

Not long after the delegates had been instructed to vote for liberty, Maryland said good-bye to its proprietary governor in a touching and surely unique little scene. All this time Robert Eden had remained in Annapolis, living at the Government House and dining out with his friends as usual. He had always been personally popular; now many of his weaknesses, even his connection with the hated Lord Proprietary, had been greatly outweighed by his conduct during the trying last few years. He had always been liked; now he had made himself respected. "It has ever been my endeavor," he wrote home to England, "by the most soothing measures I could safely use, and yielding to storm, when I could not resist it, to preserve some hold of the helm of government, that I might steer as long as possible, clear of those shoals which

[37] Rowland, *Life*, I, 178, quoting the convention journal.
[38] James McSherry, *History of Maryland* (1904), p. 195.

all here must, sooner or later, I fear, get shipwrecked upon." [39]
How well he had succeeded was evidenced by the reception
the Council of Safety gave Congress's well-meaning suggestion that Eden ought to be arrested. Congress had read an
intercepted letter to Eden from Lord George Germaine, and
promptly passed a resolution requesting Maryland to eliminate
a man whom they considered a dangerous enemy.[40] Maryland had no idea of doing so, and the Council of Safety wrote
Congress a rather sharp note to that effect.[41] "The council
. . . acted on this critical occasion with the utmost moderation and delicacy," Governor Eden's secretary admitted.[42] He
was required only to give his parole not to leave the continent.
He agreed, and relations between governor and patriots continued as cordial as before. Next month, however — the letter
had been intercepted in April — even his old friends realized
that it was no longer possible for Eden to remain in Maryland.
He had received definite orders to take an active part in British
armament.[43] On May 23rd the convention tactfully suggested
that the governor's departure for England would be welcome; [44] and, as soon as he could get his affairs in order, he
embarked on a British warship. Large numbers of his neighbors came to see him off, and a spokesman for the crowd made
a pleasant little speech asserting the general admiration for
Governor Eden and the hope that he would come back to
Annapolis one day. (And, after the war, he did!)

Now that it was definitely committed in favor of independ-

[39] To Lord Dartmouth, date not given; Dictionary of American Biography, VI, 17.
[40] Eddis, Letters from America, pp. 278–82. A copy of the letter from
John Hancock, President of Congress, to the Maryland Council of Safety
is found in the unpublished Maryland archives, Red Book I, 46.
[41] Archives, XI, 349–50.
[42] Eddis, Letters from America, pp. 280–1.
[43] Lord George Germaine to Robert Eden, December 23, 1775; Red
Book I, 42. This letter (printed in Force, American Archives, IV, 440–1)
mentions "a great deal of very useful information" which Germaine had
received from Eden, and orders him to "give facility and assistance" to "An
armament consisting of seven regiments, with a fleet of frigates and small
ships, . . . now in readiness to proceed to the Southern Colonies, in order
to attempt the restoration of legal Government in that part of America."
[44] Eddis, Letters from America, pp. 281–2.

ence, the Maryland convention made choice of what the Tories called "a pack of damn'd Radicals" to Congress. Among the new delegates was a man who a few years before would have been considered totally ineligible, and who even more recently had considered himself so.

This time, Charles Carroll of Carrollton did not refuse to represent his province in Continental affairs. His change of front was significant, for the circumstances in which he found himself had not much changed since 1774. It was true that sentiment against Roman Catholics, occasioned by the Quebec Act, had grown less bitter with the passage of time; it was true also that many of the most prejudiced members of Congress had changed their minds about Mr. Carroll's fitness to hold public office. Although the mission to Canada had been a failure, it was generally recognized now that the scheme had never had a chance for success, and Mr. Carroll had been commended on all sides for his capable handling of an impossible situation. There remained enough bigotry, however, for him still to reason that somebody else would represent Maryland more advantageously than he. Only one circumstance made him feel that he could be of special use if he accepted a seat in the Congress. This was the fact that America was trying to negotiate an alliance with France.

The same qualifications which had made it desirable for Carroll to join the commission to Canada made it desirable for him to take a part in this vitally important matter. His long residence in France, his fluency in the French tongue, his Catholic religion and his understanding of the French point of view all contributed to his usefulness. Various members of Congress, over a social glass in Philadelphia, had hinted pretty broadly to Mr. Carroll that if the Maryland Convention should see fit to elect him again as a delegate — and everybody knew that the First Citizen could get anything he wanted out of that same Maryland Convention — Congress would welcome him with considerable enthusiasm.

As at the time he had been asked to go to Canada, some of Carroll's family and friends resented the left-handed compliment which sought to make use of a man who otherwise would not have been considered a suitable member. Carroll himself did not resent it at all. "If men would lay aside little bye views & party disputes It would be a pleasure, as well as a duty, to serve the Public," he wrote when his election to Congress was in the wind, "but men will be men." [45] He understood exactly what he was getting into. Where public service was concerned, however, he apparently had no pride. He had stayed out of Congress in previous years because he had conceived that he would serve Maryland best by doing so; but now that he had decided that it was his duty to enter Congress no amount of urging could keep him away from Philadelphia.

Personally he found it a very inconvenient duty. He had not liked his first venture into national affairs. For one thing, he was not used to being away from home for any length of time and he missed his father and his books and his favorite horse and the unobtrusive comfort of his big brick house on Spa Creek. He even became a little sentimental about Molly and the children. Although he had not broken over to the extent of writing most of the letters home to his wife instead of to his father, he did send "dear Molly" his love with more enthusiasm than usual, actually sent a message to "kiss little Poll" for him,[46] and admitted that he wished he "could hear a little of two shoe's prattle." [47] He saw it as a distinct disadvantage that it was out of the question for Molly and the babies to accompany him to Philadelphia. Molly would have loved to go; she was not the kind of female who appreciated being left behind and had been sadly disappointed not to be taken on the Canadian commission, a journey full of hardships which most ladies of her day would not have thought alluring. In Philadelphia, of course, she would have had the time of her life. But she was simply not well enough to stand the pace. Already broken in health, she was expecting her fifth child; Doctor Scott had shaken his head when he heard about it.

[45] To Charles Carroll of Annapolis, June 28, 1776; Carroll Papers, IV, 351.
[46] To Charles Carroll of Annapolis, March 4, 1776; Carroll Papers, IV, 320.
[47] To Charles Carroll of Annapolis, March 29, 1776; *ibid.*, IV, 330.

Business duties presented another problem. Though in most people's eyes Charles Carroll of Carrollton was to be envied as a gentleman of leisure, actually he was overwhelmed with private business. He took care of all the details of the great Carroll fortune — a full-time job. Nor could he readily hand it back to his father, now that he was going into Continental politics. His father was seventy-four. Finally, there was the fact that Charles Carroll of Carrollton had discovered, from his familiarity with the workings of previous sessions of Congress, that he would not find a political career very agreeable. He was not fatuous enough to think that the gentlemen already in Philadelphia would take kindly to any attempts of his to correct the faults in their assembly, but he did dislike the welter of inefficiency and thick-headedness and pomposity he knew he was getting into. He still thought public service was a privilege as well as a duty, but he had lost any illusions he had had about its being a pleasure.

The new delegates to Congress had been chosen on July fourth, the same day that Congress was voting for independence. As the Maryland Convention was still in session, Carroll did not go at once to Philadelphia; but he took his seat there July eighteenth.

Mr. Carroll of Carrollton was politely received and promptly placed on certain committees. The very day he got there he was one of three gentlemen appointed to examine and report on some intercepted letters from Lord Howe to the colonial governors. On the nineteenth, he was made the sixth member of the Board of War, one of the most important, if not the most important, of the committees in Congress. This group had charge of all the executive business connected with the military department. Carroll, of course, had some experience along this line in Canada, and he was cordially welcomed by the overworked Board as (to quote Chairman John Adams) "An excellent member whose education, manners, and application to business and to study, did honor to his fortune, the first in America." [48]

[48] *The Works of John Adams*, edited by Charles Francis Adams (1850–6), III, 60.

The most momentous business before the Congress, at the time Charles Carroll took his seat, was the matter of the Declaration of Independence. Though Congress had voted in favor of it on July fourth, the document had to be engrossed on parchment and was not ready for signature until the second day of August. Charles Carroll of Carrollton, as befitted the newest delegate, was the last to sign for Maryland, recording his customary signature in his customary small, firm hand.

(It should be unnecessary to deny again that most familiar Charles Carroll story. As firmly rooted in American history as George Washington's cherry-tree, it goes usually like this:

"Will you sign?" John Hancock asked Carroll, offering him the quill. "Most willingly," he replied, and, coming forward, wrote "Charles Carroll" at the bottom of the parchment. "There go a few millions!" remarked one of the bystanders. He voiced the general opinion, that Carroll was a patriot indeed to hazard the greatest fortune in America; but another gentleman was more cynical. "Oh, no, he will get off!" the latter assured him *sotto voce*. "There are so many Charles Carrolls." Our hero heard him. Full of pride and injured dignity, he stepped forward to take up the quill again, this time to add "of Carrollton" to his signature. The world in general, and George III in particular, might make no mistake about him!

This is one of the nicest bits of grandiloquence in our glorious history. It is a real pity it is not true; but we have seen already that, ever since his return to America, Charles Carroll had consistently written "of Carrollton" after his name. It was quite as much a part of his signature as the Charles or the Carroll.

It is probable, however, that the legend is founded on fact, and that the recorded remarks really were made by gentlemen who were not familiar with Mr. Carroll of Carrollton's writing habits, and who were politely refraining from looking over his shoulder.)

Though extremely busy with his duties as a member of the Board of War, in addition to attending the sessions of Congress, Carroll had no idea of lessening his activity in Maryland politics. "I hold my resolution of being at our Convention provided I am chosen of it," he wrote a few days after his arrival in Philadelphia: "if I should be left out, I shall remain here till I am superseded, or a new deputation made out." [49] He judged, and correctly, that he was more indispensable in the affairs of his own state than in those of the nation. In Annapolis, the First Citizen was a person of the greatest influence; in Philadelphia he was merely a cadet member of Congress whose weight as a man of wealth, education, and devoted purpose did not quite make up for the fact that he was a Roman Catholic. But there shows also here the distressing tendency that Carroll always had, and that he shared with most of the patriots from Washington on down, to feel loyalty and duty to his state before he felt it to his country, and to put the former unhesitatingly first whenever he was confronted with a choice. It will appear again and again in his political career, even when he is most loudly asserting his belief in the necessity for a strong central government.

Most of the Maryland delegates, sharing Carroll's views, returned to Annapolis with him, leaving Thomas Stone as the state's sole representative in the Continental assembly. The Maryland Convention met August 14, 1776, and William Paca and Charles Carroll of Carrollton were elected the new delegates from Annapolis. Before this convention was the important business of framing a form of government for the State of Maryland. Charles Carroll of Carrollton, of course, was one of the seven gentlemen chosen to prepare a Maryland Declaration of Rights and Constitution.[50] Accordingly prepared and presented to the convention August 27th, these were referred to the October session, and the convention closed September 17th. On the last day it voted that the members of Congress should immediately return to Philadelphia.

Those were the days when politics really inconvenienced politicians. Back to Philadelphia after only a month in Annapolis, back again to Annapolis, over the terrible roads whose

[49] To Charles Carroll of Annapolis, July 23, 1776; Carroll Papers, IV, 356.
[50] Force, *American Archives*, I, 1054-5.

ruts had just been accented by the first frost, when he had
hardly rested from his journey. At the October session of the
Maryland Convention the Bill of Rights was reported on October 31st and as amended agreed to November 3rd. The Constitution was taken up November 1st and adopted a week later.
Carroll thought this was rushing things a bit. "Our affairs are
in a very critical situation," he had written to his father October 4th: "whether we shall go into ye consideration of our bill
of rights & form of govt I know not: to judge from ye temper
of the house I think we shall tho' I think that matter had better
be postponed till there is greater certainty, than we have at
present, of possessing a country & People to govern. . . ." [51]
    It is fairly sure that the famous Maryland Bill of Rights was
first drafted by Charles Carroll the Barrister,[52] who was also a
member of the committee. This gentleman was a distant cousin
of Charles Carroll of Carrollton, saw much of him socially, and
was connected with him in private business. From the historian's point of view, it is a thousand pities that on top of
this they felt a simultaneous urge to serve their state politically. As a result they have been mixed up for more than a
hundred and fifty years. They are indexed improperly in almost every source book. Charles Carroll the Barrister was an
extremely capable man, even though he was not of his cousin's
stature either actually or potentially. There are still a few
die-hards who credit the Bill of Rights to Charles Carroll of
Carrollton, not so much from the evidence in this particular
case as from the fact that the Signer usually did the work, by
himself, of any committee he happened to be placed on. The
greater bulk of the evidence weighs for the Barrister. We do
know, however, that Charles Carroll of Carrollton was in great
part responsible for the writing of the Constitution, his pet
clause being that which set forth the manner of electing the
members of the State Senate. "I was one of the Committee,
that framed the Constitution of this State, and the mode of
chusing the Senate was suggested by me," he wrote many years

[51] Carroll Papers, IV, 366B.
[52] 1723–1783.

later; "no objection was made to it in the Committee, as I remember, except by Mr Johnson, who disliked the Senate's filling up the vacancies in their own body. I replied that if by the mode of chusing Senators by election were deemed eligible, the filling up of vacancies by that body was inevitable, as the Electors could not be convened to make choice of a Senator on every vacancy, and that the Senate acting under the sanction of an oath and l'esprit de corps, would insure the election of the fittest men for that station, nor do I recollect while I was in the Senate, that the power intrusted to it in this instance was ever abused or perverted to party views. . . ." [53] This system was in use till 1837.

In the midst of the important session which dealt with the Constitution and the Bill of Rights, Charles Carroll of Carrollton had had to obtain leave of absence "on account of the indisposition of his family." [54] This was poor Molly again. They were beginning to be really anxious about her. She had always been delicate; four children in six years had not improved her state of health and she had not yet fulfilled her duty as a colonial mother. Anne Brooke Carroll was born in this year, 1776, and there were two more babies yet to follow. Molly had been in almost constant pain for many months; now the "pain in Her Breast" became much worse.[55] Over and over again she "set a resolution not to take any more opium," [56] but each time found herself unable to keep it. Her father-in-law thought she was too ill for her husband to leave at any time, but Charles Carroll of Carrollton's devotion to public business would not let him agree. He was promptly in his seat when the Continental Congress met in December 1776. But this session was conveniently held at Baltimore, for Congress, afraid that the capital was about to be captured by the British, had moved out of Philadelphia bag and baggage.

[53] To Virgil Maxcy, December 29, 1817; Rowland, *Life*, I, 190–1.
[54] Rowland, *Life*, I, 188.
[55] E.g., Charles Carroll of Annapolis to Charles Carroll of Carrollton, April 22, 1779; Carroll Papers, VI, 516.
[56] E.g., Charles Carroll of Carrollton to Charles Carroll of Annapolis, May 8, 1779; *ibid.*, VI, 525A.

Congress was still in session when, on February 5, 1777, the first assembly of the State of Maryland convened at Annapolis. .This assembly was called together by the Council of Safety, the committee which had governed Maryland pending the declaration of liberty and the establishment of a more formalized government and which was now meeting for the last time to yield up its authority to its successor.

Like the other new states, Maryland in setting up a form of government for itself had retained many of the features of the old colonial government. The system of courts remained practically the same, and the administration was carried on by a governor, a governor's council, and a bicameral assembly of which the upper and lower houses were now called the Senate and the House of Representatives.

The members elected to the first Maryland Senate were Charles Carroll of Carrollton, George Plater, Daniel of St. Thomas Jenifer, William Paca, Thomas Stone, Joseph Nicholson Jr., Brice Thomas Beale Worthington, Turbutt Wright, Samuel Wilson, James and Matthew Tilghman, Robert Goldsborough, Charles Carroll the Barrister, Thomas Johnson, and Thomas Contee. Edward Tilghman was elected in the place of James Tilghman, who refused to serve; and, he also refusing, Thomas B. Hands was chosen. Charles Graham was elected in place of Thomas Johnson, who also declined. Johnson was elected to the governorship February 13th.

Charles Carroll of Carrollton, along with the other gentlemen who were delegates to Congress, was not eligible to be considered for governor. Nor was he eligible for membership in the governor's council, for the same reason. The latter prohibition his friends gracefully recognized by electing his father, Charles Carroll of Annapolis, a councillor. It was a foregone conclusion that his age would keep him from accepting, and in a few days he did "politely decline," but the old man greatly appreciated the compliment.[57]

An explosion was certainly averted by the refusal of Charles

---

[57] Charles Carroll of Carrollton to Charles Carroll of Annapolis, February 13, 1777; Carroll Papers, IV, 374A.

Carroll of Annapolis to take an active part in political affairs. His son had in the fall session of 1776 served on the committee "to prepare a scheme for the emission of bills of credit, to enable the State to carry on its defence against British invasion." Now the first State Assembly passed "An Act to make the bills of credit emitted by Acts of Assembly and resolves of the late Convention a legal tender." Carroll of Annapolis had already expressed himself strongly on the subject: "Should a Law pass to make the Continental & Our Currencies a legal Tender in all cases, it will Surpass in Iniquity all the Acts of the British Parlamt agt America," he wrote on March 13th. "The Parliament only declares it has a right to take away Our Property the duties they have imposed are trifling, But the Act wh you say will Pass, takes away a Reall & Universall Medium of Commerce by Substituting a Medium wh Eventually may be of no Value." [58]

Charles Carroll of Carrollton heartily agreed. He thought the spirit of the law was good, but thought also that the law as framed was unjust and would fail to serve its purpose. Certainly it would be a severe financial blow to the Carroll fortune. Much of the family money was put out at interest, and the tender bill made it possible for the persons to whom good hard money had been loaned before the Revolution to cancel the obligation by payment in the paper money issued by the new and not too stable government. The phrase "not worth a continental" was to become one of the most expressive of the day, and the state emissions could not be flatteringly described either.

It was not surprising that the Carrolls should personally oppose the law; nor was it surprising that Mr. Samuel Chase, who was always up to his ears in debt and not too scrupulous about making his creditors' lives a misery, should be one of the tender bill's warmest supporters. Carroll of Annapolis had never got much fun out of trying to pick a quarrel with his son, who always remained calm and always pointed out that cool dispassionate reasoning would accomplish more than heat. But

[58] To Charles Carroll of Carrollton; Carroll Papers, IV, 377.

Samuel Chase was a different matter. He gave as good as he got, and, like the elder Carroll, welcomed any opportunity to give his temper a workout. Much to the distress of the younger Carroll the two exchanged fiery letters over a period of months, very nearly a year. Even when Chase, who was coming out second-best in the controversy, would have let the matter drop his adversary would not permit it. "I have heard You should say yr Freindship for my Son prevented yr exposing my former letters on ye Subject of the Tender Bill," he wrote Chase November 1, 1777: "As you promoted & voted for So iniquitous a Law you may be as little influenced by a sense of Freindship as by a regard to Honesty & Justice. . . . I plainly tell you the Law is a Pickpocket Law . . ." and so on through four full pages of cracks.[59]

To add insult to injury he sent these letters to Chase in care of his own son, to be delivered by him. Charles Carroll of Carrollton simply neglected to do it. He was getting desperate. His father now was threatening to publish his correspondence with Chase and affirmed that he would gladly go to jail for the pleasure of doing so. "There is a time," the younger Carroll tried to convince him, "when it is wisdom to yield to injustice, and to popular frensies & delusions: many wise and good men have acted so."[60] But his father wrote stiffly back: "I am sorry my letter to Chase was not delivered as I first directed. I look upon yr fears & Prudence as Idle & out of Season. . . . Are you not too fond of Popularity & has not that Fondness biased yr Judgment?"[61] Charles Carroll of Carrollton replied as stiffly: "I assure you I am not fond of popularity, because I am convinced it is often gained by the unworthy: I would wish to deserve the good opinion of the good & discerning; now I am sure the bulk of mankind are neither good, nor discerning, and 'tis for this very reason I wish you to avoid all publications relative to ye tender bill . . . . I am never for shewing my teeth till I can bite."[62]

[59] Carroll Papers, v, 438A.
[60] November 13, 1777; Carroll Papers, v, 444.
[61] November 14, 1777; *ibid.*, v, 445.
[62] November 15, 1777; *ibid.*, v, 447.

It was the first time that father and son had ever been at odds. They patched it up, but the subject rankled for years. In 1780 Carroll of Annapolis was still railing at the tender law with the same enthusiasm he had shown in 1777.[63]

The first Maryland Assembly adjourned April 20, 1777, but Carroll of Carrollton did not return to his seat in the Congress till May 5th, "domestic & plantation affairs" detaining him. The domestic affairs were, of course, Molly's continued bad health. He had had to ask for another leave of absence during this session.

When his duties on the Board of War — to which he was reappointed four days after he returned to Philadelphia — did not take him away from the meetings of Congress, Carroll lodged at the house of a Mrs. Yard, in Second Street opposite the City Tavern. It was a popular boarding-house which received no little luster from the several celebrities who lived there. Among them was General Benedict Arnold, one of the most capable officers of the Revolution and an acquaintance of Carroll's since the futile mission to Canada. Carroll admired his abilities very much, though they had personally very little in common. He thought Arnold had a brilliant future. Certainly he had a remarkable grasp of the military situation in America, and his conversation was of great value to Carroll, who, acting in a semi-military capacity as a member of the Board of War, now realized more sharply than ever the scantiness of his knowledge of military science and tactics. He was valuable to the Board, however, because he could approach its problems not as a soldier but as a business-man, a good manager who had made a great fortune greater because he would never tolerate laziness or dishonesty or inefficiency. His chief value was his capacity for hard work. He was always in bad health and had the unhappy faculty of catching cold every time he slept in a strange bed; his wife and at least one of his delicate children were always ill back in Annapolis; his private business affairs were suffering badly from his neglect of them;

[63] E.g., to Charles Carroll of Carrollton, December 9, 1780; Carroll Papers, VII, 629.

but, nevertheless, Mr. Carroll faithfully continued to travel from one camp to another, checking on the abuses too prevalent in the American armies. On his "large map" Charles Carroll Senior traced his son's progress from Baltimore Furnace to "Johnson's Ferry on Susquehanna Cecil County," and from "G. Washington's head quarters at ye yellow springs" to "Reading Furnace" in Pennsylvania.[64] He moved on to Potts Groves and then to Lancaster, where the Congress met September 27, 1777. This last move was specially inconvenient in that it interrupted his duties for the Board of War; but "Mr. Smith, one of our delegates, being returned home I must proceed to Congress to keep up a representation from our State." [65] He found that Congress "still continues the same noisy, empty & talkative Assembly it always was since I have known it." [66] This from York, where Congress had moved "not thinking themselves secure from light parties of the Enemy at Lancaster." [67]

Carroll's low opinion of the Congress was shared by a member of the clearest thinkers of the day, some of them members of Congress themselves. He was a statesman by instinct — he could never have been a soldier — but all his other instincts constantly revolted against the wasted time and wasted opportunities for which the Congress was always notable. Up to this time Carroll along with most other people had charitably laid Congress' many mistakes and incidents of mismanagement to inexperience, but by the fall of 1777 it was plain that something far more organic was the trouble. A definite conspiracy was under way to displace the commander-in-chief.

It was a gigantic tragi-comedy played by ambitious men. Congress and the army were not crowded — and never had been— with political green carnations like Charles Carroll of

[64] Charles Carroll of Carrollton to Charles Carroll of Annapolis, September 11 and 18, 1777; Carroll Papers, v, 418 and 420.
[65] To George Washington, September 22, 1777; Burnett, *Letters of Members of the Continental Congress*, II, 499.
[66] To Charles Carroll of Annapolis, October 5, 1777; Carroll Papers, v, 427.
[67] To Charles Carroll of Annapolis, September 29, 1777; *ibid.*, v, 425.

Carrollton, who counted it a privilege to serve, and asked nothing for himself. Circumstances had kept Carroll's political attitudes from developing naturally, and because of his abnormal background he was always an abnormal public servant; but it was only reasonable that the members of Congress and the officers of the army, while sufficiently interested in the sweet principles of liberty, should be interested too in the personal opportunities the war presented. Washington, himself a normally ambitious male, showed himself a first-rate psychologist too when he wrote Congress, September 24, 1776: "When men are irritated and the passions inflamed, they fly hastely and chearfully to Arms; but after the first emotions are over, to expect . . . that they are influenced by any other principles than those of Interest, is to look for what never did, and I fear never will happen. . . ." [68] He spoke in generalities, but he would have been the first to admit that the American Revolution had opened unusually splendid vistas. Such as opportunity for career-making had not presented itself, literally, for centuries. Though it was by no means a foregone conclusion that the colonies would win the war, the cause of liberty was a chance well worth the taking, and many a respectable gentleman led charges or sat on congressional committees, as the case might be, all the while with Caesar in the back of his mind.

As commander-in-chief Washington had the inside track; all the ambitious gentlemen, remembering their history, admitted that. It was an inevitable human corollary that some of the military ones should try to jockey him out of that position. It was as inevitable that others, who knew that the job of commander-in-chief was not in their line, should put their money on Washington's rivals and try to get Washington disqualified.

There had been a party in opposition to Washington from the moment Adams nominated him as commander-in-chief, in June 1775. John Hancock, who as President of Congress was sitting up in front where everybody could see him, let his face fall appreciably; he had been practically sure that Adams was

[68] Fitzpatrick, *The Writings of George Washington*, VI, 107.

about to name him. Weren't they both from Massachusetts, and hadn't Massachusetts always presented a solid front against the pretensions of Virginia? But Hancock quickly grasped Adams' point that it would have been bad, very bad, to appoint a New Englander commander-in-chief. So far the war had been a New England war, but if it was to hope for any success at all it must have the support of the south. The army was a New England army; placing a Virginian at the head of it would neatly solve the problem. Later, if Washington should not give Congress complete satisfaction, perhaps someone more acceptable to Massachusetts . . . Yes, Mr. Hancock saw. He was an excellent personal loser, and he stepped gracefully out of the military picture. Later on, he decided that he would rather be a congressman than a general anyway.

The two most prominent pretenders to Washington's job were soon identified in Major-General Charles Lee and Brigadier-General Horatio Gates, gentlemen who were about equally acceptable to the anti-Washington group in Congress. In the course of their attempts to ingratiate favor and get congressional support (Gates in particular was an accomplished lobbyist, and devoted several months' stay in Philadelphia to exercising his talents) they had made it pretty plain to this group that the powers behind the Revolution, once the Revolution had been won, would not be forgotten. And both Lee and Gates, in their own opinion and in the less valuable opinion of the anti-Washingtons, seemed well fitted to undertake the high command. Both of them were experienced soldiers of fortune, ex-officers in the British army, and far better trained in the formal art of war than Washington was. Washington's biographer Woodward makes no bones of thinking that between them they taught Washington "most of whatever he knew of strategy and battle tactics." [69] But the advantage the commander-in-chief derived from these helpful officers (both of them with him almost from the first moment, Lee as his second-in-command and Gates as adjutant-general) was offset. It is never good policy for the head of an army to be the pupil

[69] W. E. Woodward, *George Washington*, p. 270.

of the officers under him. And in this case the officers were those two, out of all the rest, who most dearly would have loved to step into Washington's boots, and who were the favorites of that powerful clique in Congress.

It is characteristic of the whole affair that it does not take its name — the Conway Cabal — from any of the powerful members of that powerful clique but from an obscure soldier of fortune who wrote indiscreet letters. That is because it turned out badly. Had it succeeded — had Lee or Gates replaced Washington as commander-in-chief, and had the men behind them got political control of Congress — Thomas Conway would never have got that namesake in default of a biographer to defend him. And the cabal would have been considered now, as it was then, just another piece of politics, neither messier nor more discreditable than politics often are. It all depended on the point of view. To Washington's friends and supporters it was infamous, because they were Washington's partisans, but to many admirable and conscientious gentlemen it was a plan of patriotic expediency. It is true that their views got out of style — as out of style as last year's isolationists'. But that does not make them the villains of the piece, and their admiring biographers have done them a disservice in trying to explain away their connection with the Conway Cabal.

Between the zealous biographers and the contemporary diarists and letter-writers — who, because of the very nature of cabals, wrote cryptically, or were more or less in the dark — it is hard to tell just who were and who were not mixed up in the plot against Washington. Most historians agree that the Adamses and the Lees were the most important members.[70] John Adams was the thinker of the group, and probably the most ambitious of them: "Certain principles follow us through life," he declared once, in sharp unconscious self-characterization, "and none more certainly than the love of first place." [71] He had never had first place, and wanted it passionately. His

[70] E.g., John C. Fitzpatrick, *George Washington Himself* (1933), chapter xlviii.

[71] Fitzpatrick, *George Washington Himself*, p. 339.

right-hand man was his cousin, Samuel Adams, the Father of the Revolution. Samuel Adams did not like at all the way his child had grown up and did not seem to need him any more. Adams the rabble-rouser, the politician whose politics were no dirtier than his linen, the man of whom the French minister wrote that he needed factionalism and unrest about him in order to keep his influence in public affairs,[72] had served his turn, but he did not know it or refused to admit it. He had rendered, unquestionably, important services to America; now America, whether willingly or not, was going to make suitable return. That was Samuel Adams' attitude. Then there was Richard Henry Lee, an inexplicable, undependable, eccentric Virginian, born the same year as Washington and on close "visiting terms" with him nearly ever since. If his character is a riddle of contradictions to posterity, posterity need not feel obtuse; he was just as much a riddle to the contemporaries who knew him well. He was the kind of man who, meeting an acquaintance on the street, would one day smile cordially and insist on stopping for a little chat, and the next day would pass by with only the smallest, coldest inclination of his head. His politics were moody and uncertain too. At the time when most of his neighbors were exercised over tyranny and taxation without representation, he had tried to get himself appointed stamp-distributor for Virginia; and then later it was he who introduced in Congress the resolution for independence. He passed for a passionate Virginian, yet he had been intriguing with the Adamses ever since 1775. He was a clever, clear-thinking man, but not clever enough to know when he was being made use of politically. But then ambitious men are often blinded, and Richard Henry Lee was ambitious not only for himself but for his brother Francis Lightfoot Lee, who was also a member of Congress and was mildly implicated in the Conway Cabal, and also for his brother Arthur Lee, who lived abroad and did not even know most of the members, but who was in it up to his neck. Arthur Lee was the

[72] Conrad Alexandre Gerard to the Count de Vergennes, March 4, 1779; *ibid.*, p. 345.

cleverest of the brothers, the most eccentric, the most unhappy and maladjusted and self-seeking. When he joined the
Cabal in 1775 he was thirty-five years old and, using the trial-
and-error method, he was still trying rather pathetically to discover what he wanted out of life. In his youth he had wanted
to be a doctor, but no sooner had he taken his M.D. at the University of Edinburgh than he decided that he did not want to
be a doctor after all. He went home to Virginia, practiced
medicine listlessly for a little while, and gave it up. Later he
decided to study law. He went to London, spent several years
in the Temple, and finally in 1775 was admitted to the bar.
But again he seemed reluctant to begin the practice of his profession. He hung around London, waiting for something to
turn up. Something did turn up in the shape of a request from
Congress' Committee of Secret Correspondence that Lee act
as their London correspondent. The following year Congress
appointed him one of three commissioners to negotiate about
a treaty with France, and Lee was so pleased with himself
in the role of diplomat that he subsequently suggested that
the other two gentlemen be dismissed, so that he could be
sole minister to France. That sort of thing was typical of
Arthur Lee.

The motives of the cabal's leaders were, of course, complicated by personal ambition. They were the men who would
have controlled the United States' destiny, if their scheme had
succeeded. But many of its members had nothing to gain.
They honestly thought that Washington had been a poor selection for the post of commander-in-chief, and that almost anybody else, Gates, or Charles Lee, or whoever the Lee-Adams
faction wanted, would turn in a better performance than
Washington. Congress as a whole knew very little about practical warfare. Most of the experienced fighting men in America
were, logically enough, with the army. But Congress, ranking
above the military organization, was in a position to dictate
military policies and did so without appreciably suffering from
an inferiority complex. At the beginning of the war, Congress'
stupid and short-sighted militia and short-enlistment policy

gave the army a handicap it was years in overcoming, and Congress' mismanagement was more recently being responsible for the sufferings of Washington's army at Valley Forge. The relation of cause and effect remained a hopeless riddle to the gentlemen at Philadelphia. To them a victory was a victory and a defeat was a defeat, no matter what the circumstances had been. Washington suffered a number of bad defeats during the first two years of the Revolution; and when on the heels of his defeats at Brandywine and Germantown Gates turned the whole course of the war by defeating Burgoyne at Saratoga things looked very bad for General Washington and very good for General Gates.

Gates had previously outstripped Charles Lee as the outstanding contender for Washington's place. Lee, captured by the British late in 1776, was out of the running for about eighteen months (during which months, incidentally, he prepared for the British "Mr. Lee's Plan," detailing how they could win the American war); and when he did get back in the public eye it was too late. But Gates had been making his hay while the Congressional sun shone upon him. He had been given the opportunity to win the most important battle of the war, barring perhaps the smashing finale at Yorktown. Posterity, examining the facts of the case, cannot think that Gates deserves a great deal of credit for his sensational victory. He had only recently succeeded General Philip Schuyler, whose careful, months-long preparation had paved the way for success; he had under him two of the most brilliant officers of the Revolution, Benedict Arnold and Daniel Morgan (Burgoyne himself thought that Morgan's five hundred men had as much to do with winning the battle as the rest of Gates's army put together); he had at his mercy a British army which, unfamiliar with the terrain, had become ludicrously lost in the woods; and he had eighteen thousand men to Burgoyne's five thousand. But people are not inclined to rationalize in war-time, and it was only apparent to the United States that Gates had done what no other American general had managed to do, capture an entire British army along with its important commanding general, inspire new confidence and new enlistments in the American people, and bring the wavering French nation to the point of signing an alliance with the new country which looked, suddenly, as if it might win the war. He was a popular hero and, which was more to the point, the favorite son of Congress.

Washington's friends were nearly in despair, not only at the growing size and success of the cabal against the commander-in-chief, but at his dignified determination to ignore the whole thing as became a gentleman and a general. Dignity was all very well, they felt, but it was necessary to fight fire with fire; and Congress, although with malicious intent, had just given Washington the power to do so. Before leaving Philadelphia to seek safety at Lancaster and then at York, Congress had given Washington dictatorial powers for a period of sixty days. They did this ostensibly because a serious emergency existed — Philadelphia being about to be captured by General Howe — and they were actually afraid for their own skins. Nobody knew more personally than Congress how many of Washington's troubles had been caused by the lack of a free hand, and many of the most enthusiastic caballers admitted to themselves that Washington was a good man in an emergency. His biographer Fitzpatrick compares these generous grants of power "to a village board of fire commissioners who hamper their fire department chief by turning off the water, disconnecting the hose, misplacing the ladders and interfering in every way while the building is burning and when, as a result of their interference and lack of support, the blaze gets beyond control, throw all the gear and apparatus in a heap, tell the chief to take complete charge and stalk majestically away to rest under the nearest tree." [73] But there was something more to Congress' idea of giving dictatorial powers to General Washington. Put the commander-in-chief in a very bad, almost impossible position, give him enough rope, and let him hang himself. Naturally, Congress reasoned, if Washington were in full charge of the situation he would have to assume

[73] Fitzpatrick, *George Washington Himself*, pp. 313–4.

full responsibility for failure. And failure was very nearly certain.

Washington's friends, however, seized at the desperate hope that the unlimited powers conferred on him might yet be used to his own advantage: "I wish he may use them," Charles Carroll of Carrollton wrote: "unless he does, our affairs will never go well; but he is so humane & delicate that I fear the common cause will suffer from his humanity & delicacy of temper: however I believe he is determined to act with more vigor than heretofore: this man can not be too much admired. . . ." [74] And he wrote to Washington himself, respectfully admonitory, on September 27, 1777: ". . . The interest of the best and most glorious cause ought not to be sacrificed to a false delicacy. These are not times to put into competition the interests of a few with those of a great community.

"Nothing but severe punishments will, in my opinion, make the Commissaries and Quartermasters attentive to their duty! Your Excellency has the power, and I hope will not want the will, to punish such as deserve punishment. I hope your Excellency will excuse the freedom of this letter. My zeal for our country and my wishes for your success have impelled me to write thus freely on a subject which claims all your attention — the reformation of the army and the abuses prevalent in the two important departments of the Quarter Masters and Commissary General." [75]

Washington's fortunes had never been at lower ebb. While the Congress was sitting at York, his friends were able to keep him in the saddle only by the smallest majority. The opposition party managed to bring about the reorganization of the Board of War, in November 1777, with Gates as President and Conway as Inspector-General. This was a direct slap in Washington's face, for it not only made Gates, in a sense, the superior of his superior officer, but rewarded rather than censured him for the grandiose way he had taken of sending his reports directly to Congress, over Washington's head. Washington had

[74] To Charles Carroll of Annapolis, September 23, 1777; Carroll Papers, V, 423.   [75] Rowland, *Life*, I, 218.

even had to learn about the Battle of Saratoga at second hand. At the same time the Board was reorganized, Congress, going directly against Washington's recommendation, promoted Thomas Conway to the rank of Major-General. Thomas Mifflin, one of the secondary members of the cabal, continued as head of the much-abused quartermaster's department, and another secondary member, Jonathan Trumbull, was placed on the Board, along with Timothy Pickering, whose allegiance to Washington was noticeably wobbling. The commander-in-chief's friends in Congress were able to get loyal Richard Peters on the Board as the last member, but Charles Carroll, that outspoken and uncompromising supporter of Washington, was pointedly left off.

Seeing a brilliant future ahead of it, the new Board of War, with the exception of Peters soon a solid clique against Washington, urged that a committee "to Inquire" now be sent to Valley Forge. It was a foregone conclusion that the inquiry would be a prejudiced one, and the real purpose of it not to correct existing conditions but to cast discredit on the commander-in-chief, but nevertheless Washington replied politely and respectfully when the news was broken to him: "The methods suggested by you of having a Committee of Congress or from the Board of War sent to camp . . . will be approved." [76] The opposition group, of course, managed to get a majority on this committee, but the friends of Washington rallied their forces and after a hard fight Gouverneur Morris and Charles Carroll of Carrollton were placed on the committee too.

It was a real victory for the Washington party and one which the caballers did not attempt to minimize. They knew that Mr. Morris and Mr. Carroll did not constitute a safe minority. They were among the most enthusiastic supporters the commander-in-chief had, and they were besides most devilishly clever, both of them. Either of them, alone, would not have been able to accomplish much, but together they might prove a real nuisance.

[76] W. P. Cresson, *Francis Dana* (1930), p. 42.

It was with some pleasure, therefore, that the caballers heard, just on the eve of the committee's departure, that Mr. Carroll was suddenly called back to Maryland. His wife was extremely ill. Wonderful! Not that anybody had anything personally against Mrs. Carroll of Carrollton. She was said to be a very charming and gracious lady, and it was admittedly a shame that she should die so young. But the Lord giveth and the Lord taketh away; and, that being the case, He certainly seemed about to take poor Mrs. Carroll at a very opportune time. The caballers were suddenly quite confident of the outcome of the investigating committee's "great business." James Lovell of Massachusetts, writing from Congress to Samuel Adams, said plainly that the gentlemen were going to Valley Forge "to rap a Demi-G— over the Knuckles." [77]

Arriving at Washington's winter quarters, even the committee-members who opposed him were honestly shocked at the conditions they saw around them. The commander-in-chief with his staff, as he had indicated in his letter to Congress, was only too glad to show the investigating gentlemen around the camp. They took a grim pleasure in pointing out men who had not tasted meat for three or four days, men whose feet were wrapped in bloody rags against the cold, men whose shirts hung in tatters (few of them, Washington commented trenchantly, had "more than one shirt, many only the moiety of one, and some none at all") [78] and were stiff with dirt because the quartermaster's department had not seen fit to send the soap allowed by Congress. And they were delighted to have the "Committee to Inquire" dine at the commander-in-chief's table, where "pasnips" were the pièce de résistance, with a "small quantity of potatoes and cabbage, less of turnips" completing the menu.[79] Washington, blandly ignoring the torn tablecloth and the absence of wine, played the gracious host quite as if he were entertaining his friends at Mount Vernon.

[77] January 20, 1778; Burnett, *Letters of Members of the Continental Congress*, II, 42.
[78] To the President of Congress, December 23, 1777; Fitzpatrick, *Writings of George Washington*, x, 194.
[79] Cresson, *Francis Dana*, p. 45.

His courtesy was complete. There was nothing in his manner to indicate that he suspected the existence of a cabal against him. On the contrary, he was giving the investigating committee every facility in his power — access to his military papers and accounts, and aide to explain whatever was necessary, and a comfortable building in which the committee might hold its sessions undisturbed. The regret that he expressed for the illness of Mrs. Carroll of Carrollton was, as far as anybody could tell, purely social.

Poor Molly was really desperately ill. They thought for some days that she was going to die. Her husband's place was, of course, with her, but the presence of her adored "Mr. Carroll" did not give Molly unalloyed comfort. It added to her distress to know that she was keeping him from the important committee-work at Valley Forge. Probably her surprising and rapid recovery (at least to the indifferent state of health which was the best she had enjoyed for years) was due in great part to her determination not to interfere with her husband's career. Molly was always more interested in that than he was. And she knew that he was feeling the call of "duty and Privilege," at that particular moment, more urgently than ever before. Washington's destiny, which Carroll thought was inextricably mixed with the destiny of America, certainly hung on the findings of that committee at Valley Forge.

As soon as Molly was out of immediate danger, then, Carroll made haste to join the other gentlemen at headquarters. Too bad Molly could not have enjoyed, too, the expressions on the anti-Washingtons' faces — as if they tasted something very bad — when they congratulated him on Mrs. Carroll's remarkable recovery.

Their worst fears were soon to be realized. They had been afraid that Carroll and Gouverneur Morris, together, would be able to swing a majority of the committee to their way of thinking. Carroll and Morris did just that. They chose Francis Dana, the chairman of the committee, as being more open to conviction than either Nathaniel Folsom or Joseph Reed, and energetically went to work on him. Dana must have paid par-

ticular attention to the arguments of Charles Carroll, who had
been for many years a personal friend of Washington and
knew whereof he spoke. At any rate, it was not long until
Morris and Carroll had the pleasure of watching Francis Dana
change his mind. Dana was one of those well-meaning members of Congress who had judged Washington by his defeats
and Gates by his sensational victory, without bothering to inquire deeply into either. He was a conscientious and thoroughly capable man, big enough to admit that his judgment
had been mistaken, fearless enough to turn traitor to that powerful group in Congress who had made him chairman of the
committee because of his known prejudice against the commander-in-chief. Not all the credit for overcoming it went to
the friends of Washington, hard as they had worked to show
him their point of view. Some of it went to Washington himself, who, without trying at all, had commanded Dana's unwilling admiration. During the three months at Valley Forge
Dana and Washington actually got to be friends, so much so
that Washington on one occasion lifted the mask of impassive
dignity he wore with almost everybody. Dana, "taking a
breath of air," one night when the camp was asleep, found
Washington pacing back and forth outside his modest headquarters. He turned abruptly to Dana: "Congress, sir, does
not trust me — I cannot continue thus." [80]

Washington had had a harder winter at Valley Forge than
any of the frostbitten sentries with no shoes on their feet. For
that matter, he had had a pretty thin time of it ever since his
appointment as commander-in-chief. He was heartsick of
trying to make bricks without straw, of doing his excellent
best and getting censured for it, of being kept in office only
by dramatically small margins at the last minute. But now the
Washington luck was changing. The report of the committee
"to Inquire" not only disposed in forthright terms of the
charges against Washington's conduct of his army, but placed
the blame for the conditions at Valley Forge where they belonged, squarely on the shoulders of that veteran caballer,

[80] Cresson, *Francis Dana*, p. 46.

quartermaster-general, and member of the Board of War, Thomas Mifflin. As a result, Mifflin resigned. He would have tried a little earlier to brazen it out, but the new Board of War had shown itself sadly deficient in departments other than the quartermaster's. A badly planned attempt to invade Canada made the Board ridiculous, and laid open to serious question the value of President Gates's military abilities. Finally, the drunken maunderings of Wilkinson, one of the caballers, had thrown the conspirators into confusion, and they were so busy denying accusations before they were made, and trying to lie out of their respective parts in the affair and throw the blame on each other, that they appreciably lowered themselves in the esteem of their friends in Congress. It became apparent who some of the conspirators were; and the motives of some of the known ringleaders were shown up; but the slip of the tongue which Wilkinson had made "during a convivial hour" was not what caused the Conway Cabal to collapse, as is generally asserted. It was purely incidental. The main points were Washington's steadfast and ethical conduct as contrasted with Gates's far from ethical conduct and the bad generalship he had shown in the matter of the Canadian fiasco, and the findings of the committee at Valley Forge.

By spring the Conway Cabal seemed about petered out. Gates had been ordered by Congress back to the army, and Wilkinson resigned as secretary of the Board of War. Mifflin had already given up the quartermaster's department, and in May Baron von Steuben replaced Conway as inspector-general. Most of the trouble-makers were out of the way, or at least had had their stingers drawn, when General Charles Lee returned to the army.

Monmouth was the first battle in which Lee participated after Washington had arranged to have him exchanged. It is a pity that Washington bothered. He knew quite well, by this time, that Lee had been one of the early conspirators against him; but he was a forgiving soul and besides, with Congress really back of him for the first time since the beginning of the war, he felt able to handle this one malcontent. Lee soon made it plain that he still was a malcontent. Washington had already promised Lafayette the honor of leading the attack, but Lee pointed out that he was the senior major-general of the two, and therefore ought to be given preference. And he wanted to lead the attack himself.

Washington thought it over and, with apologies to Lafayette, decided to humor the eccentric prodigal son. After all, there was something in Lee's argument. So he gave him five thousand troops and Lee accordingly led the attack, Washington's forces pressing close after him. Lee had, at first, more men than the enemy, but he hesitated, and the British had time to send up reinforcements, whereupon Lee, without notifying Washington, who was behind him, and without attempting to contest the ground, gave the order for retreat. His men turned back, of course, and the most complete confusion was occasioned by their trying to march one way when Washington's men, close behind them and knowing nothing of General Lee's plan, were still trying to march the other. Fortunately, Washington was able to control the situation. Learning from some of the men under General Lee's command that the latter was falling back, he hastily threw two regiments in the path of the British, and himself sought out Lee. Lee's cowardice, or stupidity — he did not know, of course, that it was really treachery — had made him angrier than the members of his staff had ever seen him. Just then Lee rode up, and Washington let loose his wrath. "My God, General Lee!" he shouted. "What are you about?" Lee tried to advance some explanation, but Washington had things to say himself, and he said them. One bystander said that he "swore till the leaves shook on the trees." Lafayette said that Washington called Lee a "damned poltroon"; this is the only one of the "singular expressions" which Lee said Washington used toward him which has authentically survived, but undoubtedly it was *e pluribus unum*, and not one of the most striking examples at that. Damned poltroon by itself would not shake the leaves on a lilac bush.[81]

[81] This is the traditional account of Lee and Washington at the Battle of Monmouth. I have told it as John Hyde Preston (for instance) tells it on

The upshot of the matter was that Monmouth was a drawn battle, instead of the decisive victory it would otherwise have been for the Americans, that Lee wrote Washington an impudent letter, and that Washington promptly called his bluff and had him put under arrest. He was tried by court-martial for disrespect to Washington, disobedience to orders at the Battle of Monmouth, and misbehavior before the enemy by making an unnecessary and disorderly retreat, and was convicted on all three counts. As far as the Americans were concerned, exit General Lee.

He had failed in his plan to render much service to the British cause, and the British had no more use for him than the Americans did. He was not offered a commission in His Majesty's army. So Lee retired, not very gracefully, to private life on his Virginia plantation (the same plantation the Continental Congress had given him when he first came to America), varying its monotony by a round of visits. He was heard from no more officially, but Charles Carroll of Carrollton may have shown to some of his associates a letter from Molly: "I was in great hopes to have it in my power to give you an account of General Lees departure, but am sorry to find there is no prospect of so much joy, the wretch is perfectly recover'd goes singing about the house, rides out every day, abuses General Washington. . . . I have not a doubt but Papa will be

---

pages 147–8 of his extremely readable book *A Gentleman Rebel: The Exploits of Anthony Wayne* (Farrar and Rinehart, 1930). It is based on the accounts of supposed eyewitnesses, but eyewitnesses were quite as unreliable in the eighteenth century as they are now, and most modern historians think that the matter of Washington's swearing at Monmouth is open to question. This issue is further clouded by the fact that there is some disagreement as to what swearing is. Thus Washington's biographer Woodward (*George Washington*, pp. 352–3) devotes some space to the thesis that the Father of his Country did not swear at Monmouth; yet he too quotes Washington as I have done. If he thinks that "My God!" is not swearing then General Washington's biographer was brought up less strictly than Mr. Carroll of Carrollton's. Whether he actually used these words or not, I rather think that General Washington did swear at General Lee; certainly I rather hope that he did. It seems to me that, in this case, the much-tried commander-in-chief might have cited one of his clerical acquaintances (Bennett Allen to Horatio Sharpe, June 6, 1768: *Archives of Maryland*, III, 502): ". . . they accuse me of Swearing by God I wod Shoot him, & I believe I did swear, wch was better than praying just then."

obliged to give him a *broad hint* that his Company is disagreeable." [82]

Molly, you see, had not lost her spirits during her recent serious illness. Nor did she appear to hold against him, as her father-in-law did on her behalf, her husband's too wholehearted absorption in public affairs. It was true that he had come home from Valley Forge the time they thought that Molly was actually dying, but he had gone back as soon as she was out of immediate danger. Indecent promptness, Charles Carroll of Annapolis thought it was. He was no less devoted to Molly than to his own son, and he had no idea of standing by and seeing her slighted. And indeed she was slighted! — duty or no duty to the country. Outsiders noticed it, too. It kept him busy slapping down the people who implied, tacitly but no less definitely, that politics was the only thing Mr. Carroll of Carrollton cared much about. "If Mr. Carroll should pay Annapolis a visit first in order to sound his Brethren of the Senate," John Ridout suggested to Carroll Senior, in a letter regarding the possible repeal of the Tender Law, "Mrs Ridout will when he returns to the Mannour accompany him & stay some time with Mrs. Carroll Whom she is very anxious & impatient to see." [83] Charles Carroll of Annapolis wrote back in brief reproof: "My Son cannot leave Mrs Carroll." [84] So it was embarrassing when he did leave, after only a little while, to go back to Congress.

This was to be, however, Carroll's last Congress. When it adjourned, June 27, 1778, he had already decided that he would not go again to Philadelphia. He resigned at the Maryland Assembly's fall session, writing to his good friend Doctor Franklin: "The situation of my domestic concerns, and the little use I was of in that Assembly, induced me to leave it altogether. The great deal of important time which was idly wasted in frivolous debates, disgusted me so much, that I thought I might spend mine much better than by remaining

[82] Undated; Carroll Papers, VII, 621.
[83] March 11, 1778; Carroll Papers, V, 466.
[84] March 13, 1778; *ibid.*, V, 467.

a silent hearer of such speeches as neither edified entertained or instructed me." [85]

A more important reason, and one which with characteristic reticence Carroll failed to mention even to Doctor Franklin, was the fact that the particular work which he had been doing in Congress was now finished. When he had accepted his election to that body, back in 1776, he had done so because, and only because, he had felt that he would be of special use in the matter of negotiating the French alliance. Franklin and Washington had both favored him as commissioner to the Court of France, and the indications are that Carroll really wanted to go. Something happened to prevent it. To this day nobody knows exactly what it was, though every once in a while a historian assumes the virtue of knowing and sets down as solemn truth what is really no more than his own opinion. Perhaps it was nothing more politically portentous than poor Molly's illness — for Charles Carroll of Carrollton, no matter what his father and Molly's friends might say, was not really an unfeeling monster, and, even though he might leave his sick wife to go to Congress and to Valley Forge and such places, probably would have been reluctant to go beyond calling distance. It is probable, too, that Carroll as the outspoken friend of Washington was not acceptable to the opposition party then powerful in Congress. Arthur Lee, it must be remembered, had been since 1775 the "Committee of Secret Correspondence" 's correspondent abroad, and Arthur Lee was in close sympathy with the opposition. He wanted the commission to France himself, and got it, along with Franklin and Silas Deane. It is puzzling and contradictory, however, to read a letter Lee wrote at the height of the Cabal, at a time when sincerely or otherwise he was convinced that Franklin was mishandling the business in France. Detailing the need the post of minister had for "a man of sense, of honor, of integrity and education," he wrote: "In many respects I should think Mr. Carroll, the Catholic, a fit man to send in his [Franklin's]

---

[85] December 5, 1779; Burnett, *Letters of Members of the Continental Congress*, IV, 239n.

place. What objections there may be to him I do not know. If the honor, the principles, the salvation of America be dear to you, take away the man that is endangering, and, if permitted, will ruin them all." [86] He wrote this letter to Mr. Samuel Adams, of all people. Even more puzzling is the remark which Charles Carroll of Carrollton's biographer Leonard quotes as his own: "I am the one man that must be kept entirely in the background. It must not be known to a single soul that I am personally active in this matter." [87] Why not? And if he really were "personally active," in spite of not going to France with the commission, why is there so little record of his activity? Persistent tradition has it that Carroll was highly instrumental in bringing about the alliance with France; but there are precious few bits of documentary evidence to indicate that he had anything at all to do with it.

But in any case the French alliance was successfully consummated February 6, 1778, when treaties of amity and commerce were signed by the representatives of France and America. As for the business which had engaged Carroll's attention for the last eighteen months, the Washington party's efforts to keep Washington in the saddle as commander-in-chief, it was finished too. Washington was firmly established, not only in the position of commander-in-chief but in the esteem of his fellow-Americans, civilians as well as soldiers. One almanac, published for the year 1779, already was speaking of him as "The Father of His Country." [88]

Charles Carroll had rendered a very special service in Congress even though it was not the special service he had had in mind when he accepted his seat there. But he felt that there was no longer any work in Philadelphia which another man could not do as well.

Ironically, Carroll was withdrawing from Continental politics just at the time when, at long last, he was about to be fully accepted in spite of his uncongenial religion. He had

[86] May 22, 1779; Joseph Gurn, *Charles Carroll of Carrollton 1737–1832* (1932), p. 104.
[87] Lewis A. Leonard, *Life of Charles Carroll of Carrollton* (1918), p. 175.
[88] Francis Bailey, *Lancaster Almanac*, 1778.

been two years accomplishing it, but finally the members of Congress, even the most prejudiced, even the ones he had fought in the matter of the Conway Cabal, had come around. "Congress is at present embarrassed with the choice of a new President," the newly arrived French minister wrote home in November 1778. ". . . For that office a man active and talented is required, and with a fortune that would permit him to make some appearance. Mr. Carroll of Maryland is the one thought of — he is a Roman Catholic — but it is feared he will not accept." [89]

No, he had no idea of accepting. He would listen to none of the arguments of his friends — the same friends, some of them, who had been championing his career ever since 1773, though without much encouragement from him. They thought he was being ridiculous. Hadn't he been working two whole years in Continental politics, and finally hadn't he succeeded in proving to Congress, as he had proved five years before to Maryland, that a Roman Catholic could be just as useful and capable and conscientious a public servant as anybody? Well, then, didn't he want to reap the harvest of his labors? Here was the presidency of Congress being handed to him on a silver platter, and, instead of accepting it as any sensible man would do, he was turning it down as if it were a little thing! Didn't he have any ambition? Didn't he know opportunity when it knocked so hard it was nearly knocking the door down? But Carroll's answers were still the same. No, he didn't have ambition. He never had had. Yes, he realized that he was being offered an excellent opportunity to push himself forward, but he didn't want to push himself forward. He thanked the gentlemen for the honor that they would have done him; he was deeply grateful to them for thinking that he was capable of filling such an important post. But he thought that he would just stay in Maryland.

Up in Philadelphia, the gentlemen of Congress shook their powdered heads. Too bad about Carroll. Fine statesman,

---

[89] Conrad Alexandre Gerard to the Count de Vergennes, November 10, 1778; quoted in the *Maryland Historical Magazine*, xv, 342.

valuable and capable and conscientious man. All the qualifications for holding public office. Delightful company, too, after you got to know him. Remarkable chess-player, good talker, good judge of horseflesh. But something very queer about him. Didn't seem to care whether he got to be a great man or not. Funny — but, then, it took all kinds of people to make a world.

"...at Length Decided by Arms"

1778–1787

H ISTORIANS commonly divide the American Revolutionary War into two periods. About the time
Charles Carroll of Carrollton came home from his
last Continental Congress — and that was in June 1778 — the
second period was just getting under way.

It was as different as possible from the first. During the
early part of the war America had enjoyed prestige neither
at home nor abroad. National sentiment was far from being
unified. Quite aside from the Toryish Americans who believed that the British ministry had done nothing to provoke
a rebellion and that anyway it was wrong to take up arms
against His Sacred Majesty, there were large numbers of in-
subordinate Americans, some in the State assemblies, some in
the Continental Congress, and some in Washington's army,
who neither anticipated nor really wanted independence from
England. As they conceived it, the colonies were fighting for
the redress of certain grievances. They wanted to force the
British ministry to remove these causes of complaint and to
realize that the colonies were not to be similarly imposed upon
for the future. But that was all they did want. Independence
sounded radical to them, and they thought of the people who
advocated it as radicals.

It was far from sure, then, that the new United States would
not "die a-borning." The established nations of the world

would have looked pretty silly recognizing a country which might itself decide against being a country after all. If they did recognize the United States, and thereby tacitly approved and supported their rebellion against Great Britain, they would find themselves in an extremely embarrassing position in case the move for independence petered out. They might even involve themselves in war with Great Britain, and this not one of the European nations was willing or indeed able to risk. If they could have some reasonable assurance that the United States might win their revolution, might attain actually the status of independence which they now possessed only on paper — well, that might be another matter. The French statesman Vergennes voiced the sentiments of all Europe when he said: "The time for giving the Americans aid depends upon their success. . . ." [1]

It was France that the American revolutionists had most counted on, though of course nobody thought she would be likely to help America out of regard for the holy principles of liberty. That would have been expecting rather too much from a monarchy — a tyrannical monarchy at that. It was very reasonably hoped, however, that the French would be pleased to fight side by side with the Americans against the British for the same reason that they would have fought side by side with the Chinese or the Hottentots or the Australian bushmen, if any of these peoples had started a promising little war with England. The traditional enmity between England, with back of it the time-honored principle of the balance of power, was always solidly to be counted on, and some of the radical Americans had been counting on it ever since Stamp Act days. "Cast ye Eye on a Map of America," Charles Carroll of Annapolis had written a decade before. "Consider ye prodigious Rapidity with which it is setling Will England in time to Come be able to Compell Such an immense Country Peopled by Miriads to Submit to Arbitrary Laws or despotick Ministeriall orders. . . . Look on ye inconsiderable Spot which Constitutes the

[1] Meade Minnegerode, *Jefferson Friend of France* (1928), p. 28.

Seven United Provinces. The People of that Spot Bafelled ye Power of the House of Austria & Shook of the Spanish Yoke. It is true France assisted them. Should English America ever be unfortunately forced to take up Arms & be unable of Herself to Vindicate her freedom, Will not France Spain & even the Dutch Lend Her a Helping hand? . . ." [2]

And sure enough, ever since the month before the Declaration, a steady stream of money and arms had been coming from Europe. Some of it was Spanish, but more of it was French. Working through the playwright Beaumarchais, who in turn hid his identity behind the mercantile name of Roderique Hortalez et Cie., the French government managed to give very considerable help to America in the first two years of the war. Beaumarchais had standing permission to take whatever he wanted from the royal arsenal, making payment whenever it suited him. He borrowed money from the royal treasury a million livres at a time. The royal navy saw to it that his "mercantile ships" — full of arms, munitions, uniforms and supplies — got out of port under the very noses of a British fleet which, though ordered to keep an eye out for suspicious shipping, could find nothing suspicious about Roderique Hortalez et Cie. The French were being very clever. Though the British ambassador reported an "unrestrained spirit" at Versailles, they managed for two years to keep surface relations with England smooth, all the while steadily giving aid and comfort to the enemy.

But during those two years they as steadily refused to consider a diplomatic treaty with the United States. The American agents at the French court, Benjamin Franklin, Silas Deane, and Arthur Lee, ran into a polite and immovable wall whenever they suggested such a thing. Even the wildly popular Franklin did not seem able to get beyond a certain point. The French government had its agents in America, and nobody knew better than the French that the war was not, so far, particularly successful, that there were friction and mismanagement and conflicting ambitions in the army, that the

[2] To William Graves, December 23, 1768; Carroll Papers, II, 120 A & B.

American people were discouraged and getting more and more
out of the notion of independence, and that there had been a
number of unfortunate defeats which seemed to indicate that
there could be no independence anyway. The year 1777
changed all that. To be more specific, the Battle of Saratoga
did it. Beaumarchais happened to be dining with Benjamin
Franklin when, early in December, two months after the
battle, a messenger from America brought the sensational news
that Burgoyne and his whole army were taken prisoners of
war. Beaumarchais's active mind supplied the implications.
He did not wait for details; he rushed from Passy to Versailles
in such a hurry that his coach upset and he dislocated his arm.
He picked himself up and went right on.

Beaumarchais's enthusiasm was justified. As he had expected, the successful battle made all the difference. The
French government officials were impressed; Vergennes admitted that "the Power that will first recognize the independence of the Americans will be the one that will reap the fruits
of this war." [3] Franklin, striking while the iron was hot, sent
an address to the French king, thanking him for the loan of
the 3,000,000 francs America had already received, and asking
that an alliance between France, Spain, and the United States
be considered. This was on December 8th; on the 17th the
king agreed to conclude a treaty as soon as he heard from
Spain.

By the time they signed it, on February 6, 1778, the big
news had, of course, leaked out. The French court had been
swarming with British spies for the last two years; the British
government listened to their latest reports in horror. The news
of Saratoga, the capture of an entire British army by the in-
significant colonials, had been bad enough, but the prospect
of an alliance between the colonies and France was infinitely
worse. The ministry decided that it was time to forgive and
forget. Lord North read in Parliament — February 17, 1778
— a bill for the repeal of the tax on tea and the acts against the
constitution of Massachusetts. It passed amid much ill-feeling,

[3] Minnegerode, *Jefferson Friend of France*, pp. 28–9.

but it passed. The colonies were actually told that the matter of their sending representatives to the British Parliament would be considered. Even George III ate dirt. He whose insistence on taxation had made him the personal cause of much of the trouble between England and her colonies (the ministry had wanted to repeal the tea tax along with the other Townshend duties, but George III said no) now asserted that anybody who thought taxing the Americans justifiable was "more fit for Bedlam than a seat" in the Parliament.[4] Bedlam was, of course, a famous English insane asylum; it is interesting to remember, in connection with the king's remark, that he himself was crazy for the last ten years of his life.

On March 11, 1778, three British commissioners were appointed to notify Congress about last month's parliamentary concessions, and to arrange the terms of a treaty of peace. The British were a little late. Fortified by the alliance with France, Congress said to the commissioners no thank you, we think we'll just fight this war out to the finish. General Washington commented: "Nothing short of independence . . . can possibly do."[5] Nobody called him a dangerous radical, either, as people had called Mr. Carroll of Carrollton when he voiced the same sentiment two years back. It was a sure sign that the American Revolution had entered its second, its grown-up, stage. Everything was changed. Not only was there, at long last, the real, intelligent prospect of victory, but there was a definite change in national sentiment. The United States no longer considered even the remote possibility of reconciliation with the mother country; they had been offered an honorable peace and a moral victory, and they had turned them down. The United States were fighting at last for freedom.

The war was still a long way from being won, there was still much to worry about. But Charles Carroll of Carrollton, for one, was pretty well satisfied with the way things were turning out.

[4] Homer C. Hockett, *Political and Social History of the United States* (1931), p. 154.
[5] Lucretia Perry Osborn, *Washington Speaks for Himself* (1927), p. 101.

He found it good to be back in Annapolis. The sessions of
the Maryland Assembly, at this time on a much higher level
than the sessions of the Continental Congress, were a pleasant
change. He could attend them, too, without neglecting his
private business, his father, and his wife who was now a confirmed invalid. Two years in national politics, his fellow as-
sembly-members found, had not changed him much. At the
spring session, 1779, he voted against the resolution that the
legislators each be allowed "three pounds current money per
day . . . and three pounds a day for itinerant charges" during
attendance; he gave his reasons as "1st. Because this resolve
sets a dangerous precedent for future legislators to vote the
people's money into their own pockets. . . . Secondly, Because this resolve plainly discovers a disposition to relieve ourselves from the effects of a depreciated currency, while private
creditors, and the public, remain unredressed. . . . Thirdly,
because this resolve appears to be a manifestation of that spirit,
which there is reason to apprehend, influenced too many to
pass the tender law, viz., the preference of private to the public
interest. . . ." [6] He still itched to reform politicians who did
not want to be reformed. He still had the quaint idea that
public service, with all its disadvantages, was a privilege and
that accepting pay for it was gilding the lily to suffocation.

As a rule he was scrupulously regular in his attendance
at the Assembly; when he missed the special session which was
convoked July 15, 1779, and lasted into the following month,
he had a reason. Charles Carroll of Carrollton, as the foregoing
quotation shows, still opposed the Tender Law and still hoped
for its repeal, but he was not thick-skinned enough to court a
repetition of the embarrassment which had been his at the last
two sessions. In November 1778 his father, in the face of all
his pleadings and warnings, had insisted on getting permission
to make a speech before the House of Delegates. It was, of
course, about the Tender Law — the elder Carroll had been
fuming about that law for nearly two years, and far from
silently — and now he found himself unable to lay his so-called

[6] Rowland, *Life*, II, 16–7.

"humble Petition" silently upon the table.[7] His accompanying speech was so full of sarcasm and plain speaking that he was severely rebuked by the House. Nothing daunted, Carroll proceeded to pay Printer Green to publish as a pamphlet speech, petition, and legislative rebuke, adding to them a lively "Letter . . . to the Reader . . ." which stepped on a good many legislative toes.[8] In March, at the next meeting of the Assembly, he presented another petition as full of plain speaking as the first. Like the first, which had been "censured . . . as highly indecent & justly exceptionable," this petition was resolved to "be in several parts scurrilous & abusive, etc." [9] Now, in July 1779, the special session of Assembly was about to have the pleasure of reading still another petition from the pen of Charles Carroll of Annapolis. He sent it to William Fitzhugh, Speaker of the House of Delegates, with the request that the language be ignored and the facts of the petition alone be voted on.[10] But he simply could not resist putting it in strong language.

All this was, of course, extremely unpleasant for the younger Carroll, who had no more influence over his stubborn old father than he had over the blowing wind. He was afraid, too, that his political enemies in the House would take the opportunity to strike at him thus indirectly, especially since his father was going about Annapolis declaring that he had been in jail before and would be delighted to go again for a good cause such as the privilege of denouncing the Tender Law. The two Carrolls had always stuck together and it was impossible for the son actively to oppose his father, so he decided to absent himself gracefully from the Assembly. July would be a good time to take Molly to the Springs to drink the waters.

It was the first vacation, expedient or voluntary, that Mr.

---

[7] Charles Carroll of Annapolis to William Fitzhugh, Speaker of the House of Delegates, July 15, 1779; Carroll Papers, VI, 537.

[8] *A Letter from Charles Carroll, Senior, to the Reader. With His Petition to the General Assembly of Maryland; His Speech in Support of it; and the Resolution of the House of Delegates thereon* (1779).

[9] Charles Carroll of Annapolis to William Fitzhugh, July 15, 1779; Carroll Papers, VI, 537.

[10] *Ibid.*

and Mrs. Carroll of Carrollton had taken since their marriage eleven years before. The whole family had been trying, over a period of months, to induce Molly to take the babies and quit Annapolis for some place not only healthier but safer. Off and on, ever since the beginning of the war, there had been rumors that the British were coming to burn the town. There had been no fighting on Maryland soil but it was reasonable to suppose that the British were not deliberately neglecting one of the most important cities in North America, and as the war moved south and the Virginian cities of Portsmouth and Monmouth were disastrously sacked Annapolis prepared again for emergency. "I have my books all packed up," Carroll wrote in May of 1779, "household linnen, cloaths, Blankets &c are ready to be removed on an alarm." [11] Molly, however, flatly refused to leave town. She had packed the "material papers, books of acct, Library, Plato &c" [12] too many times in the course of the war to be greatly excited over the British. Besides, she thought "Mr. Carroll" 's company worth a few risks. She knew she was unwell and needed a change; but she knew also what the First Citizen thought of patriots who took holidays in wartime. And she had firmly made up her mind not to go one step without him. Like all the rest of the family, Molly was stubborn enough to enjoy biting off her nose to spite her face; besides, in an age when according to persistent tradition the husband and the wife were one and that one was the husband, she was one of the many ladies who did just exactly as they pleased.

The Carrolls stayed several weeks at the Springs. "The Springs" were at Bath in Virginia, for many years a fashionable resort for Maryland gentry. Old Mr. Carroll had a house there but more often than not it was loaned out to some of his friends. So the younger Carrolls rented a house which proved to be infested with bloodthirsty fleas. [13] In spite of her fleas and her illness Molly managed to enjoy herself — there were balls

[11] To Charles Carroll of Annapolis, May 22, 1779; Carroll Papers, VI, 529.
[12] Charles Carroll of Carrollton to Charles Carroll of Annapolis, March 12, 1776; ibid., IV, 322.
[13] Charles Carroll of Carrollton to Charles Carroll of Annapolis, July 24, 1779; Carroll Papers, VI, 542 A & B.

and tea-parties and congenial company, including General Riedeisel and his wife — and the waters began to benefit her health. Carroll, however, was bored to death. "I hate this idle sauntering life," he complained in a letter to his father — "Dancing & tea-drinkings take up the time of the ladies, & gaming that of the gentlemen — I mean the generality of them." [14] He meant, of course, to except himself. He spent a good part of his holiday waiting impatiently for the mail and the newspapers with bulletins from the army.

Much of the war news was bad. General Clinton, who had succeeded General Howe for the British, unfortunately lacked the latter's predilection for staying in winter quarters. While continuing to hold New York, he was doing considerable damage with a series of plundering expeditions sent to Connecticut and the coast of Virginia. The British still held Savannah and Augusta, too, and had reinstated royal government in Georgia. The assistance of a French fleet had not made successful General Sullivan's attempt to regain Newport.

What good news there was, however, was of a promising type. The high spot of the summer, Mad Anthony Wayne's storming of Stony Point, was notable not only because it was a definitive victory but because it proved that the American armies were able now to meet as tactical equals the trained European troops they had to fight. Wayne's men showed the progress the army had made under the tuition of that painstaking tactician Baron von Steuben. His specialty was bayonet-drill. When he came to America in 1777 — one of France's pre-alliance aids to the American cause — Steuben had found the soldiers using the bayonet only to roast meat over a campfire. He taught them to use it on the British as the British mercenaries had used it on Wayne's men at Paoli. Not a bullet was fired by the Americans in the victorious assault on Stony Point.

Carroll also heard from his indignant old father that his petition about the Tender Law had not even been delivered to the Assembly. Samuel Chase — who had voted for the petition in

[14] August 19, 1779; *ibid.*, VI, 553.

the first place and had been in the Carroll bad books ever since — "insisted it ought to be presented by a Member on the floor, the house were of Chases Opinion." [15] Old Mr. Carroll, paying no attention to this obvious snub, had promptly sent the petition to "Mr John Hanson desiring Him to present it on the floor." [16] Hanson (that neglected patriot who had served as first president of the Continental Congress) was sorry to imperil his lifelong friendship with the elder Carroll but thought it would be far worse if the latter's interference in politics should imperil his son's career. Fortunately for the peace of the Carroll household, old Mr. Carroll never found out that there had been a little necessary collusion. He simply wrote to the Springs, in white-hot wrath: "Jon Hanson did not deliver my Petition. . . ." [17]

That being settled, Charles Carroll of Carrollton returned to Annapolis with Molly, who really seemed to have benefited from her trip. Not organically, of course. The "pain in her Breast" was no better but her appetite had improved and she had again resolved not to take any more laudanum. [18] Carroll, on the other hand, was not well and looked pale and thin, even for him. But he plunged into the business of the fall session of Assembly. "I fear you take too much of the Publick business on yourself, druge not, let others draw, you may correct," his father wrote him anxiously, "nothing is dearer to me than yr Health." [19]

At the fall session the senate passed a bill for the suspending of the Tender Law, which was rejected by the House. The leader in getting this bill through the Senate had been Charles Carroll of Carrollton; the leader in getting it rejected in the House was Samuel Chase. Carroll wrote in the midst of the controversy: "The Delegates have done nothing in pursuance of ye resolution of Congress for revising the tender laws — I

[15] Charles Carroll of Annapolis to Charles Carroll of Carrollton, August 10, 1779; Carroll Papers, VI, 548.
[16] *Ibid.*
[17] August 17, 1779; *ibid.*, VI, 554.
[18] Charles Carroll of Carrollton to Charles Carroll of Annapolis, May 8, 1779; Carroll Papers, VI, 525A.
[19] December 8, 1779; *ibid.*, VI, 571.

wish to God the Session may end well: but Chase's violence I fear will throw all into confusion." [20]

"Chase's violence" had come to be a byword in Maryland. Already there was a feeling of regret that Mr. Chase had been one of those to sign the immortal declaration, since posterity, examining his record, might not find him a very glorious example. There was no doubt about his intellect and energy, but he was of an unfortunate disposition and controlled his passions no better in public than in private life. He was a born instigator of rebellion for rebellion's sake. His enemies had called him, years ago, a "busy, restless incendiary, a ringleader of mobs, a foul-mouthed and inflaming son of discord"; [21] and his friends could not help admitting that the words were well chosen, even while they pointed out Mr. Chase's several virtues. A tall, vigorous, loud-laughing, red-faced man — the Maryland bar's nickname for him (behind his back, be fully assured) was "Old Bacon-Face" [22] — he was likeable in spite of his faults and immensely popular with the common people. But even these had turned a little away from him when, toward the end of 1778, his reputation for honesty began to leave him. Always stony broke, always only a few jumps ahead of his creditors and desperate to make a little money, Chase had used information which had come to him as a member of Congress and had entered a combine to corner the market in flour. The scandal broke and Chase found himself in national disrepute. He was omitted from the list of delegates to Congress, but his friends managed to reëlect him to a seat in the Maryland Assembly, where he continued to stir up trouble. He had set the spring session (1779) by the ears by accusing several members of the senate of treason; but at the special session he "again appeared in the Senate and made a poor figure, and has almost denied everything the Senate has recorded against him, altho the Clerk minuted down his words as they fell from him." Thus Daniel of St. Thomas Jenifer, an ex-member of the pro-

[20] To Charles Carroll of Annapolis, April 8, 1780; Carroll Papers, VI, 574A.
[21] Sanderson, *Biographies of the Signers*, IX, 191.
[22] A. J. Beveridge, *Life of John Marshall* (1919), III, 184.

prietary governor's council who had in 1777 become president of the patriot senate. "He was desired to deliver in writing by way of explanation what he meant by the Charges he made against particular Members of the Senate. He has done so — and the poor Wretch has lost much ground, indeed in the opinion of all thinking men sunk even below contempt. I wish his Scheme may not have been deeper laid than has been immagined." [23] The "poor Wretch" was, however, not as humiliated as he should have been, and in less than a year Charles Carroll of Carrollton, speaking of the Maryland House of Delegates, commented bitterly: "Chase rules there without controul." [24]

The two men who had been fellow members of the Homony Club, before the war, co-commissioners to Canada, successful conspirators in the movement to make Maryland vote for independence, were now politically far apart. They had first split upon the merits and demerits of the Tender Bill; at the fall session of 1779 they were even more estranged on the question of the confiscation of British property. Chase advocated it violently; Carroll opposed it, "because," as he said in a letter to Franklin, "I think the measure impolitic, contrary to the present practice of civilized nations, and because it may involve us in difficulties about making peace, and will be productive of a certain loss, but of uncertain profit to this State, for as the business will be managed, it will be made a job of, and an opportunity given to engrossers and speculators to realize their ill-gotten money." [25] The recent defection of Mr. Chase had confirmed the lesson long since learned in public service, that

> . . . should war and hell have the same dimensions,
> Both have been paved with the best intentions
> And both are as full of profiteers.[26]

[23] To Charles Carroll of Annapolis, August 2, 1779; Carroll Papers, vi, 546.

[24] To Charles Carroll of Annapolis, May 6, 1780; *ibid.*, vii, 583.

[25] December 5, 1779; Burnett, *Letters of Members of the Continental Congress*, iv, 239n.

[26] Stephen Vincent Benet, *John Brown's Body* (1929), p. 158. Quoted by permission of Doubleday, Doran & Company.

Carroll's opinion of Continental politics was being reluctantly extended to the politics of his own state: "I have nothing but disagreeable news to write," he said in April 1780 — "an empty treasury, very little probability of filling it, inattention to public business, waste of time, & want of principle, and empty magazines form but too true a description of our present situation, & circumstances." [27]

Even his enemies had to admit that in this increasingly inattentive and inefficient assembly Mr. Carroll of Carrollton stood out. He was as enthusiastic about liberty as he had been in the first days of rebellion; he still did most of the work of every committee on which he was placed (and, naturally, he was still much in demand as a committeeman); and in his practice he had not deviated a hair's breadth from his own strict ideal of public service. His friends said that he stuck to his principles; his enemies said that he was merely stubborn, as stubborn as his father had ever thought of being. But whatever the case, as the Maryland Assembly went from bad to worse as far as enthusiasm and energy were concerned, the phrase "Mr. Carroll of Carrollton dissenting" became so common that people made jokes about it. They said it was a foregone conclusion he would hold out against the other members of the Senate. Frequently he did, as when at the special session of 1780 eight out of nine senators voted for the "act for sinking the quota required by Congress of this State of the bills of credit emitted by Congress" [28] Carroll was the ninth one who voted no, the only one of the previous session's majority who stuck by his guns. But he did sometimes reverse a decision. For example, he finally voted in favor of confiscation, which he still thought ought to be "contrary to the present practice of civilized nations," [29] because it seemed to be a necessary expedient of war. It had occurred to him, perhaps, that really civilized nations do not fight wars.

[27] To Charles Carroll of Annapolis, April 29, 1780; Carroll Papers, vi, 581.
[28] Rowland, *Life*, ii, 39.
[29] To Benjamin Franklin, December 5, 1779; Burnett, *Letters of Members of the Continental Congress*, iv, 239n.

The progress of the current war continued unfavorable to the American side. There were a few successes to leaven the lump — John Paul Jones, for example, won a brilliant naval victory over the British, and beyond the mountains the settlers of that Virginian county which was called "Kentucke" had under George Rogers Clark made considerable headway against the British system of forts in the vast northwest territory — but in 1780 most of the war news was bad. The key cities of Georgia were still in the hands of the British; an American attempt to recapture Savannah, though strengthened by the assistance of French naval power, had been blackly unsuccessful. The important seaport of Charleston had surrendered to the British May 12th, and General Lincoln, commanding the American army in the south, had surrendered with all his men to General Sir Henry Clinton. Taking advantage of the fact that there were more loyalists in South Carolina than in any one of the other states — about half the population, in fact — the British annexed large numbers of militia companies to their regular armies and had high hopes of forcing the whole state into allegiance to the king. General Gates, succeeding the captured General Lincoln in the command of the American forces, did little to interfere with the British ambitions. His genius for making mistakes, which he had been lucky enough to conceal during the early part of the war, made his southern campaign a failure from start to finish. Finally in August his ignominious defeat at Camden, under circumstances which should have resulted in an American victory, made it very plain that the hero of Saratoga was a greatly overrated general. It was small satisfaction to Carroll to see the man who had plotted against his friend Washington lose his military prestige; the American cause had too much at stake. Then, with the whole country cast down by the news of the disaster in the south, word came from the north of the treachery of General Benedict Arnold and his flight on a British warship. This was nearly the last straw. If there was a capable soldier in the American armies it was General Arnold; if there had been a soldier whom his commander-in-chief trusted to the last extremity it was he. Carroll too, having known him in Canada and later occupied rooms in the same house with him in Philadelphia, had thought him exceptional. Now he had not only gone over to the British but had got the plans of the important fortress of West Point into British hands, threatening disaster in the northern as well as the southern departments. Congress was still thick-headed and fumbling, and the future looked black indeed.

There was a general feeling that something had to be done, at once, to improve the general tone of the Congress. Everybody knew it no longer attracted the same class of men who had been at Philadelphia in '75. Maryland was one of the states that tried to do something constructive about it. In November, while Charles Carroll of Carrollton was absent on a few days' leave — Molly was gravely ill again — he was elected a delegate to Congress.

He refused, but not without a good deal of thought. There was much to keep him in Maryland, but if he could convince himself that he would be of real use again in Congress he would certainly accept the post. He worried a great deal about adequately serving his country. Anyone less of a devotee to the cause of liberty would have said that he was already doing enough, and he himself thought that the work he was best fitted for lay in Maryland. He had no idea of cutting himself off from the politics of his native state; that was one of the reasons why he had refused, the year before, to be considered as American minister to the court of France, replacing Doctor Franklin. He had, however, managed before this to combine the sessions of Congress and the sessions of the Maryland Assembly and he was willing to try it again if it seemed advisable. How thoroughly he studied that question is partly evidenced by the fact that he did not take any action on his election to Congress until the third of January, nearly two months later.

He refused for a very old reason, one which he had hoped would not arise again — religious prejudice. Maryland had in 1776 granted full civil and religious liberty to Catholics, and Marylanders had for three years before that, ever since the

days of the First Citizen letters, been willing to accept Mr.
Carroll of Carrollton's religion as something which they did
not understand his having, perhaps, but which was perfectly
all right since he did have it. Other Americans were not so
broadminded. They never forgot that Carroll was a Catholic,
and they obtruded the fact of his religious belief at the most
irrelevant times. On the occasion of his first official service,
the mission to Canada, Congress appointed him with grave
apprehension; and, though willing that he should flaunt his
religion before the Catholic Canadians whose political allegiance they were trying to win, were more than a little
ashamed to have a Catholic known in America as their ambassador. John Adams wrote to a friend in 1776: "Your prudence will direct you to communicate the circumstances of
the Priest, the Jesuit, and the *Romish* religion, only to such
persons as can judge of the measure upon large and generous
principles, and will not indiscreetly divulge it." [30] He implied
that there were not many people with such large and generous
principles, and he was quite right. Anti-Catholic sentiment
had cropped out at various times and in various places ever
since the beginning of the war. In 1777 the Reverend Jacob
Duché, chaplain of the Continental Congress who changed his
mind about independence and turned Tory when the British
took his home-town of Philadelphia, wrote a letter to Washington urging that he too see the error of his ways and do
something about it. "Take an impartial view of the present
Congress. What can you expect of them?" Duché wrote
urgently. ". . . Maryland no longer sends a Tilghman and a
Protestant Carroll." [31] Charles Carroll the Barrister, a Protestant, was then out of Congress and his cousin of Carrollton,
the Catholic, was in; this was quite true. Less accurate was
Benedict Arnold's handbill, issued after his treason, urging
others to do as he had done: "What security remains to you
even for the enjoyment of the consolations of that religion for

[30] To James Warren, February 18, 1776; Force, *American Archives*, IV,
1184.
[31] October 8, 1777; Gurn, *Life of Charles Carroll*, p. 133.

which your fathers braved the ocean, the heathen, and the wilderness? Do you know that the eye which guides this pen, lately saw your mean and profligate Congress at Mass for the soul of a Roman Catholic in purgatory, and participating in the rites of a church, against whose antichristian corruptions your pious ancestors would have witnessed with their blood." [32]

Up to 1778 anti-Catholic sentiment had, however, not been very generally outspoken. And it had reached an all-time low when, in the autumn of that year, Charles Carroll of Carrollton had had his chance at the presidency of the Continental Congress. But the French alliance had brought it out into the open. Tory politicians went into ecstasies of propaganda against the French (just as they had done twenty years before, in the French and Indian War), using their old tried-and-true weapon to show that France was determined to convert the Americans to Catholicism, by means of medieval torture-machines if necessary. Even some of the outstanding patriots opposed the alliance on religious grounds. "What a miraculous change in the political world!" Elbridge Gerry wrote. "The Ministry of England advocates for despotism, and endeavouring to enslave those who might have remained loyal subjects of the king. The government of France an advocate for liberty, espousing the cause of protestants and risking a war to secure their independence." [33]

The months since the signing of the French treaties had shown, too, that Americans in general were not too pleased to be allied to France. Though the financial help had been welcome indeed, and the French troops very acceptable in time of battle, the alliance had been purely a practical one. It went against the grain for the Americans — who had, remember, been English all their lives until 1776 — to accept the French as comrades-at-arms. There was a good deal of feeling in the

[32] *Rivington's Gazette*, November 1, 1780. The Spanish agent, Juan de Miralles, had died while visiting Washington's camp at Morristown; according to diplomatic practice, several American dignitaries, including Arnold, attended his requiem mass at a Philadelphia church.

[33] May 26, 1776; James T. Austin, *Life of Elbridge Gerry, with Contemporary Letters* (1828), I, 276.

army about the preference given to some of the French officers, and "French ways" were not popular with the rank or
file.

And since the glorious American privilege of free speech
was already well established halfway through the Revolution,
our French saviors were left in no doubt as to the pleasant
American opinion of them. Beaumarchais's agent in 1778 noticed "a prejudice, a national contempt" for the French to be
prevalent in America: "The people generally regard the
Frenchman as a degenerate being, as an animal of the second
order, unworthy to be compared with them. With very slight
modifications this is the view of most Americans. . . . I shall
never believe in there ever being that union of interests between us with which they flatter themselves. The treaty
pleased them because it insures their independence." [34] The
Abbé Robin, who came with Rochambeau in 1780, noted the
"strange idea the Americans had of the inhabitants of France,
prior to the war; they looked upon them as a people bowed
down beneath the yoke of prejudice, mere idolators in their
public worship. . . ." [35]

Annapolis had its share of the French troops in 1781, when,
at different times, both Rochambeau and Lafayette made their
headquarters in the Maryland capital. The southern campaign
which was to end at Yorktown made Annapolis a logical base
for military forces and supplies, and the townspeople — who in
their hearts almost resented that there had never been a single
battle fought on Maryland soil, and had felt themselves cheated
out of the more pleasant aspects of war — thoroughly enjoyed
the excitement. The presence of the French troops was welcome, too, because Annapolis was having one of its perennial
scares about the British. Lafayette arrived in March to find
two British sloops, the *Hope* and the *Monk*, blockading the
town; it was not known whether they had any designs on the
town itself, but everybody suspected the worst. Lafayette
was surprised and pleased at the warmth of his reception. He

[34] Minnegerode, *Jefferson Friend of France*, p. 30.
[35] Claude C. Robin, *New Travels through North-America* (1784), p. 18.

was on his way to Virginia, where Cornwallis and the traitor Arnold at the head of a British force were making things sufficiently hot for the Americans, but everybody urged him to stay as long as he would. He should have been met by a French squadron coming from the north; but this, he learned, had been forced back by the British and he must rely on his own resources. Eventually he set boldly out with two hastily fitted ships, with only two eighteen-pounders on board, and *mirabile dictu* the *Monk* of eighteen guns and the *Hope* of twenty were fooled into retreating hastily before him.

Of course, social Annapolis had managed a good deal of entertainment in honor of the marquis. The Carrolls — Molly was feeling a little better — led the way. Though Lafayette was a number of years younger than Charles Carroll and they were as different as two people well could be, they had a common outlook on the war and they shared a background in France. Lafayette, too, had received his education at the College of St. Omer.

It is purely irrelevant to wonder whether the distinguished guest had had smallpox before he reached Annapolis. If not, the Carrolls hospitably afforded him an opportunity. All of the little Carrolls — a nurseryful by this time, for Molly had dutifully produced Catherine in 1778 and another Elizabeth in 1780 — had been inoculated with the disease several days before, and by the time Lafayette came to dinner "the pocke" had "come finely out" on all of them.[36] Young Charles was especially well covered with blotches. The medical authorities of the day tried to save people from severe cases of the nearly inevitable smallpox by infecting them with a small amount of the virus and standing by to keep the disease as mild as possible. The theory did not always hold, though, and sometimes very bad cases of smallpox — not to say epidemics — resulted from inoculation. Dr. Upton Scott, still the Carroll physician and family friend in spite of his stubborn Tory refusal to "take ye oath prescribed by ye Act of Assembly, or even ye oath pre-

[36] Charles Carroll of Carrollton to Charles Carroll of Annapolis, April 5, 1781; Carroll Papers, VII, 643.

scribed by ye Delegates with a small & immaterial altera-
tion," [37] came to stay at the house for several days, but even
so Molly was very much worried about her children and entertained Lafayette with most of her mind in the nursery. She
does not seem to have worried about Lafayette at all. This
thing of giving dinner-parties while there was smallpox in the
house — it was a sizable dinner-party, too, complete with General Smallwood and a whole collection of French staff-offi-
cers — [38] would seem to indicate that the Carrolls were not
quite bright, but it was one of the nonchalant customs of the
times. Washington had caught smallpox years before at just
such a dinner-party.[39] He had been afraid to go but he was a
brave soldier and a Virginia gentlemen and went anyway.

Molly never had eyes for any gentlemen but her ungrateful
"Mr. Carroll," but the other Annapolitan ladies, the married as
well as the unmarried ones, were very much in a twitter over
the French officers in their beautiful white uniforms — such
a pleasant change from American rags and tatters! — especially
as " 'Tis all marquises, counts, etc." [40] True, their educations
were often unequal to the strain and sometimes they did not
know what to call the so-polite and elegant gentlemen who
gathered around their tea-tables, having to content themselves
with such mentions as "a Count Somebody with a hard
name." [41] But all the ladies were having a marvelous time, and
so were the officers.

[37] Charles Carroll of Carrollton to Charles Carroll of Annapolis, November 28, 1780; *ibid.*, VII, 627.
[38] Charles Carroll of Carrollton to Charles Carroll of Annapolis, April 5,
1781; *ibid.*, VII, 643.
[39] Accompanying his sick brother Lawrence to Barbados, nineteen-year-
old George was invited to Major Gedney Clarke's house to breakfast and
to dine. According to Sparks, whom Fitzpatrick quotes (*Diaries of George
Washington*, I, 22n), he went "with some reluctance, as the smallpox was in
his [Clarke's] family." This was on November 4, 1751; for November 17th
George's entry reads: "Was strongly attacked with the smallpox . . ."
(*ibid.*, I, 25). He bore no grudge, however, and within the month he was
safely and happily dining again with Major Clarke.
[40] Henrietta Margaret Hill Ogle to —— Lowndes, March 1781; "Maryland
Women and French Officers," by Kate Mason Rowland, *Atlantic Monthly*,
November 1890, LXVI, 653.
[41] Ann Dulany to —— Lowndes, December 29, 1781; *ibid.*, p. 656.

The common soldiers of the army, though, assumed the proportions of a local nuisance. "The soldiers are very troublesome," Charles Carroll of Carrollton wrote to his father; "they have stolen the Chickens that were sent down from Dooheragen. . . . The soldiers are a great nuisance, & I heartily wish they were gone: they have burnt a great many of ye rails of my lotts in town. . . . It is uncertain how long the soldiers will remain, or wh way they will go — I am heartily tired of them." [42] Other Annapolitans, no doubt, had far greater cause for complaint. Soldiery who had no reverence for the chickens of a Signer of the Declaration of Independence could hardly be expected to be considerate of the possessions of common people.

Carroll was far less disgusted with the soldiers, though — they were only a passing annoyance — than with the Maryland Assembly, which continued to meet regularly but apathetically. At the spring session of 1781 it took nineteen days to obtain a quorum of senators. The fall session, scheduled to meet the fifth of November, did not reach a quorum until the seventeenth. The spring session of 1782 took fifteen days to get a quorum. When it opened there was only one senator there — Edward Lloyd — in addition to Carroll. The First Citizen, it went without saying, was always in his seat the very first day.

The only bright spot that Carroll could see, in regard to the Assembly, was the fact that it had finally ratified the Articles of Confederation. Maryland was the last of the states to do so, and Carroll, as a strong talker for the necessity of a strong, organized central government, felt personal shame at the circumstance. "We have not yet confederated," he had written from Philadelphia in August 1777, "but almost every member of Congress is anxious for a Confederacy, being sensible, that a Confederacy formed on a rational plan will certainly add much weight and consequence to the united States collectively and give great security to each individually, and a credit also to our paper money: but I despair of such a confederacy, as

[42] April 5, 1781; Carroll Papers, VII, 643.

ought, and would take place, if little and partial interests could be laid aside. . . ." [43] His same old plaint! This letter was written to Carroll's good friend Doctor Franklin, whose pet theory of American government was the necessity for real union. Franklin had been the author, as far back as 1754, of the Albany Plan for the confederation of the American colonies then under the Crown; he had submitted a similar plan twenty-one years later at the meeting of the second Continental Congress. No action was taken on it by that body at the time, but in the following year Richard Henry Lee, introducing a resolution that "the United Colonies are, and of right ought to be, free and independent States," [44] brought up the question again by introducing a second resolution urging a permanent confederation. This time a committee was appointed to draft articles. The chairman was John Dickinson, by then a representative from Delaware but in earlier years that "Pennsylvania Farmer" whose letters about the Townshend Acts had established him as one of the great men of the Revolution. Dickinson and his committee used as the basis of their work Franklin's plan of 1775, adding a few new points; they turned in their report promptly, a few days after the Declaration of Independence was adopted. But in characteristic fashion Congress concentrated on less important matters and it was not until November 7, 1777 — sixteen months later — that a final vote was reached. Even then it was necessary to submit the Articles to the legislatures of the various states, ratification by every one of those states being necessary before the Articles could go into effect. Some of the states ratified promptly, but Maryland held up matters by objecting to Virginia's claim to the western lands. Maryland and Virginia had been quarreling over land questions, off and on, ever since King Charles I had created Maryland out of land previously given to Virginia, and there was not overmuch political cordiality between the two states. Other states, jealous of Vir-

[43] August 12, 1777; Burnett, *Letters of Members of the Continental Congress*, II, 450.
[44] June 7, 1776.

ginia's power, contributed to Maryland's delinquency and finally Congress had to appeal to Virginia to withdraw her claims so that the Articles of Confederation could go into effect. Having got her own way, Maryland finally ratified in 1781.

Charles Carroll of Carrollton, usually tenacious of Maryland's rights and claims, had in this instance warmly supported the idea that nothing was more important than a central government for the thirteen so-called United States. As late as January 28, 1781, he had been stubbornly voting in the minority for an act to empower the delegates of Maryland in Congress to ratify the Articles of Confederation. He was jubilant over his final victory.

The war was going favorably too, for a change. Nathanael Greene, newly appointed chief in command in the south, was turning in a magnificent performance. By the simple expedient of reversing the tactics of his predecessor General Gates (whose "northern laurels," as Charles Lee had warned him, really had changed into "southern willows") [45] he had turned despair into victory. He suited his tactics to the circumstances in which he found himself. Instead of taking the offensive with the enemy he tried to avoid pitched battles, at the same time annoying the British all he could and maneuvering them into unfavorable positions. Greene's forces were too small and too badly equipped and clothed and rationed to make battle desirable, and when it was forced upon the Americans they had to depend on generalship to see them through. Usually it did see them through. Nathanael Greene, most military authorities now agree, was the most capable general of the Revolution, and there were other hardly less brilliant officers under him. Notable among these was Daniel Morgan, the unofficial hero of Saratoga. On January 17, 1781, Morgan was attacked by Tarleton at Cowpens, South Carolina, and taught the British in one easy lesson that they were up against a better commander than the Gates whom Tarleton had twice recently defeated. The British were put to rout and the Americans

[45] Fiske, *The American Revolution*, II, 186.

chased them enjoyably for twenty-four miles; besides, more than three-fourths of the British were either killed, wounded, or captured, while the American losses were hardly worth mentioning. A few weeks after this victory Greene himself, cleverly retreating from South into North Carolina, met Cornwallis at Guilford Court House, and after a bloody battle with considerable loss on both sides succeeded in driving the British back. Cornwallis claimed the victory, for Greene, too weak to continue battle, had to withdraw from the field; but he had bought victory at the price of a ruined army.

Greene next met the British under General Stuart at Eutaw Springs, South Carolina, not far from Charleston. Tactically, it was a drawn battle, but morally it was a decisive victory for the Americans. Again the American loss was far less than the British, and again the American troops had the pleasure of pursuing the enemy as they retreated slowly toward Charleston. In every such battle he fought, Greene was effectively paving the way for the Battle of Yorktown, the climax not only of the southern campaign but of the war.

The last honors were reserved to the commander-in-chief, General Washington. Cornwallis, maneuvered by Greene's persistency into retreating northward, came at last into Virginia. Lafayette was in Virginia but Cornwallis felt that he had little to fear from "the boy," and his three thousand men. Cornwallis himself had seven thousand. No, he had nothing to fear — if he had used his head. Instead he allowed Lafayette to jockey him into the vicinity of Yorktown, which stood on a little peninsula. Lafayette seized the opportunity and, placing his own army across the only landward exit, sent word to Washington to hurry down and help him. Washington did. It was as simple as that. It took him more than a month to get there, though, and in the course of that time Cornwallis could perfectly well have done battle with Lafayette and got out of his unfavorable position. He had more than twice as many men as the Frenchman. Cornwallis, however, did not see the necessity. He stayed right in Yorktown and was neatly trapped there between Washington and Rochambeau, coming from the north to cut him off by land, and Admiral de Grasse, hurrying from the West Indies to cut him off at the edge of the Chesapeake. The whole chain of events was lucky for the Americans. De Grasse arrived in time to defeat a British fleet — under Admiral Graves, whom Charles Carroll had known as a captain in London — on its way to Cornwallis' assistance. This was on September 5th. The latter part of that same month Washington and Rochambeau arrived and, joining their armies to Lafayette's, began the siege of Yorktown. There were now 16,000 Americans to 7,000 British. Cornwallis had no chance. On October 17, 1781, he was ready to discuss terms of surrender; on October 19th he sent Brigadier-General O'Hara with his sword. Historians have always said that Cornwallis "feigned illness," but doubtless he did feel pretty sick. He knew, as the Americans knew, that this was the end of the war. Rochambeau received the sword for Washington, and the British marched out of Yorktown to the familiar strains of an old march called "The World Turned Upside Down." [46] Whoever had charge of the drum corps had a satirical sense of appropriateness. Poor bewildered British die-hards, their world was upside down indeed.

The messengers had not waited for the final formalities of victory. The news that Cornwallis was ready to discuss terms had been enough to send them galloping out of Yorktown in all directions. "I give you joy in the surrender of Ld Cornwallis ye 17th instant," Carroll of Carrollton wrote his father on the twentieth: "this glorious news is just come to town & I have had ye pleasure of communicating it to ye Public by turning into English Count de Grasse's letter to the Governor dated on board la ville de Paris ye 18th instant. . . ." [47] It was the high-spot of the impromptu celebration with which Annapolis greeted the virtual end of the war — gun-firing, toast-drinking, and red flares burning on State-House Hill. And how they cheered the First Citizen, when he stood before them to translate the dispatch!

[46] Fiske, *The American Revolution*, II, 283.
[47] Carroll Papers, VIII, 679.

But this celebration was nothing to the one which waited for General Washington when, on his way north after York-town, he arrived November 21st in Annapolis. Nothing impromptu this time; high and low had spent about a month in getting ready. Quoth the local paper:

"When the citizens received the pleasing information of his Excellency's arrival, all business ceased, and every consideration gave way to their impatience to behold their benefactor, and the deliverer of his country. On his appearance in the streets, people of every rank and every age eagerly pressed forward to feed their eyes with gazing on the man, to whom, under Providence; and the generous aid of our great and good ally, they owed their security, and hopes of future liberty and peace; the courteous affability, with which he received their salutes, lighted up ineffable joys in every countenance, and diffused the most animated gratitude through every breast.

"You would have thought the very windows spoke, so many greedy looks of young and old through casements darted their desiring eyes upon his visage; and that all walls, with painted imagery, had said at once, 'God save thee, Washington.'

"The General's arrival was marked by the discharge of cannon, and he was accompanied to his Excellency the Governor, by the honest acclamations of the whigs; a few tories, to expiate their crimes and shuffle off the opprobium of their characters, feebly joined in applauding the man whose successes had annihilated their hopes, and whose conduct was a satire on their principles. The President of the Senate, Speaker of the House of Delegates, Members of the House of Delegates, Members of the General Assembly and Council, and many of the citizens, hastened to offer their tribute of affection, which was richly repaid by the engaging frankness and affectionate politeness of the reception. The evening was spent at the Governor's elegant and hospitable board with festive joy, enlivened by good humour, wit, and beauty.

"On the next day the General partook of a public dinner given by the legislature, as a mark of their respect, and to render the participation of his company as general as possible. In the evening the city was beautifully illuminated, and an assembly prepared for the ladies, to afford them an opportunity of beholding their friend, and thanking their protector with their smiles.

"His Excellency, to gratify the wishes of the fair, crowned the entertainment with his presence, and with graceful dignity and familiar ease so framed his looks, his gestures, and his words, that every heart overflowed with gratitude and love, and every tongue grew eloquent in his praise. When he retired from the assembly — with one united voice, all present exclaimed,

'Unrivalled and unmatched shall be his fame,
'And his own laurels shade his envied name.' " [48]

It was all over but the shouting, after Yorktown. Everybody knew that the British would not continue the war, though King George still thought it ought to be done. This time he was getting no coöperation whatever from his parliament. Englishmen remembered how he had stubbornly insisted on keeping the tea-tax, at the time the other Townshend duties were repealed, and could not help reflecting that a good deal of trouble might have been avoided if Parliament had paid no attention to him then. England's national debt was nearly doubled; she had lost her colonies in America; she was weakened not only by her war with the United States and France, but by simultaneous wars with Spain and the Netherlands who, true to old Charles Carroll's prophecy years ago, had found the opportunity too good to miss. [49] Other European countries, under the leadership of Catherine the Great of Russia, had banded together against England in an "Armed Neutrality." No wonder that when the House of Commons resolved to "consider as enemies to his Majesty and the country" everybody who favored prosecuting the war with the colonies — a thousand pardons, with the United States of America! — the

[48] Ridgely, *Annals of Annapolis*, pp. 200–02.
[49] To William Graves, December 23, 1768; Carroll Papers, II, 120 A & B. See pp. 189–90 above.

measure passed without question. The wartime prime minister, Lord North, resigned and his successor's first move was to open negotiations for peace.

The two years after Yorktown, and before the signing of the formal treaty, were anticlimactic. Washington, a fighting man who now spent most of his time going from one ovation to another — the Annapolitan splurge was a fair sample — put it on record that those years were the dullest he ever spent. Everybody, indeed, was restless. The Articles of Confederation had been found, in practice, to be exceedingly inadequate and yet, pending the treaty of peace, there was little to be done about the formation of a more perfect union. In the meantime affairs were in the wildest confusion, dissatisfaction and dispute everywhere. The thirteen new states quarreled among themselves; the state assemblies were more apathetic than ever. Soldiers clamored for their back pay, and there was not enough money to pay them. Even some of the officers threatened to mutiny. Most startling of all the aftermaths of the war was the growing desire of the men who had fought for liberty to establish an American monarchy, with Washington as King George I. Critically analyzed, this was not out of character, for the American people had always lived under the rule of kings and the Articles of Confederation were certainly not providing a satisfactory form of government in substitute. But it was bitterly discouraging to men like Washington and Charles Carroll of Carrollton to realize that the Americans, after six years of war, neither understood nor valued the principles of liberty.

For Carroll these years before the treaty of 1783 held grief as well as political worry. In the summer of 1781 Molly's mother, Mrs. Darnall, died. This was the "Cousin Rachel" who had been like Carroll's own mother for nearly twenty years, and he mourned her sincerely. He and Molly tried to get old Charles Carroll of Annapolis to move to town with them, after her death, but he still stubbornly asserted that in-laws had no business living with young married people. Not that Charles and Molly Carroll were young married people any more — forty-four was not young for a man who, always in poor health, had noticeably overtaxed his strength during the war years, nor thirty-one for a woman who had borne seven children and seen three of them buried. However, there was no arguing with Papa. There never had been. And now that peace was assured and his most extravagant prophecies about a free Maryland vindicated, he was more sure of himself than ever. He had wanted to live in a free country before he died, hadn't he? His family delighted in his childlike delight that he was doing it. True, he was eighty years old, but he was still physically as well as mentally vigorous. "He is the greatest comfort of my life, & I do all in my power, to render him happy & easy," his son had written a few years before.[50] Not a very gallant remark from the husband of a devoted wife and the father of several attractive children, but that was just how Carroll felt, and he never wasted his famous tact on his family. He cared more for his father than for anyone else on earth, and the old man's splendid health encouraged him to think that he could enjoy his companionship for many years to come.

On May 30, 1782, old Mr. Carroll was standing on the porch of the Annapolis house, focusing his spy-glass on a sailboat on Spa Creek. His attention on the little spot of white, he took a careless step, missed his footing, and fell heavily to the ground. When they picked him up he was already dead.

Molly saw him fall. She was not well, and she never recovered from the shock.[51] She had adored "Papa" only less than she adored her kind, unresponsive husband. She never left her room after the accident, and died less than two weeks later, on the tenth of June.

The double loss was a stunning blow to Charles Carroll of Carrollton. His personal world was in ruins about him. He was left with four young children to plan for, the eldest twelve, the youngest only two years old. Obviously he could

[50] To the Countess of Auzoüer, September 20, 1771; *Maryland Historical Magazine*, XXXII, 203.
[51] *Appleton's Journal*, September 1874.

not cope with this domestic problem alone, so Miss Nancy Darnall, who thanks to the interweaving branches of the Carroll family tree was related to him as well as to Molly, came to live at the Annapolis house and take care of the children. The three older ones, though delicate as their father had been in childhood, flourished under her supervision; but the baby Elizabeth — named, like the first child of his marriage, for Carroll's mother — died in 1783.

Carroll's infinite capacity for hard work now stood him in good stead. During the war years he had got so used to putting politics first that politics seemed now his logical escape. But the circumstances were against him. There was not much surcease to be found in attending a Senate where, as likely as not, he would be the only member present. Mr. Edward Lloyd had kept him company, among the empty chairs and unsullied sand-boxes of the Senate Chamber, at the openings of both the sessions of 1782; but he did not find the experience sufficiently interesting to repeat in 1783. Charles Carroll was the only member present when the Senate was supposed to meet April 21st, and a quorum was not reached until some time in May. Again at the fall session Carroll, this time with two companions, appeared dutifully on November 3rd. He grimly continued to appear every morning for ten days, but when on November 13th there was still no quorum he left town to attend to some private business. He was sick of being a good example, and few of us will blame him.

His private business certainly needed looking after. The Carroll estate had not been one of those which had profited through the war with the mother country. Much of the money which had been out at interest at the time of the Tender Bill's passage had to be written off as nearly total loss, for creditors had flocked to take advantage of the law that let them repay good honest pounds sterling with worthless paper money. The plantations had suffered under the less conscientious management of hired "overlookers," and especially the Baltimore Iron Works, which in the years before the war had provided a good living for each of the stockholders, had been so neglected and poorly managed that they were barely making expenses.[52]

Carroll was still rich enough, though, to play host to the entire community when Annapolis heard the news of the signing of the treaty at Paris. "Tomorrow we celebrate Peace," one Annapolitan lady wrote, April 23, 1783. "I hear there is to be a grand dinner on Squire Carroll's Point, a whole ox to be roasted & I can't tell how many sheep & calves besides a world of other things. Liquor in proportion. The whole to conclude with illuminations & squibs, &c. I had liked to have forgot to mention the Ball which I think had better be postponed. I am horribly afraid our gentlemen will have lighter heads than heels." [53] A wonder if they did not, for it was quite a party. On Carroll's Green, part of the estate which sloped down to Spa Creek on the edge of Annapolis, a large temporary shelter was built and dinner, "an elegant dinner," provided for a large number of private gentlemen as well as for the Governor and his council, the members of the Senate, and the members of the House of Delegates. No ladies were present, for the gentlemen were really much too busy drinking toasts to be bothered

[52] You may be wondering why the Baltimore Iron Works did not boom during these war years, especially in view of Carroll's pre-war and post-war reputation for making money on even slight provocation. In this case the opportunity had practically thrust itself upon him. As early as 1775 Carroll, with Charles Wallace and Daniel of St. Thomas Jenifer, had been "empowered to contract for the making and Delivery of any number not exceeding 1000 good substantial proved Musquets. . . ." (*Archives*, XI, 77.) Other opportunities to provide orders for the Baltimore Iron Works presented themselves throughout the war. But Carroll's attitude in such matters was clearly presented in a letter to William Carmichael, May 31, 1779 (Burnett, *Letters of Members of the Continental Congress*, IV, 238): "The faction of the Lees is industriously propagating, I hear, that their opponents, or most of them, are engaged in mercantile connections with Dean and others. I hope this is not true, for be assured, if it should turn out so, that party will lose the con[fidence of] the People. If members of Congress should engage in trade, their votes in that assembly, it is to be feared, will be often guided by their particular interest. Mr. Chase was excluded from Congress on the current report of his being a speculator. I have heard it said that G. Morris is in trade. I hope the report is groundless. I have a high opinion of that gentleman's abilities, and integrity; the latter may be warped by the prospect of amassing great wealth — ceci entre nous."
[53] Mary Grafton Dulany to Walter Dulany, Jr., April 23, 1783; Elizabeth Hesselius Murray, *One Hundred Years Ago, or the Life and Times of the Reverend Walter Dulany Addison 1769–1848* (1895), p. 67.

with them. There was wine along with the dinner, of course, and when dinner was over there were thirteen toasts — symbolic of the thirteen United States — drunk to the roars of thirteen cannon which had been set up on the green. The ladies, however, had their turn that evening, when they joined the celebration at the brilliant ball held at the Assembly Rooms; and such was the greatness of the founding fathers of Maryland that not a single drunken casualty was recorded for history.

In this same year, 1783, Congress began holding its sessions at Annapolis and Trenton, New Jersey, until the new federal buildings could provide a roof over Congress' head. It was Annapolis' turn that fall, and so it was to Annapolis that General Washington came, in December 1783, to resign his military commission. Everybody crowded to see the great man; the ovations of 1781 were repeated. The Senate Chamber was filled with Maryland celebrities as well as with the members of the national Congress and the officers attached to Washington's staff, and the gallery swarmed with ladies — even Tory ladies. As one of the important tableaux in American history, the scene has been duly painted by Trumbull; you may see it in the Capitol at Washington. There is an excellent study of Charles Carroll of Carrollton. He had an important place in the assemblage, of course, both because he was a Maryland senator and because he had signed the Declaration of Independence; and it is interesting to note that the solemn occasion was not so formal that he was refused permission to bring his children. Everybody was being very kind, since Molly's death, to the three little Carrolls; even though the Custis children had to stay with Madam Washington in the gallery, the Carroll children watched the historic ceremony from the floor of the hall, wedged among celebrities.

Charles Carroll of Carrollton was not used to taking his children about with him. He loved them, now, a great deal more than he had been able to love them when they were babies, but he still did not enjoy their company or find coping with them any less of a problem. He did not understand children and never pretended to. He had grown accustomed to leaving all their problems to Molly. Every once in a while, now that Molly was dead, he would tell himself sternly that he must be both mother and father to his son and daughters, and would conscientiously take them somewhere with him or give them some of his time at home. Probably he even went so far, every once in a while, as to leave his library door open. But these attempts to establish contact with his children were never as successful as they should have been.

It was the partial solution of a problem, therefore, when in 1785 Charles Carroll the Fourth was ten years old, old enough to be sent away to school. Though there was no longer any religious necessity for his going abroad, his father liked the idea of young Charles's going to the College of St. Omer, where both he and his own father had been educated. His own French schooldays had been very happy, in spite of the separation from his mother and father; Charles Carroll of Carrollton honestly felt that boarding-school would be a pleasant change for the motherless little boy whose father — he acknowledged it humbly to himself — had not much talent as a parent.

Young Charles Carroll sailed for Liège in August 1785. It was an important occasion, from the family point of view nearly on a par with General Washington's resigning his commission. Important enough, anyhow, to be recorded in a painting. This one (with portrait-heads, traditionally, by Pine) shows the young traveler surrounded by his father, his big sister Mary, his little sister Kitty, and a lady who has never been certainly identified but who was probably Miss Nancy Darnall. In the background there is a likeness of the little boy's body-servant, black as the ace of spades.

Sister Mary soon took it on herself further to alter the family circle. At the age of seventeen she calmly informed her father that she was engaged to Mr. Richard Caton, a young Englishman of whom the family knew little and approved less. Charles Carroll of Carrollton was aghast. Also he was conscience-stricken. He remembered how carefully and exhaustively his own father had gone into the subject of matrimony, when he himself had approached a marriageable age.[54] And here was Mary, grown up almost before he knew it, getting herself engaged without a word to her father. Young ladies didn't do that in the eighteenth century, even in an enlightened country which had just successfully staged a revolution. Besides, he had always taken it for granted that Mary would marry her cousin, young Daniel Carroll of Duddington. Carrolls had been marrying "family" ever since the Attorney-General first came to Maryland. Cousin Daniel himself — "Cousin Long-legs," Kitty called him —[55] was so sure of the outcome of his courtship that he was complacently taking a tour of France; to him it now became necessary to write a kind and tactful letter.

"Dear Cousin," Charles Carroll of Carrollton wrote to Daniel Carroll: "I am favored with your letter of the 20th September. As the intelligence I am going to give you may make some alterations in your plans, I must impart it to you. My daughter, I am sorry to inform you is much attached to, and has engaged herself to a young English gentleman of the name of Caton. I do sincerely wish she had placed her affections elsewhere, but I do not think myself at liberty to control her choice, when fixed on a person of unexceptionable character, nor would you, I am sure, desire that I should. My assent to this union is obtained on these two conditions, that the young gentleman shall extricate himself from some debts which he has contracted, and shall get into a business sufficient to maintain himself and a family. These conditions he has promised to comply with, and when performed there will be no other impediment in the way of his marriage. Time will wear away the impression which an early attachment may have made on your heart, and I hope you will find out in the course of a year or two, some agreeable, virtuous, and sweet-tempered young lady, whose reciprocal affection, tenderness, and good-

[54] Charles Carroll of Annapolis to Charles Carroll of Carrollton, September 1, 1762; Carroll Papers, I, 84.
[55] Charles Carroll of Carrollton to Daniel Carroll of Duddington, March 13, 1787; Rowland, *Life*, II, 105.

ness of disposition will make you happy, and forget the loss of my daughter. . . ." [56]

As he wrote this fatherly, sensible letter — dignified as all his letters were — he was no doubt remembering a young man who had been unsuccessful with another seventeen-year-old, and wondering: What ever became of Louisa?

Perhaps Carroll had a sneaking hope that young Mr. Caton would not meet the requirements he laid down in his unaccustomed role of stern parent. They were certainly not unreasonable — indeed, solvency and a means of support would seem to be negative virtues in a young man contemplating matrimony — but in a century when it was quite the fashion to be in debt young Mr. Caton's debts were truly magnificent. His fiancée's wealthy father did not lift a finger to help him, but by the autumn of 1787 Richard Caton was out of debt and into business, and he and Mary Carroll were married. Charles Carroll of Carrollton was not one to break his word, though he still could not help regretting Cousin Daniel. But he rose to the occasion with his blessing and the gift of a handsome brick house in Baltimore, and as time went on and he visited there more and more often, he was pleasantly surprised to find that he was really quite fond of Mr. Caton.

But he mentally resolved to keep more of an eye on Kitty. One could not always expect such luck. Perhaps a convent school would be a good idea, later on; he himself, as he had demonstrated, was totally unfit to cope with daughters. He loved them, but he never expected to understand them; and anyway there were more absorbing matters — books to read, and business to see to, and sessions of the Maryland Assembly to attend. Even if nobody else showed up.

[56] March 13, 1787; Rowland, *Life*, II, 104.

CHAPTER VIII

The Federalist

1787–1800

THE MARYLAND ASSEMBLY's devotion to duty had not returned with the return of peace. At the fall session, 1784, it took exactly twenty days to get a quorum in the Senate. In the fall of 1785 it took more than ten days, in the fall of 1786 twenty-four days. And even when enough members had straggled in to permit the Assembly to be declared "in session," the lack of interest in public business had been, to say the least, profound.

But the Assembly which met in November 1787 was very different from its lackadaisical predecessors. The business before the house was the question of the proposed Federal Constitution, and there was hardly a legislative gentleman in Maryland who was taking the matter calmly.

Peace had found the United States in one of the worst messes since the dawn of history. "We have as much to fear from victory as a defeat,"[1] Charles Carroll of Carrollton had said back in 1774; and his gloomiest apprehensions had been realized. The war had been followed by a depression and the "Panic of 1785." The public debt was appallingly large, and even the interest on it could not be paid. Public opinion in favor of an American monarchy increased rapidly; by 1786 Washington was noting that "even respectable characters speak

[1] To Charles Carroll of Annapolis, September 7, 1774; Carroll Papers, III, 258.

of a monarchical form of government without horror." [2] American paper money was hardly worth the paper it was printed on; "hard money" was painfully scarce. Great Britain went to great pains to point out to the United States the disadvantages of being no longer her colonies. She placed a high tariff on all American exports to that country; worse, she forbade the United States to trade in British West-India ports. She no longer gave preference to American products such as tobacco in the English markets; she no longer paid bounties on the production of such crops as rice. Diplomatically, America had very little status at the court of Great Britain. This was not surprising, but her status at the courts of the "friendly" European nations was hardly better. "We are the lowest and most obscure of the whole diplomatic tribe," Jefferson wrote from France.[3] No country had much to gain by being nice to the struggling young United States, which under the Articles of Confederation were united by name but not by nature.

The Articles of Confederation were, in fact, directly responsible for some of America's most harassing difficulties. Inherently weak, they were entirely inadequate in a trying situation.

As Carroll of Carrollton had feared, back in 1777, the thirteen states had not been willing to enter into "such a confederacy, as ought, and would take place, if little and partial interests could be laid aside. . . ." [4] The Continental Congress would never have approved a really strong confederation, nor would any, much less all, of the thirteen states have ratified it if they had. It all went back to the lamentable fact that nearly everybody, whether he admitted it or not, cared more about his state than he did about the country as a whole, and was still intensely conscious of the jealousy and rivalry that had held over from the time the states were colonies. Also, it is necessary to remember that the Articles of Confederation had been prepared five years before they ever went into effect;

[2] To John Jay, August 1, 1786; Sparks, *Writings of George Washington*, IX, 189.
[3] H. C. Hockett, *Political and Social History*, p. 179.
[4] To Benjamin Franklin, August 12, 1777; Burnett, *Letters of Members of the Continental Congress*, II, 450.

and a great deal had happened between 1776 and 1781. The whole American picture had changed. Possibly the Articles would have worked well enough in the America of 1776. They had been designed to meet the needs of that America. The America in which they finally went into effect, when Maryland ratified in 1781, had quite outgrown them.

And the states, in the meantime, had worked out their own salvation. All thirteen had wisely decided to base their state governments on the old tried-and-true, before-the-war colonial political organizations. Eliminating lord proprietaries and kings, of course. In the five years before the Articles of Confederation were finally ratified, the little difficulties incidental to newness had mostly been worked out, and thirteen state governments were functioning with accustomed ease.

Naturally they had little respect for the new national scheme. Congress' lack of power, under the Articles of Confederation, weakened it in all its dealings with them. Congress could make requisition for revenue from the states, for instance, but since it had no authority to collect the money if it failed to come in promptly this did little good. The states contributed to the national government when and if they pleased; Congress usually got about a twentieth of what it asked for. Congress could not force the states to abide by national treaties; so, naturally, no foreign nation cared about making a treaty with the United States. Congress could not checkmate the English commercially by fixing American tariffs; it could not even regulate commerce among the states. Congress could not maintain a standing army, as the Articles of Confederation said it should, because it had no money. Congress could not settle the interstate disputes which constantly arose. The states had hung together, after a fashion, during the war, but now that peace was restored they seemed to imagine that the danger was over.

Across the ocean, England watched the quarreling Americans with poorly concealed interest.

By 1787 the situation was fruitful of real alarm. Washington, who had commented mildly the year before: "The Confederation appears to me to be little more than a shadow without the substance, and Congress a nugatory body, their ordinances being little attended to," [5] now put it strongly: "I do not conceive we can exist long as a nation without having lodged somewhere a power, which will pervade the whole Union in as energetic a manner as the authority of the State governments extends over the several States." [6]

This was obvious to any halfway enlightened layman. It was especially obvious to Alexander Hamilton. So a convention had met at Annapolis, in September 1786, to talk about ways and means of altering the Articles of Confederation. But after the characteristic manner of the Continental Congress and too many of the State assemblies, most of the delegates did not show up. Only five states were represented. The Annapolis Convention adjourned without having done much but resolve to ask Congress to call another convention. Congress did, and a much larger group of gentlemen assembled in Philadelphia the following May. Charles Carroll of Carrollton, rather to the general surprise, was not one of them. He had, indeed, been elected a delegate from Maryland — there were five in all — but he declined. So did three of the other gentlemen. Four new delegates had to be hurriedly elected in the place of the four who had been first choice.

Carroll stayed home because he was needed in Maryland. There it was again. It kept cropping out at all the critical moments, that tendency of the times — even among men who warmly advocated a stronger central government and spared no pains to bring it about — to place state ahead of country whenever a choice became necessary. "This is a most pernicious mistake and must be corrected," Alexander Hamilton, father of the Federal Convention, exclaimed. He always found it extremely irritating that "Each State, in order to promote its own external government and prosperity, has selected its best members to fill the offices within itself, and conduct its own affairs . . . and local attachment falsely operating has

[5] To James Warren, October 7, 1785; Sparks, *Writings of George Washington*, IX, 140.
[6] To John Jay, August 1, 1786; *ibid.*, p. 187-8.

THE RICHARD CATON HOUSE
BALTIMORE, MARYLAND

made them more provident for the particular interests of the State to which they belonged, than for the common interests of the Confederacy. . . ." [7]

We who are a century and a half removed from the beginnings of the republic, and three-quarters of a century from the American Civil War, find this tendency nearly as irritating as Hamilton did. Couldn't they see, these brilliant great men, that it was one of the reasons why the Continental Congress had, through the war, been a weak and ineffectual body compared with the various state legislatures? Couldn't they see that it was one of the reasons why the Articles of Confederation had failed?

Irritating as the tendency might be, though, it was natural. Americans had been Rhode Islanders and Virginians and New Yorkers and Marylanders before the United States had ever been dreamed of. Though most of them, after the United States became a fact, tried honestly to relegate old loyalties and prejudices to their proper place, they still forgot and said "my country" when they meant only a part of America. In fact, Hamilton himself was about the only prominent patriot who put America first — and the reason for that was that he was only an American by adoption. He had been born in the British West Indies and did not owe allegiance to any of the thirteen states.

The spring session of the Maryland Assembly coincided with the convention in Philadelphia, and the important business before it was the question of emitting paper money. This measure had passed the Lower House in last fall's session, mainly through the influence of Samuel Chase; Chase and his partisans were now lobbying earnestly to get it through the Senate. "The partisans in favor of the measure in the lower House threaten, it is said, a secession if it is rejected by that Branch of the Legislature," Washington noted; and he added with weary satire: "Thus are we advancing." [8]

[7] To George Clinton, February 13, 1778; *The Works of Alexander Hamilton*, edited by H. C. Lodge, VII, 1886, 536–40.
[8] To Henry Knox, December 26, 1786; Fitzpatrick, *Writings of George Washington*, XXIX, 123.

Nobody who knew Chase well — as Charles Carroll of Carrollton did — doubted for an instant that he was perfectly capable of leading a rebellion much more efficient than Daniel Shays's, which had recently been put down in Massachusetts. But he considered this the lesser of two evils. A rabid opponent of inflation, Carroll as a successful business man believed that the worst thing that could happen to Maryland would be the Assembly's adoption of Mr. Chase's scheme for flooding the state with still more worthless paper money. Besides, he was not at all sure about Chase's personal motives. Most people had forgiven if not forgotten Old Bacon-Face's flier in wartime flour, but Carroll had never trusted him since. It was bad enough to see Chase so influential in the Lower House; he was grimly determined that he should not extend his influence to the Senate, and he knew that there was only one man in Maryland important enough to tip the scales against him. And he, Charles Carroll of Carrollton, was that man. He felt he had to stay, no matter what was going on in Philadelphia. His contemporaries — whatever we may think of him — thought he was exactly right. They would have done the same thing if they had been in his place; some of them did follow his example. Thomas Johnson, also a delegate to the convention, stayed to help him, as he had loyally helped him at other times during the last ten or twelve years. Together they "declined quitting Maryland even upon the important business of new framing the national Government, Mr. Chase having just before menaced the Senate for rejecting an emission of paper money and appealed to the people against them. They had joined in that general issue and could not venture to relinquish to a violent and headstrong party their active influence in the Senate, as well as in the Lower House, at the very moment when it was so essentially needed to stem the torrent of the populace and for the paper. Those gentlemen, therefore, remained at home, convinced their fellow citizens of their superior rectitude and wisdom, and defeated that favorite measure of Mr. Chase." [9]

[9] John B. Cutting to Thomas Jefferson, July 1788; Gurn, *Charles Carroll*, p. 116.

Charles Carroll had really wanted to go to Philadelphia, too. It was one of the few times in his political life that he felt defrauded and disappointed. Just as he had considered signing the Declaration a privilege, so would he have liked a part in forming the new and more perfect union. And he would have been interested to watch — even if he did not entirely approve — the birth of rival political parties.

Federalists and Republicans. Later there would be other differences between them, but for the moment the simple distinction lay in the fact that the Federalists were those who favored the adoption of the Federal Constitution. The Republicans (or Antifederalists, as their opponents preferred to call them) thought it would have to be drastically amended before it would do. The country promptly split in two on the issue. There were exceptions, of course, but generally speaking the Federalist Party included those seaboard merchants, lawyers, and wealthy planters who had been influential as a class back in the days before the Stamp Act, while the Republicans drew their strength from the people who only in recent years had been heard from politically. These were the small farmers and business men in such districts as the western half of Pennsylvania and the Piedmont Valley of Virginia; also to be reckoned with were the pioneers who were rapidly settling the Ohio country, Kentucky, and Tennessee. A fraction of the latter group would under other circumstances have found themselves in the Federalist camp, for they had been born into the old prewar governing class and had inherited its traditions; but since they were mostly younger sons or confirmed ne'er-do-weels, and comparatively if not actually poor, they did well to cast their allegiance on the side of the Republicans, who in opposing the Constitution as written purposed to protect the interests of the average American.

Aside from the fact that the richest man in America was no average American, Charles Carroll was bound to be a Federalist. He considered the Constitution a masterly document, worth working hard to have ratified. The endorsement of nine states was necessary — and not at all sure. Maryland was one of the "doubtful" states. Even before the Constitutional Convention had closed in Philadelphia, a lively movement against ratification had got under way in Maryland. Its leader was Luther Martin, who had stalked out of the convention hall declaiming: "I'll be hanged if ever the people of Maryland agree to it!" [10] and, having hurried home, was doing his best to see that they did not.

Martin was one of the most colorful, not to say gaudy, figures in all Maryland history. He was attorney-general for twenty-seven years, having secured the post in 1778 through the influence of Samuel Chase. He was drunken, extravagant, ribald, and exceedingly brilliant. Although he was never involved in any actual scandal during his long career, he was not pointed out as a shining example to young gentlemen who wished to become statesmen rather than politicians; and he did not scruple to govern his political credos by his personal animosities. After having viciously attacked the Federalists for a period of years — and given them any number of bad moments, for he was unquestionably a formidable opponent — he suddenly turned Federalist himself, simply because he could not bear to stay in the same party with Jefferson.

Martin, with John Francis Mercer, another of the Maryland delegates, had published on his return home an essay called *The Genuine Information, Delivered to the Legislature of the State of Maryland, Relative to the Proceedings of the General Convention Lately Held at Philadelphia*,[11] in which he set down his criticisms of the proposed Constitution. Unfortunately for the Federalists, they had little information of their own with which to refute it. The Constitutional Convention had met behind closed doors, and precious little of the proceedings had been allowed to leak out. Delegates who kept notes did not publish them till many years later. Except for the tangible result of the finished Constitution, the Federalists were unpleasantly in the dark as to what had gone on in Philadelphia. They reflected bitterly that, if it had not been for Mr. Chase and his questionable scheme of emitting paper

[10] Hockett, *Political and Social History*, p. 220.
[11] Philadelphia, 1788.

money, Mr. Johnson and Mr. Carroll of Carrollton would have been there to see. To add insult to injury, Chase had of course allied himself with the radical party and Chase was a host in himself. Maryland never bore any son more talented at calling names. In later years he and Martin were to quarrel and Martin was to fling at him: "I never prostituted my talents till I defended you and Colonel Burr — the two greatest rascals on earth"; [12] but in 1787 they worked smoothly together, so smoothly that they were an almost unbeatable machine. They succeeded in staving off the ratification vote till spring.

The only record of the convention which met in Annapolis April 21, 1788, to vote on the Constitution is an *Address to the People of Maryland*,[13] prepared by the Republicans and so violently partisan that it cannot be relied on as a source of information. Surely the Federalists were not quite the double-tongued black-hearted devils this pamphlet would have us believe. They were excellent vote-getters, though; they chalked up sixty-three votes to their opponents' eleven. No wonder Washington had said thankfully, touching upon the uncertainty that Maryland would ratify the Constitution, "Mr. Carroll of Carrollton, and Mr. Thos. Johnson, are declared friends of it." [14] Johnson was still the *fidus Achates* and Carroll still, after fifteen years, the First Citizen of Maryland. He had won again, hands down.

The last Maryland Senate to meet under the old Confederation convened at Annapolis November 3, 1788. Charles Carroll of Carrollton was, as always, promptly in his seat. When the session adjourned for the Christmas holidays he and John Henry had been elected senators to sit in the newly organized Federal Congress — the first United States Senators from Maryland.

There seemed no reason why he should not accept. He

[12] *The Private Journal of Aaron Burr* (2 vols., 1838), edited by M. L. Davis, II, 68.

[13] Annapolis, 1788. This pamphlet is very possibly the work of Samuel Chase.

[14] To James Madison, November 5, 1787; Fitzpatrick, *Writings of George Washington*, XXIX, 305.

wanted to accept; the question of religion was *passé*, thank
heaven, and Congress under the new and more perfect form
of government should not be the spineless, bloodless, helpless
body he had known before. Certainly there were few ties to
keep him in Annapolis. Papa and Molly and Cousin Rachel
were all dead, little Molly was married, little Charles at school
in France. He had been thinking for some time of sending
Kitty, too, away to school; the big lonely house on Spa Creek
was no place for a lively ten-year-old. He would shut it up,
or turn it over to the pleasure-loving young Catons to use
during the season, if they wanted to come down. Annapolis
was still a "metropolis" with a "season," even though Baltimore had forged commercially far ahead. Richard Caton
would look after his plantations and his business affairs for
him. He had come to place more and more confidence in the
young Englishman he had disapproved of as his daughter's
suitor; Caton would never be as canny as his father-in-law in
money matters, but he was conscientious and hard-working in
a manner after Carroll's own heart. Carroll himself would
spend part of his time in Annapolis, where he would continue
to attend the sessions of the Maryland Assembly. He had no
idea of giving up his seat there, for even in the midst of his
enthusiasm over the new federal government he was not forgetting that he had been a Marylander before he became an
American. But he hoped that the sessions would be better
attended under the Federal Constitution.

Pending the selection of a permanent national capital, the
first Congress' sessions were held in the city of New York.
Charles Carroll traveled north in April, and was in his seat on
the thirteenth. On that same day he was named on the Judiciary Committee; shortly thereafter he was made one of the
committee to receive General Washington, who was expected
to arrive within a few days to be inaugurated first president of
the United States. The great man left Mount Vernon April
16th, stopping in every city, as he traveled north, to receive
ovations from the assembled citizens, tread on flowers scattered
by flowered-wreathed young ladies, and reply politely to the

terrible heroic poetry of the local bards. April 30th was the "great, important day. Goddess of etiquette, assist me while I describe it," wrote the literary Senator from Pennsylvania.[15]

". . . The President advanced between the Senate and Representatives, bowing to each. He was placed in the chair by the Vice-President; the Senate with their president on the right, the Speaker and the Representatives on his left. The Vice-President rose and addressed a short sentence to him. The import of it was that he should now take the oath of office as President. He seemed to have forgot half what he was to say, for he made a dead pause and stood for some time, to appearance, in a vacant mood. He finished with a formal bow, and the President was conducted out of the middle window into the gallery, and the oath was administered by the Chancellor. Notice that the business was done was communicated to the crowd by proclamation, etc., who gave three cheers, and repeated it on the President's bowing to them.

"As the company returned into the Senate chamber, the President took the chair and the Senators and Representatives their seats. He rose, and all rose also, and addressed them (see the address). This great man was agitated and embarrassed more than ever he was by the leveled cannon or pointed musket. He trembled, and several times could scarce make out to read, though it must be supposed he had often read it before. He put part of the fingers of his left hand into the side of what I think the tailors call the fall of the breeches, changing the paper into his left hand. After some time he then did the same with some of the fingers of his right hand. When he came to the words *all the world*, he made a flourish with his right hand, which left rather an ungainly impression. I sincerely, for my part, wished all set ceremony in the hands of the dancing-masters, and that this first of men had read off his address in the plainest manner, without ever taking his eyes from the paper, for I felt hurt that he was not first in everything. He was dressed in deep brown, with metal buttons, with an eagle on them, white stockings, a bag, and sword.

[15] *The Journal of William Maclay* (1927), p. 6.

"From the hall there was a grand procession to Saint Paul's Church, where prayers were said by the Bishop. The procession was well conducted and without accident, as far as I have heard. The militia were all under arms, lined the street near the church, made a good figure, and behaved well." [16]

Carroll found among the new Senators and Representatives many of the old acquaintances he had made in Continental Congress days. Apparently they had never heard of such an old-fashioned and un-American thing as religious intolerance, for they were extremely cordial. Many of them had brought their wives and families and had taken houses in New York for the session; the round of balls and levees and tea-drinkings was reminiscent of Annapolis in the old days. Mr. Carroll as an extra man — and a very polished, agreeable, and well-mannered extra man — was greatly in demand among the ladies of the "Republican Court"; servants were always knocking at 52 Smith Street with notes of invitation. In between engagements, the Senator from Maryland could relax very comfortably in this fashionable boarding-house, which sheltered also the Maryland representatives, George Gale, William Smith, and his cousin Daniel Carroll.

In May he made a brief trip to Maryland to see Kitty off. She sailed on the twentieth from Baltimore, accompanied by a maid, to enter the English convent school at Liège.

Of course Mr. Carroll stayed at Mary's house while he was in Baltimore, and Mary plied him eagerly with questions about New York. She was Molly's own child; she had already heard many glowing tales of the new federal society at the capital, and what her father had to tell her confirmed her determination to have a taste of it. It was too late in the season to plan a visit to New York, but when her father returned for the second session of the First Congress, some months later, Mary went with him. New York was everything she had expected. As the daughter of a Senator and a Signer of the Declaration of Independence she had an assured position in the new noblesse, and she was a beauty in her own right. She was one of

[16] Maclay, *Journal*, pp. 8–9.

the outstanding belles of the season. In fact she had such a good time that her father had to remind her she did have a nice husband and little daughters back in Baltimore.

"Were I to indulge my own feelings and inclinations, I should always wish you with me," he wrote after he had tactfully effected her departure from New York, "and I shall ever be happy, when you can visit me without rendering your absence from home inconvenient to your husband; he is tender and affectionate, and deserves from you a return of all those little attentions and tender solicitudes which render the marriage state happy." Since Molly's death he had been wondering if he had not frequently been at fault as a husband; he had arrived at the conclusion that he had. Mary should not, if he could help it, make the same mistake.

"I am sure," he went on to tell her, earnestly, "without the mutual performance of those civilities attentions and endearments, I have just spoken of, there can be but little happiness in the married state; and without being happy at home, it is vain to look for happiness abroad. I cannot help thinking there is, particularly in this place, a great deal of precious time wasted in the most frivolous amusements; the chit chat of the tea table, dress and morning visits seems to be almost the sole employment of those ladies, whose parents and husbands are in circumstances to admit the abuse of such silly indulgences.

"Perhaps you may think this too serious and preaching a letter. I wish your happiness, you are often in my thoughts; if you practise those duties, I have glanced at, you will be happy; if you should neglect them, your conscience will reproach you with the neglect of them; and what becomes of happiness when the mind is not at ease?" [17]

This letter among others shows how much, at fifty-two, he had grown like his father, old Charles Carroll of Annapolis. (Eliminating the lack of control; Mr. Carroll of Carrollton's magnificent command of himself had, if anything, increased with his years.) People who had known them both commented on the growing resemblance, and Carroll always felt

[17] Undated; Field, *Unpublished Letters*, pp. 168-9.

flattered and grateful. His father had been the most admirable and important person in his world; his death had put a period to the most intimate human relationship he had ever enjoyed. After a few years his son-in-law, Richard Caton, became more or less his confidant, but the several important years after his father's death are significant in their absence of revealing letters. Lacking his father, there was nobody Charles Carroll of Carrollton talked to intimately on paper.

This is particularly regrettable when added to the fact that Congress was evidently not interested in preserving its doings for posterity. The few notes that were made officially were skimpy and unsatisfactory. Congress met behind closed doors, and if it had not been for those members who were in the habit of keeping diaries we should know practically nothing.

Premier diarist of his day was the Honorable William Maclay, United States Senator from Pennsylvania. His account of Washington's inauguration, previously quoted, is a fairly typical excerpt. Maclay wrote without his gloves on. He had a keen eye and a keener wit; though he obviously preferred certain members of the Senate to others he always tried to be just and almost always succeeded, and he made the august members of the First Congress "come alive" as few writers, contemporary or modern, have succeeded in doing. They all got their due in the diary, and "Mr. Carrol" was one of those whose name frequently appeared.

Maclay liked Carroll, which was a real feather in the latter's liberty cap. A plain farmer-lawyer from the interior of Pennsylvania — where the land and the people and the outlook in general were decidedly different from that part of the state around sophisticated Philadelphia — Maclay was from the first suspicious of Federalists and all they represented. Carroll was one of the most outspoken Federalists in Congress, and his part in bringing the reluctant Maryland convention into line was not unknown in New York. But he was not, as Maclay soon found, one of those Federalists who were advocating certain measures one-tenth for the advantage of their country and nine-tenths for the advantage of themselves. Also Maclay was glad to discover that the richest man in America, who was also among the most socially secure, was not in the least a snob. He was thus a refreshing change from, for example, Mr. John Adams. Adams had been middle-class Massachusetts all his life and was so thoroughly enjoying his elevation to the political aristocracy that he could hardly fulfill his duties as vice-president. Maclay was not the only one who was disgusted with the airs and graces of "This son of *Adam,*" but no one touched him up more neatly than did Maclay in his entry of March 17, 1790. We shall be less interested in the exposé of Mr. Adams than in the fact that Mr. Carroll of Carrollton is there, too, to the life:

"Before the Senate was formed this morning, Mr. Carrol, of Carrolton, happened to be sitting next to me. We were chatting on some common subject. The Vice-President was in the chair, which he had taken on the performance of prayer. He hastily descended, and came and took the chair next to Mr. Carrol's. He began abruptly: 'How have you arranged your empire on your departure? Your revenues must suffer in your absence. What kind of administration have you established for the regulation of your finances? Is your government intrusted to a viceroy, nuncio, legate, plenipotentiary, or *chargé d'affaires?*' etc., etc. Carrol endeavored to get him down from his imperial language telling him he had a son-in-law who paid attention to his affairs, etc. 'Twas in vain. Adams would not dismount his hobby. At it again; nor was there an officer, in the household, civil, or military departments of royal or imperial government that he had not an allusion to. I pared my nails and thought he would soon have done, but it is no such easy thing to go through the detail of an empire. Guardian goddess of America, canst thou not order it so, that when thy sons cross the Atlantic they may return with something else besides European forms and follies? But I found this prayer ruffled me, so I left them before Adams had half settled the empire." [18]

Carroll was more polite a listener than Maclay. But it was

[18] Maclay, *Journal,* pp. 210–1.

not just that. He had known Adams long enough to realize some of the good qualities which balanced off his petty ones. Nevertheless as the session proceeded even Carroll's tolerance was sorely tried. Entirely too much of the Congress' time was taken up with questions of precedence and place, the proper titles for the president and his lady, the vice-president and his lady, and so on. If Adams had had his way we should have had a "Republican Court" indeed. Carroll stubbornly balked him at every turn. "Mr. Carrol, of Maryland, showed he was against titles," is the first mention of him in Maclay's diary, April 24, 1789.[19] "Mr. Carrol got up to declare that he thought it of no consequence how it was in Great Britain; they were no rule to us, etc.," on April 30th. "Mr. Carrol rose and . . . spoke against kings," on May 8th.[20] "Mr. Carrol expressed great dislike at the fore part of the motion, which stated the acts of the Senate to be in favor of titles, when, in fact, no such resolution ever had passed the Senate. I rose and moved a division of the motion. Was immediately seconded by Mr. Carrol. Now a long debate ensued. . . . Mr. Carrol declared that . . . it was well known they [the Senate] were not all for titles. He was opposed, and so were sundry other gentlemen. He wished only for a fair question, that it might be seen who were for them and who were not. He wished the yeas and nays, and let the world judge. . . . Mr. Carrol called for the yeas and nays. None rose with him but Mr. Henry [the other Senator from Maryland] and myself, and for want of another man we lost them." [21] This was the Carroll the Maryland Senate knew, willing to fight everybody single-handed, if necessary, whenever he was convinced in his own mind. Even in that snobbish Congress his earnestness made some impression. By June 4th, "Up now rose Grayson, of Virginia, and gave us volley after volley against all kinds of titles whatever. Louder and louder did he inveigh against them. Lee looked like madness. Carrol and myself exchanged looks and laughs of con-

[19] Maclay, *Journal*, p. 2.
[20] *Ibid.*, pp. 7, 23.
[21] *Ibid.*, pp. 34-5.

gratulation. Even the Vice-President himself seemed struck in a heap — Izard would have said *rotundity*. Grayson mentioned the Doge of Venice in his harangue, as he was mentioning all the great names in the world. 'Pray, do you know his title?' said the Vice-President from the chair. 'No,' says Grayson, smartly, 'I am not very well acquainted with him.' " [22]

Carroll was made one of the members of the committee on titles. He was decidedly in the minority, most of the gentlemen holding it necessary that "all the world, civilized and savage, called for titles." [23] In his extreme simplicity, Carroll would have liked to hear the president called, simply, "The President of the United States," feeling that this was title enough. Finally the gentlemen compromised on "His Excellency," which, though a bit pretentious, was not ridiculous as "His Highness" or "His High Mightiness" would have been. Some months later the admiring Maclay recorded in his diary: "Carrol, of Carrolton, edged near me in the Senate chamber and asked me if I had seen the King of France's speech and the acts of the 'Tiers États,' by which the distinctions of the nobility were broken down. I told him I had, and I considered it by no means dishonorable to us that our efforts against titles and distinctions were now seconded by the representative voice of twenty-four millions. A flash of joy lightened from his countenance. . . ." [24]

Maclay was not given to throwing words around. It is interesting to note that the word he used here was "joy," not "complacence" or "gratification."

This was the sort of thing that must have made Charles Carroll regret his father's not being there to see. And how proud the old man would have been of the first of the ten amendments which Congress approved for the new Constitution: "Congress shall make no law regarding an establishment of religion, or prohibiting the free exercise thereof. . . ." Perhaps Charles Carroll of Carrollton did not actually push this part of the Bill

[22] *Ibid.*, p. 63.
[23] Maclay, *Journal*, p. 22.
[24] *Ibid.*, p. 227.

of Rights. That is one of the things about the first Congress
that we do not know. But in any case he was there in his seat,
a useful object lesson, as he had been every day of his life
for sixteen years.

From the amount of time they had devoted to discussing
titles you would have thought the First Congress had little
important business on hand. The very reverse was true. Unfortunately for harmony, the most pressing questions to be
decided were Federalist measures, and the session degenerated
into a contest between Federalists and Republicans. First there
was the matter of a permanent capital of the United States —
finally, in large part owing to the work of Charles Carroll of
Carrollton, located on the Potomac on ground that had been
part of Maryland — the judiciary bill, and the tariff. Alexander Hamilton, the brilliant Federalist leader, was the author of
three schemes: the first, to fund at face value all the United
States' continental debt and to transfer to the Federal Government all the individual war debts of the individual states;
the second, to establish a United States Bank; and the third,
to raise money through the establishment of certain customs
duties. It was contended by the Republicans — and with some
justice — that the Federalists' proposed measures regarding the
bank and the funding of the depreciated debt would benefit
the wealthy Americans who, either by circumstance or design,
held large quantities of paper money, and would work a hardship on the small farmers and business men who had sent Republican representatives and senators to Congress. Carroll, as
an experienced and successful money-maker in private life,
thought plans of Hamilton's sort inevitable if the United States
were to be put on any sound financial basis. His point of view
nearly broke Maclay's heart. He was used to having Carroll
support him in opposition to petty snobbery, used to making
entries in his diary such as this one: "Attended at the Hall.
And now the report of the committee on the Compensation
bill was taken up. As I knew there was a dead majority against
everything I could propose, I had determined not to say a
word; but flesh and blood could not bear them. The doctrine

seemed to be that all worth was wealth, and all dignity of character consisted in expensive living. Izard, Butler, King, Morris, led boldly. They were followed by the bulk of the Senate, at least in the way of voting. Mr. Carrol, of Maryland though the richest man in the Union, was not with them. . . ." [25] Now he sadly made entry in his diary for July 15, 1789: "Senate met. Mr. Carrol . . . spoke a considerable length of time. The burden of his discourse seemed to be the want of power in the President, and a desire of increasing it. Great complaints of what is called the *atrocious assumption of power in the states.* . . . How strangely this man has changed!" [26] A year later he wrote: "Since I am obliged to give up Carrol's political character, I am ready to say, 'Who is the just man that doeth right and sinneth not?' " [27]

Maclay was mistaken. Carroll had not changed. Maclay had at the first encountered only one side of him — the aristocrat who preferred simplicity, because he had no need to affect anything else, the patriot who supported the cause of the soldiers who had fought through the war. Now he was meeting a financier who was quite as sharp as Alexander Hamilton.

Carroll and Maclay were still congenial, however, in that they were both soon disgusted with the United States Senate. Maclay, whose first experience in politics it was, by his own admission "came here expecting every man to act the part of a god; that the most delicate honor, the most exalted wisdom, the most refined generosity was to govern every act and be seen in every deed. What must my feelings be on finding rough and rude manners, glaring folly, and the basest selfishness apparent in almost every public transaction? They are not always successful it is true; but is it not dreadful to find them in such a place?" [28] Carroll, with long years of public service behind him, was of course not so naif, but he was incurably hopeful that the Congress under the new Federal

[25] Maclay, *Journal*, p. 136.
[26] *Ibid.*, pp. 110–1.
[27] *Ibid.*, p. 313.
[28] *Journal*, p. 140.

Constitution would lack the most glaring faults of the old governing body. When he found that it was not a great deal better he did not resort to Maclay's rhetoric; he did not rail against the way things were going because it was no use. He simply wished that he were out of it. "I can't at present form any opinion when Congress will adjourn," he wrote to his daughter Mary Caton, April 14, 1790; "some think about the end of next month or the middle of June; I suspect that the Session will last till the end of September, and if it terminates in funding the foreign and domestic debt of the Union, I shall not regret its length, tho' I am already tired of my situation and wish to be at home, where I could employ my time more to my satisfaction than in this place." [29]

In spite of the fact that he was tired of serving in the Senate, he accepted without protest his reëlection to that body in November 1790. He felt there was still work for him there. He had taken up his place in national politics about where he had left it in 1778, when he was so well established that he had been offered the presidency of the Continental Congress. He was a person of real influence in the Senate, and his particular kind of influence was sadly needed. The Senate was too sharply divided between Republicans who opposed on principle whatever the Federalists suggested, and Federalists whose sound financial measures were leavened by their lack of democratic principle and practice. Already there were distinct monarchical leanings in the Federalist Party. Mr. Carroll, a sound financier, backed by the unavoidable prestige of his reputation as the richest man in America, was needed to take the monarchists down a notch, every once in a while. He was especially needed in the Senate, too, because he was one of the few patriots whose faith in the principles of American liberty had survived fifteen trying years. Maclay had recorded in May 1789: "The discourse was general on the subject of government. 'If our new government does well,' said our Vice-President, 'I shall be more surprised than ever I was in my life.' Mr. Carrol said he hoped well of it; it would be sufficiently

[29] Field, *Unpublished Letters*, p. 161.

powerful. 'If it is,' said Mr. Adams, 'I know not from whence
it is to arise. It can not have energy. It has neither rewards
nor punishments.' Mr. Carrol replied the people of America
were enlightened. Information and knowledge would be the
support of it. Mr. Adams replied, information and knowledge
were not the sources of obedience; that ignorance was a much
better source. . . ." [30]

During all the time that he had been serving as United States
Senator, Charles Carroll had been serving also in the senate
of his own state. He was one of the committee appointed in
1790 to revise the state constitution; in the same year he had
industriously if ineffectively opposed voting the irrepressible
Samuel Chase two hundred and fifty pounds "for his services
in defending the State of Maryland in the English Chancery
suits." Family affairs called him home less often than in the inconvenient days of the old Continental Congress, but neither
roads nor means of transportation had been improved since
then, and New York was many weary miles farther from Annapolis than Philadelphia had been. And Carroll's health was
much worse than it had been at the beginning of the war. He
had been delicate from childhood and had reached the middle
fifties only by taking the most constant care of himself. By
eighteenth-century standards he was, in any case, on the down-
ward slope; he himself said: "The infirmities of age are coming fast upon me." [31] Everybody took the statement quite
seriously and sympathetically; how could anyone know that
this delicate son of a delicate father (who, incidentally, had
lived to be eighty and then died from falling off the front
porch) would celebrate ninety-five birthdays? Mr. Carroll's
friends had in the past few years increasingly regretted that he
felt it his duty to hold two political posts at the same time —
and none of them regretted it more than Mr. Carroll himself.
It was with obvious relief that he wrote to John Henry, his
colleague in the United States Senate, on December 3, 1792:
"Last Friday, the law disqualifying members of Congress from

[30] *Journal*, pp. 52–3.
[31] To George Washington, January 5, 1793; Rowland, *Life*, II, 199.

holding seats in our Legislature, &c, passed the Senate, myself
and Mr Worthington only voting in the negative. On the same
day I resigned my seat in the Senate of the United States.
Tomorrow my successor will be appointed — three persons
are mentioned, Mr Potts, James McHenry and Col. Stone.
Thus I have got rid of a trust which I really accepted with
reluctance and which, I assure you, hung heavy on my
mind. . . .

"If anything new and interesting turns up, drop me a line or
two. Though not a player myself, I shall find myself interested in the game that is played." [32]

Apparently, he had never considered the possibility of
sacrificing his seat in the Maryland senate to his seat in the
Senate of the United States. From his point of view it was not
really a possibility at all.

The retirement of Mr. Carroll of Carrollton from national
politics was the occasion for great regret among his Federalist
friends. The Republicans could not be expected to mourn —
he was too formidable an opponent — and yet some of them
did.

President Washington hastened to try to draw him back into
the national spotlight. He quite understood his old friend's
reluctance to give up his connection with Maryland politics
but no one knew better than he that capable and conscientious
statesmen were rare among the crowd of politicians and op-
portunists with whom he found himself still surrounded as he
began his second term. Asking Carroll to undertake the commission of treating with the Western Indians — who had been
massacring white pioneers right and left in the newly colo-
nized territory of the Ohio — he wrote candidly: "It is necessary, that characters be appointed, who are known to our
citizens for their talents and integrity, and whose situation in
life places them clear of every suspicion of a wish to prolong
the war; or say rather, whose interest in common with that of
their country is clearly to produce peace. Characters, uniting
these desiderata, do not abound." [33]

[32] *Ibid.*, 189–91.
[33] January 23, 1793; Sparks, *Writings of George Washington*, x, 313-4.

Carroll refused the commission on account of his health and advanced also the old excuse which he had produced every time he had ever been asked to take any public office, his fear that he was not sufficiently well qualified. His contemporaries, often of lesser talents, appear to have been seldom afflicted with this reluctance; but Carroll wrote quite feelingly and honestly to Washington: "The anxiety . . . of mind I should experience from the responsibility of the station and dread of not answering your and the public expectation and wishes . . . really might disqualify me for the business." [34]

Not only Washington, but the whole Federalist Party, was interested in seeing Carroll back in public affairs. In 1792 they had been prepared to offer him the Federalist candidacy as President of the United States. Up to almost the last moment it had been uncertain that Washington would be willing to run again. His first term of office had not been an unqualified success. The growing unpopularity of his party had reflected on him too; even the great man's military record and his undoubted integrity did not save him from criticism. Washington had not liked the way many people had treated him as a demigod, but, being quite human, he had found even more unpleasant the Republican attitude toward him as a battle monument that had no further use in active politics. Our old friend Maclay spoke for his party when he said: "Republicans are borne down by fashion and a fear of being charged with a want of respect to General Washington. If there is treason in the wish I retract it, but would to God this same General Washington were in heaven! We would not then have him brought forward as the constant cover to every unconstitutional and irrepublican act." [35] Washington's own cabinet was torn in two in the dispute between Hamilton, Secretary of the Treasury and the leader of the Federalists, and Jefferson, Secretary of State and the leader of the Republicans. Washington himself was heartily tired of trying to make peace between them and tired of being a bone of contention. He would have been thankful to quit public office at the close of his first term

[34] January 28, 1793; Rowland, *Life*, II, 199.
[35] *Journal*, p. 341.

and go back to quiet Mount Vernon. Even his own party-members, some of them, thought that this might be a good thing. However, Washington's candadacy, if he would consent to it, would at least insure the Federalist Party another term in office. The General's prestige was still such that he would probably be unopposed out of courtesy; if anyone else were to be the Federalist candidate it was probable that Jefferson would run against him. Jefferson was already politically strong and growing stronger. It would take a big man to oppose him. James McHenry wrote to Hamilton August 16, 1792: "I mentioned Mr. Carroll as proper to be brought forward to oppose a man whom I suspect the antifederal interest will unite in supporting, in case of an opportunity." [36] He meant Jefferson, in case Washington chose not to stand again for office. And the all-powerful Federalist leader replied: "Your project with regard to the Presidency, in a certain event, will, I believe, not have an opportunity of being executed. Happily for the public tranquillity the present incumbent, after a serious struggle, inclines, if I mistake not, to submit to another election. If it turns out otherwise, I say unequivocally — I will cooperate in running the gentleman you mention, as one of the two who are to fill the two great offices. Which of the two may turn up *first* or *second*, must be an affair of some casualty as the Constitution stands.[37] My real respect and esteem for the character brought into view will insure him my best wishes in every event." [38]

If Hamilton had supported Carroll it goes without saying that he would have received the Federalist nomination. If so, he would very probably have been able to defeat Jefferson, who though gaining rapidly was not yet fully established and even four years later was defeated by John Adams, a much less

[36] Bernard C. Steiner, *Life and Correspondence of James McHenry* (1907), p. 136.

[37] Under the old scheme the runner-up got the vice-presidency.

[38] A letter from McHenry to Hamilton, October 20, 1792, encloses these words in quotation marks, stating that they are from Hamilton's letter to McHenry "of the 10th ultimo." Hamilton, *Works of Alexander Hamilton*, v, 536.

likely Federalist than Carroll. But no use to speculate. Carroll probably would have refused this too, as he had refused most of the political opportunities that had come to him. Poor health, he would have said. Talents unequal to the task.

Back in Annapolis, Carroll welcomed home his two younger children, Charles and Kitty. Charles at nineteen had, if he had not exactly finished his education, at least absorbed all he seemed likely to absorb from foreign founts of knowledge. To his father's deep regret and considerable puzzlement (for he believed in heredity) young Charles was not in the least a scholar. He was not inclined to ponder for hours over the philosophical works of Cicero, as his father and grandfather had so enjoyed doing; he found the comedies of Molière only mildly amusing; and he took no pride whatever in being able to quote the Aeneid. Nor did he show any serious purpose in life or, indeed, any desire for one. There was no doubt that he would get along well in the world — he had enough good looks and charm for half-a-dozen young men — but his serious-minded father could not help regretting his outlook. Young Charles Carroll felt quite sure that the world owed him a good time; he was vague about having, in his turn, any duty to the world.

Kitty, for her part, was sixteen and though hardly more erudite than her brother had acquired quite as much knowledge as was either necessary or desirable in a well-born young female. She had become very pretty — not as pretty as her elder sister Mary, but quite pretty enough — and was less "puny" than she had been before she went to Liège. Her father was not in the least disappointed in Kitty. Not that he intimated to anybody that he was in the least disappointed in Charles.

The Carroll children had returned from France rather hurriedly because of the French Revolution, now well under way. Though at first approving France's bid for liberty, Charles Carroll of Carrollton was aghast at the means of securing it which the French people had resorted to. "I am happy to hear that affairs in France are going on so well," he had written to Jefferson in 1791; "on the success of the revolution in that country, not only the happiness of France but the rest of Europe, and perhaps our own, depends. I wish sincerely freedom to all nations of the earth; to France, from education and gratitude, I feel a particular attachment. With such feelings, it is not surprising that I should view with anxious care the proceedings of the National Assembly. I own my doubts of a happy issue to their new system do not arise so much from the opposition of the dignified clergy and noblesse, as from the fear of disunion, the side views and factions, combinations and cabals, amongst the popular party. God send my apprehensions may be entirely groundless." [39] They had, however, been only too thoroughly realized. King Louis XVI had been guillotined in January 1793. In June of the same year the downfall of the Girondists had ushered in the Reign of Terror. One of the outstanding sufferers during the Terror had been the Roman Catholic Church — the revolutionists having conceived against all religion that prejudice which is usually a feature of the popular uprising — and neither convent schools nor colleges operated by the Society of Jesus were very safe places, even for the children of one of America's best-loved patriots, who had been foremost in the cause of liberty. Charles and Kitty would have been even less safe if the citizens of France had known Charles Carroll of Carrollton's uncomplimentary Federalist opinion of the way they were going about their revolution.

Carroll was by this time generally accepted as an ardent Federalist, though in reality there were several Federalist measures to which he was certainly not much "attached." History too has set him down as a dyed-in-the-wool party man, and this he never was. He had, in fact, a very low opinion of political parties, all political parties, and regretted that human nature apparently made it impossible for such factions to be outlawed. He had held this view as a young man, and a long career in politics had shown him no reason to change it. He was twenty-eight when he wrote to a friend in England: "We have political parties amongst us but they are too trivial and

[39] April 10, 1791; Gurn, *Charles Carroll*, p. 147.

of too little consequence for me to relate or you to hear: I shall only observe that they seem to me to spring from the same source in which your factions have theirs: the want of a sufficient number of lucrative offices to gratify the avarice or the ambition of the 'Outs.' " [40] He was sixty-three when he declared roundly: "If our country should continue to be a sport of parties, . . . anarchy will follow." [41] Since there were to be parties, Carroll on the whole preferred the Federalist to the Republican, but there were many things about it that he strongly disliked, and he made no bones of saying so.

The nature of both parties had undergone considerable change since the adoption of the new Federal Constitution. In the beginning the Federalists had favored the Constitution and the Republicans had opposed it; but once it had been set in operation, and found to work well, the Republicans said as many kind words for it as the Federalists had ever done. It was the same with the Federalist measures which had been so violently opposed by Republicans in the first session of Congress. Hamilton's scheme for funding the national debt, for example, they had bitterly fought; but Republicans as well as Federalists were pleased to find their country benefited in every way by the establishment of a respectable national credit. There soon developed, however, a new and more important difference between the two factions — a difference which was actively debated for nearly a hundred years, was one of the chief causes of a great civil war, and still lurks in the background of the Democratic and Republican parties which have succeeded the old Republican and Federalist parties. This was the question of strong state governments versus a strong national one.

Another difference — which, too, is still harrowing their political successors today — was the question of whether the Constitution should be interpreted strictly or liberally.

Idealistically, there was little to choose between the two

[40] To Edmund Jennings, November 3, 1765; Field, *Unpublished Letters*, p. 98.
[41] To James McHenry, November 4, 1800; Steiner, *McHenry*, p. 473.

parties. Each had excellent arguments on its side. But, practically, each had its glaring faults. It did not look well, for instance, that many prominent Federalists had feathered their own nests luxuriously as a result of some of the excellent Federalist financial schemes; or that many others outspokenly cast slurs on the simplicity of our national government and praised the way they did things in Great Britain. On the other hand, the Republican Party's endorsement of what was going on in France — where crimes were being committed hourly in the name of liberty — was decidedly not to their credit.

It was the French situation which at this time was the cause of most of the animosity between the two American political parties. If conservatives — and conservatives were usually to be found in the Federalist camp — were scandalized at what the French popular party were doing, they were even more exercised over the increasing strength of the American popular party who, trading on the magic word "liberty," might turn out as badly. They worried over Jefferson's increasing influence over that party; they remembered that he had said, when a certain rebellion in Massachusetts had sought to wipe out old debts, "No country should be long without one." [42] And Charles Carroll, for one, could not forget seeing "a letter of his, in which, amongst several others, was contained this strange sentiment, — 'that to preserve the liberties of a people, a revolution once in a century was necessary.' " [43] A dangerous man, all the conservative Federalists agreed.

When it came to distrust of Jefferson, Charles Carroll was as strong a Federalist as anybody. But he was often out of step with his party. He was supposed to believe in a strong central government, for instance, and he did believe in it up to a point. But time and time again, when a personal choice became necessary, he had put Maryland first. Now in the matter of American loyalty to France he was more inclined to agree with the Republicans — who claimed that the new

[42] To James Madison, December 20, 1787; *Writings of Thomas Jefferson* (1853–4), edited by H. A. Washington, II, 331–2.
[43] Charles Carroll of Carrollton to Alexander Hamilton, April 18, 1800; Hamilton, *Works of Alexander Hamilton*, VI, 435.

United States, owing in a measure their very existence to French assistance, were morally bound — than with the Federalists who were being realistic or cold-blooded according to the point of view.

Maclay's diary records a typical incident in the Senate of 1789, which serves to illustrate the prevalent Federalist point of view: "Senate met . . . the impost was taken up. There was a discrimination of five cents in favor of nations having commercial treaties with us per gallon on Jamaica spirits. Then rose against all discrimination, Mr. Lee, Mr. Dalton, Mr. Izard, Mr. Morris, Mr. Wingate, and Mr. Strong. . . . I declared for the discrimination; that if commercial treaties were of any use at all, nations in treaty should stand on better terms than those who kept at a sulky distance; but if we now treated all alike, we need never hereafter propose a commercial treaty. I asked if we were not called on by gratitude to treat with discrimination those nations who had given us a helping hand in the time of distress. Mr. Carrol rose on the same side with me. I was, however, answered from all sides. All commercial treaties were condemned. It was echoed from all parts of the House that nothing but interest governed all nations. . . .

"I had to reply as well as I could. . . . It had been asserted that interest solely governed nations. I was sorry it was so much the case, but I hoped we would not in every point be governed by that principle. The conduct of France to us in our distress, I thought, was founded, in part, on more generous principles. Had the interest of principle solely governed, she would have taken advantage of our distress when we were in abject circumstances and would have imposed hard terms on us, instead of treating on the terms of mutual reciprocity. She likewise remitted large sums of money. Was this from the principle of interest only? . . .

"Mr. Langdon spoke, and seemed to be of our opinion. I did not hear a 'no,' however, on the question but Mr. Carrol's and my own." [44]

Something more than loyalty, too, bound the United States

[44] Maclay, *Journal*, pp. 49–51.

to support France. In 1778, in the same treaty in which France pledged her support to the United States, the United States had promised France, in time of war, the use of American harbors. The Republicans thought the treaty ought to be kept at all hazards. The Federalists replied that the hazards were too great. And — the Administration being Federalist — President Washington proceeded to repudiate the treaty. On April 22, 1793, he issued a proclamation of American neutrality.

It was a realistic thing to do, even if it was not the kind of thing that orators like to mention on the twenty-second of February. America could not have helped France much by carrying out her promise. She would have got herself into immediate and serious trouble with France's enemy, Great Britain; and the United States could not afford to be drawn into another war. It was too young, too weak, too poor, too unsure of itself and too unrecognized. The gesture toward France might have cost America her still new, still unpaid-for independence.

Thus Washington probably did what was best for the United States; certainly he thought he did. But, perversely, the United States did not appreciate it. The most unlikely people began to talk loudly about French claims and American honor. The honest bewilderment of the French Republic's envoy, young Edmond Charles Genet — who could not understand why Washington should snub him when everybody else seemed glad to see him — made him a *cause célèbre* overnight.

Following this commotion too closely for the Federalists' political good, a treaty signed with England November 17, 1794, and taking its name from Minister John Jay, caused the Administration to fall into deeper unpopularity. There were public demonstrations against the man whom, a few years before, some Americans had wanted to crown as King George I. If that idea had worried him, this worried him even more. Washington wrote to Charles Carroll of Carrollton, whom he knew he could depend on to view the matter impartially: "Every true friend to this country must see and feel that the policy of it is not to embroil ourselves with any nation what-ever, but to avoid their disputes and their politics; and if they will harass one another to avail ourselves of the neutral con-duct we have adopted. Twenty years peace with such an in-crease of population and resources as we have a right to ex-pect, added to our remote situation from the jarring powers, will in all probability enable us, in a just cause, to bid defiance to any power on earth. Why then should we prematurely em-bark (for the attainment of trifles comparatively speaking) in hostilities, the issue of which is never certain, always expen-sive, and beneficial to a few only (the least deserving perhaps,) whilst it must be distracting and ruinous to the great mass of our citizens.

"But enough of this! The people must decide for them-selves, and probably will do so. . . ." [45]

Charles Carroll of Carrollton did not entirely agree with Washington. He was as hearty an isolationist, and he saw per-fectly why Washington did not want the United States drawn into a European war; but he still thought, as he had thought in 1789 when he had opposed his fellow Federalists in the Senate, that our debt to France should not be so lightly disregarded. The nominal head of the Federalist Party had spoken, how-ever, and Carroll was too good a politician not to dread a split in the party. It was a time for compromise, since a divided Federalist Party would undoubtedly help the Republicans into power.

In 1795, therefore, the Maryland Senate went on record as approving Washington's policy and on the motion of Charles Carroll of Carrollton it was resolved that publicity be given in all Maryland newspapers to the House of Delegates' en-dorsement.

The following year Carroll was mentioned for the post of minister to France, succeeding James Monroe. He had made it pretty plain that he was not to be drawn back into national affairs, so this was more in the nature of a compliment than anything else. Charles Carroll of Carrollton would have made

[45] May 1, 1796; Rowland, *Life*, ii, 204–6.

an excellent minister to the France of a few years before, but not many imaginations could compass the spectacle of his having anything to do with the present atheistical régime. Even Washington said, in a letter to his Secretary of State: "Mr. Carroll of Carrollton, though sensible and attached to Federalist measures, would find himself on quite new ground, and, besides, he has such large concerns of his own to attend to, and is so tenacious of them, that it is morally certain he would not be prevailed on to go." [46]

Jay's Treaty had, meanwhile, done untold harm not only to Washington but to the whole Federalist Party. For many people it was the last straw. They were sick of Hamilton's administration — for it had been Hamilton's, from the first, more truly than it had ever been Washington's. Whatever Jefferson's views on revolutions, his Francomania would not be worse than the Anglomania which Hamilton so freely professed. Under his leadership, the monarchical tendencies in the Federalist Party had become dangerously strong. It was not only the common people — the people whom Hamilton had not hesitated to call "a great beast" and to ignore in his scheme of practical benefits — who were tired of living under a Hamilton régime. And many of them realized that, if Federalist John Adams should be the next president, the Hamilton régime would go forward without apparent interruption. Many of them, therefore, were swinging to the Republican Party. Hamilton admitted it was nothing short of miraculous that the Federalists were not put out of power in the third presidential election. As it was, Adams defeated Jefferson by three votes, a frighteningly small margin.

The Federalists would never have got another chance had not the French Revolution been succeeded by a revolutionary nobody named Napoleon Bonaparte. His exploits were so extensive and brilliant as to alarm even those who had espoused everything French. It became no longer popular to love our former allies and, for the moment, the balance weighed for Federalism.

[46] To Timothy Pickering, July 8, 1796; Sparks, *Writings of George Washington*, XI, 142.

THE FEDERALIST

The characteristic fault of the Federalist Party again asserted itself. Federalists took advantage of their power to push measures more dedicated to self-interest than to the interest of the United States at large.

The most unpopular of these were the Alien and Sedition Acts. A new naturalization law had made fourteen years' residence instead of five necessary before an immigrant could become a citizen; the Alien Acts empowered the president to deport any of these foreigners awaiting citizenship if he thought it best. Naturally, this power was liable to great abuses. The president was not even required to give his reasons, much less grant a trial to the unfortunate alien. The Sedition Act was even worse. Fines and imprisonment were the penalties awaiting those guilty of stirring up rebellion, uniting in opposition to governmental measures, or writing anything "false, scandalous, or malicious" against Congress, the President, or the current administration. This power, too, was open to abuses and was consistently abused. For instance, one of the Republican members of Congress was fined and imprisoned for mentioning President John Adams' "thirst for ridiculous pomp [and] foolish adulation" — something which was only too apparent to anyone who conversed five minutes with the President.[47] This bridle upon free speech was, to say the least, un-American and the prohibition against rebelling and uniting in opposition to governmental measures ridiculous when it came from a nation which had been formed by just those means. A number of prominent Federalists were opposed to these laws and only for the sake of party unity concurred in them. Many, while regretting the aristocratic tendencies which were thus showing themselves in American government, still found the Federalist preferable to the Republican Party, which continued in the championship of France. Charles Carroll of Carrollton was one of these, of course.

The new State of Kentucky now took a hand in national affairs. In November 1798 the Kentucky Legislature passed certain resolutions declaring the Alien and Sedition Acts to be illegal and of no force. Backed up by the Virginia Legislature,

[47] Hockett, *Political and Social History*, p. 263.

Kentucky in the following year "resolved that the several States who formed [the Union under the Constitution], being sovereign and independent, have the unquestionable right to judge of its infraction; and that a nullification by those sovereignties, of all unauthorized acts done under color of that instrument, is the rightful remedy." And Virginia again supported Kentucky's stand. This bold exposition of the Republican creed of states' rights raised such a storm all over the country that the Sixth Congress unwillingly decided to appoint a committee to consider repeal of the Alien and Sedition Acts. The committee reported against repeal, and their report was accepted by the House — but by the small majority of fifty-two to forty-eight. They were not necessarily discerning Federalists who saw, right then, the handwriting on the wall.

A split in the Federalist Party was still to confirm its political doom. John Adams had had enough. He had had a pathetic time of it in the presidential chair, beginning at the moment of his inauguration when people had paid more attention to the outgoing President Washington than to him. He had made the mistake of accepting ready-made the cabinet which had served Washington's second term; and, of course, he was never able to exercise any control over it. So he made the second mistake of trying to rid himself of it in mid-term. Charles Carroll's old friend James McHenry, Secretary of War, was one of those he forced to resign. Naturally, he made enemies, and some of them were important men in the Federalist Party. Then, on top of that, he was foolish enough to try to buck Hamilton himself. Washington had, in what seemed to be a national emergency, accepted for the second time the chief command of the armies of the United States. There was nothing more natural than that he should choose as his second-in-command Colonel Alexander Hamilton, his favorite staff officer during the Revolution and his political mentor ever since. There was no reason from the military point of view why Adams should not have promptly confirmed the appointment. But Adams, inevitably looking at the matter from a personal point of view, remembering all the slights he had suffered at Hamilton's hands, delayed. Tacitly he refused to approve Colonel Hamilton. It may have been good for his character for him to assert himself, even at that late date; but politically it was a grave mistake. Federalist pressure — some of the strongest of it from Washington himself — was immediately brought to bear upon him. Finally, in a towering rage, he had to sign Hamilton's commission.

The breach between Adams and Hamilton made it sure that Adams would not be successful in his bid for reelection, and the other candidates, Burr and Jefferson, were both Republicans. The Federalists did what they could to take the sting out of their inevitable defeat. As Jefferson put it, they retreated into the judiciary. With the administrative branch of government about to be closed to them, they hastened to enlarge the judicial. New judgeships were created, and new and old filled with good strong Federalists. John Adams signed commissions until nine o'clock at night, on the eve of his leaving office; John Marshall, Secretary of State and newly appointed Chief Justice of the Supreme Court, countersigned as busily. The story goes that he was still at it at midnight. On the stroke of the hour Levi Lincoln, symbolically holding Jefferson's watch, walked in on him and made him stop.

And the Federalists were out. They would never be in again. They would have candidates in several more presidential elections, and survive as a party for about twenty more years. But the turn of the new century marked the beginning of the end.

CHAPTER IX

No More Rivers

1800–1817

Bᴀᴄᴋ ɪɴ 1777, when he and his son had been near a quarrel about that matter of the Tender Bill, old Charles
Carroll of Annapolis had lost his temper and written
heatedly to his son: "Are you not too fond of Popularity &
has not that Fondness biased yr Judgment?"[1] If he had lived
to the year 1800 he would have had a satisfactory answer. He
would have seen his son leaving the state senate — severing his
last connection with politics — as one of the most unpopular
men in Maryland. All because he had put his convictions first.

Charles Carroll of Carrollton had had a long and honorable
career in politics — it was a quarter of a century since his election to that first Maryland committee of correspondence — but
nothing in all his political life had become him so well as his
leaving of it. "Patriots . . . are not always consistent,"[2] he
admitted in a letter written the year of his retirement from
politics. It was a year in which many ardent Federalists were
finding it expedient to change themselves into ardent Republicans. Mr. Carroll of Carrollton knew as well as anybody
which way the wind was blowing; but he was never one of
your unpredictable patriots. Nobody was surprised when he
stood firm in his conviction that the Republican Party would
ruin America and bring it finally to revolution. He said so as

[1] November 14, 1777; Carroll Papers, v, 445.
[2] To James McHenry, November 4, 1800; Steiner, *Life and Correspondence of James McHenry*, p. 475.

loudly as ever, even when it was pretty sure that Mr. Jefferson would be the next president. (The only ray of hope he would discover was that, in spite of Jefferson's outspoken predilection for revolutions, "possibly, were he the chief magistrate, he might not wish for a revolution during his presidency.") [3] By refusing to trim his sails to the wind he was, of course, heading for political oblivion. Republicanism was sweeping the country. He knew it and did not care. If it seemed to him hard and unjust that he should sacrifice his career, by implication at least, on the altar of the Federalist Party in which he found so many serious faults, it was not a new sensation. He had offered a similar sacrifice, long ago, to the Roman Catholic Church in the organization of which he saw as many flaws; and he might have said in 1800, as he had said in 1774: "If my countrymen judge me incapable of serving them in a public station for believing ye moon to be made of green cheese, . . . I will serve them in a private capacity notwithstanding. . . ." [4]

But in spite of his defiance Maryland's defection to the Republican Party nearly broke Carroll's heart. He had watched the Republicans' growth to rapid popular power all over the country, but he had hoped against hope for Maryland. He wrote to Alexander Hamilton August 27, 1800: "Our county (Ann Arundel), which was lately so federal, is at present much divided in the upper part of it. I suspect there is a majority for anti-federal candidates to our State legislature. . . .

"Notwithstanding the arts, and lies, and indefatigable industry of the Jacobins in this State, I am of opinion a great majority of its inhabitants are friendly to the federal government and its measures. . . ." [5]

He had so long been nearly all-powerful in his own state, so consistently looked up to and deferred to, and he had so often won against nearly overwhelming opposition, that he could

[3] To Alexander Hamilton, April 18, 1800; Hamilton, *Works of Alexander Hamilton*, VI, 435.
[4] To William Graves, August 15, 1774; *Maryland Historical Magazine*, XXXII, 223.
[5] To Alexander Hamilton, August 27, 1800; Hamilton, *Works of Alexander Hamilton*, VI, 467.

hardly realize the fact that the election of 1800 would certainly go against him. The campaign was unusually bitter. The Republicans elected a majority of the Legislature, and they were not generous in victory. They were particularly jubilant over the political downfall of the First Citizen, Charles Carroll of Carrollton.

There had been a vicious personal campaign against him. One of the Republican papers wrote: "Even old Charles Carroll, that hoary-headed aristocrat, has gone down to the Manor, no doubt with a view to influence the tenants on that place. Shall the people be dictated to by this lordly nabob because he has more pelf than some others? Has he more virtue, more honor, more honesty than a good industrious farmer? Dares he with his British monarchical and aristocratic policies, come into Frederick County to cajole, to swindle the people out of their rights? Is he, old in iniquity as he is, to be the chief director of the people on the Manor? Citizens of Frederick County, set Charles Carroll at defiance!" [6]

Carroll retired from politics a discouraged and an embittered man. He felt that he had worked hard and accomplished very nearly nothing. He worried a great deal about his country — the country he had helped to form. He could not get the political situation out of his mind, though he was no longer in a position to influence it in any way. Because he was politically pessimistic he became personally melancholy. His children actually worried about his state of mind. This is a sample of it, a letter he wrote to his son from his daughter's house in the country:

"I got here last night more than two hours after sunset. Mr. Caton accompanied me from Belvedere. We were overtaken with a thunderstorm about three miles from this place and heavy rain. We took shelter and remained upwards of an hour in a poor cottage where we sat during the height of the storm by a comfortable fire. The good inhabitant, a mother, was giving supper to her three children; it consisted of boiled Irish potatoes and milk. They ate their supper with a good appetite,

[6] Gurn, *Charles Carroll*, p. 173.

and were immediately put to bed. What do you think were my thoughts during this scene? It occurred to me that in the course of a few years I might be driven into exile by the prevalence of an execrable faction, and forced to shelter in as poor a hovel the remnant of a life, a considerable part of which had been faithfully devoted to my country's service. I reflected, however, that if this turn of fortune should fall to my lot, very little would support nature. . . ." [7]

No doubt it was fortunate that, just about this time, young Charles Carroll created a diversion by falling in love.

Charles was twenty-five, handsome, beautifully mannered, and socially a howling success but, it was to be feared, no more serious-minded than he had been at nineteen. His father had been trying vainly, during the last six years, to find some common ground on which they could meet. He was devotedly attached to his son and understood him no better than he understood Mary and Kitty; he never knew quite what to expect next. It had therefore been a pleasant relief when Charles's taste in marriageable young females proved irreproachable. In 1798 he had been calling on Miss Nelly Custis at Mount Vernon, and the Carroll and Washington families were terribly pleased about the way things seemed to be going. He did not "declare himself," however, and in 1799 Miss Custis married her step-grandfather's nephew, Lawrence Lewis. Young Mr. Carroll without appreciable delay started making visits northward instead of southward, to Pennsylvania instead of Virginia, where Miss Harriet Chew lived at Cliveden with her father the Chief Justice. This time he did declare himself, and the two were married on July 17, 1800.

Carroll became very fond of his new daughter-in-law. The wealthy Chews were as definitely "nice people" in Pennsylvania as the Carrolls were in Maryland, and Harriet was the prettiest of six pretty sisters. Her conversation was so amusing that when Washington was sitting to Gilbert Stuart for his portrait (the one that appears as frontispiece in school histories of the United States) he asked Harriet several times to

[7] October 23, 1800; Field, *Unpublished Letters*, pp. 170–1.

keep him company in order that his face might wear "its most agreeable expression." [8] The stern and rock-bound result does no great credit to Harriet's wit, though, unless we reflect on what the picture might have been if she had stayed at home.

For this new daughter-in-law and his only son Charles Carroll of Carrollton built a fine brick house on his Homewood plantation, then not far from Baltimore. (Now, of course, Baltimore has grown around and far beyond it, and the "mansion house" stands on part of the Hopkins campus.) Some people said that Mr. Carroll was setting his son up in the country because he was too much inclined to gay company who, for their part, were too much inclined to look on the wine when it was red. But there is little reason to think so. Baltimore and Annapolis were gossipy towns then as now. Charles Carroll of Homewood (as we must henceforth call him) was "a young man . . . temperate without excess . . . and with few of the vices of the age." [9] This according to George Washington Parke Custis, who as Miss Nelly's brother probably knew. Besides, Charles Carroll of Carrollton donated to the cellars of Homewood at least one "but of Madeira" [10] — which is about five hundred quarts — and it is doubtful that he preferred a son who was a solitary drinker instead of a social one.

Homewood, incidentally, is one of the finest Georgian houses in America. Some architects think it the very finest. It has always been a source of puzzlement to people interested in old houses that the name of the architect has not been preserved; a house for the richest young man in America is an important commission in any century, and such a house as Homewood should have added luster to a well-known architect's reputation and skyrocketed an unknown's to fame. The answer seems to be that no professional architect got the com-

[8] Rufus Wilmot Griswold, *The Republican Court, or American Society in the Days of Washington* (1867), p. 411n.

[9] To George Washington, April 2, 1798; G. W. P. Custis, *Recollections and Private Memoirs of Washington* (1860), p. 101.

[10] Charles Carroll of Carrollton to Charles Carroll of Homewood, July 3, 1800; Rowland, *Life*, II, 243.

mission. Professionals were becoming more plentiful than before the Revolution, but Charles Carroll of Carrollton inclined to the old ways in most matters, and no one knew better than he that good houses were not necessarily the work of professional architects. He knew too many beautiful examples which had been built in the old-fashioned way, planned by the gentlemen-owners who had studied design as part of their cultural education, and executed by skilled "house-carpenters" who were not far from being architects themselves. Besides, Charles Carroll of Carrollton was his father's own son when it came to saving money where he could — and he could have planned Homewood himself without sacrificing quality. He knew a good deal about architecture and was interested in it. We remember the young student in Paris who took "a master of design," and progressed nicely because he had "allways had a taste and turn that way: its a pretty amusement, even usefull not to say necessary in several occasions." [11] Such as planning a house, he meant, some time in the future. In London, and in the course of his travels around England and the Continent, he saw the best European examples; he returned to live in Annapolis, where there are some of the most beautiful Georgian houses in America; and as a prolific book-buyer he had on his shelves not only history and belles-lettres but a number of architectural works, including a full set of *Vitruvius Brittanicus*.[12] If these seem inadequate preparation for the building of such a house as Homewood, remember that it was as much as or more than most of the colonial builders had had, and that the eminent architects Thornton and Jefferson were similarly "untrained."

But whether he drew up the plans for Homewood or not, Charles Carroll of Carrollton went to considerable pains and expense to set his son up in a manner which would do credit to his position. Before he had time to rest from his labors he was called upon to do the same thing for Kitty. She had got

[11] Charles Carroll of Carrollton to Charles Carroll of Annapolis and Elizabeth Brooke Carroll, February 17, 1759; Carroll Papers, I, 40.

[12] Charles Carroll of Carrollton to William Graves, August 9, 1771; *Maryland Historical Magazine*, xxxii, 199.

herself engaged to Robert Goodloe Harper and, like her older sister Mary, she had neglected to speak to her father before-hand.

Charles Carroll's patience with the younger generation was sorely tried. Also, he seriously blamed himself for inattention. He remembered again how carefully his own father had seen to it that he married a young woman suitable in every way; what would he have said to his grandchildren's marrying out-side their Church? Carroll of Carrollton could well imagine. He himself did not object to Protestants as in-laws except that he felt that difference in religion furnished just another possi-bility for friction between husband and wife, particularly if there were children. He did object very strongly to the cir-cumstance that while his daughter would have a large dowry Mr. Harper was as poor as a pre-Revolutionary Catholic church-mouse. He did not doubt that he was the soul of honor and he certainly considered him an intelligent man — had he not entered Congress as a Republican and been converted there to Federalism? — but he could not forgive him his debts. Fortunately for Mr. Harper, he found an ally in Kitty's broth-er-in-law, Richard Caton, who had been in debt once himself. Now he was a prime favorite with Charles Carroll of Carroll-ton and had so much influence with him that the latter with-drew his objections to Mr. Harper and he and Kitty were married at Annapolis May 23, 1801. Cousin Jacky Carroll, now a bishop and soon to become an archbishop, came down from Baltimore to perform the ceremony.

Charles and Kitty both gone, Richard Caton managing his business affairs as capably as he could have done it himself, and the Federal and State governments operating under a Republican régime which found no use for an unreconstructed old Federalist, Charles Carroll found himself without an occu-pation. He was not yet seventy, but people thought of him as an old man and he so considered himself. He was a grand-father several times over, for Mary had a houseful of little girls and Harriet Chew Carroll produced in 1801 Charles Carroll the Fifth, the great-great-grandson of the Attorney-General.

He was as always in poor health and thought it only reasonable to assume that he would not live much longer. He had accepted his retirement from public life as final, and even though he kept abreast of the times and exchanged heated letters with his friends, detailing the foibles of the Republicans and the horrible fate which surely awaited America at their hands, he was at heart glad to be out of the messiness of politics. For the first time since the First Citizen letters had catapulted him to public notice he was free to do the things he liked to do. In the last twenty-five years, for example, he had more often than not been separated from his beloved library. "Money cannot be laid out better, in my opinion than in the purchase of valuable books," [13] he had written as a young man; and every year since then, even during the war and subsequent depression, when he could hardly collect the interest on the moneys owing to him, he had added to his collection of books. But his favorites were the old ones: his very special favorite was the dirty old volume of Cicero which he had read as a child at St. Omer. This had gone with him to New York and Philadelphia and Valley Forge; he had it now nearly by heart. Still, it was good to be back among his own bookcases. Then too he had missed his daily ride on his own horse. Strange horses were not the same, just as other people's books, however kindly loaned, were never as much pleasure to read. Back at his own estate, he rode many miles on every decent day. He was keeping open house again, not for political associates but for the friends he really cared for, the old Maryland friends of the pre-war days. He had time for the races and the theater again and he found himself not too old to look on, at least, at the dancing parties and assemblies. He took back from Mr. Caton some of the management of his plantations, and found enjoyment, as he had in his younger days, in "that state or manner of life which is least exposed to corruption, or endangered by faction. I mean that of a private gentleman, pursuing the amusements of agriculture. . . ." [14]

[13] To William Graves, August 14, 1772; *Maryland Historical Magazine*, XXXII, 215.
[14] To Edmund Jennings, August 9, 1771; *ibid.*, XXXII, 198.

The renewed close contact with his plantation people focused Charles Carroll's mind again on one of the subjects in which he had been deeply interested for years, but which had often been pushed aside by the pressure of public affairs, the question of slavery. It was a question on which he felt very strongly, and, as usual, his opinions were wholly consistent with his character and far in advance of his times. Carroll, like Jefferson (though how he would have hated to be bracketed with Jefferson, as he has to be so many times when it is a matter of public welfare instead of politics!) was a conservative abolitionist. Ever since he had come into his inheritance he had wanted to set his people free.

They spoke of their slaves as their "people," these southern slave-holders who, like Carroll of Carrollton, had helped launch the American Revolution and honestly cherished the principles of liberty. By evading the ugly word "slavery" most of them tried to evade facing the extremely awkward and embarrassing and problematic institution which had seemed hopelessly saddled on them ever since the Continental Congress, considering Jefferson's first draft of the Declaration, had struck out the clause which denounced the king for introducing negro slavery into America. It embarrassed them to know that they were practicing something which they not only did not preach, but which they definitely had preached against and fought against — something contrary to their principles of freedom and equal rights. Yet they did not know just what to do about it. Jefferson had spoken for all the South when he said that slavery was a wolf which Virginia had by the ears — to hold on was dangerous, but to let go was not so good either.

Outsiders made the situation more unpleasant by offering what they called a simple and logical solution. Abolish slavery, they said. Pretty soon they were shouting it. Set the slaves free. Slavery is all wrong. Down with slavery!

Well, of course slavery was all wrong. Men like Charles Carroll of Carrollton did not need busybodies from Massachusetts and Connecticut to tell them that. People who were unfamiliar with slavery, who had never lived in close contact with the institution, did not know how appallingly wrong it was. But such people could not realize, either, how intricately that institution was woven into the fabric of every southerner's life, whether he was black or white, slave or free. It ought to be eliminated, yes. It would have to be eliminated, sooner or later. But, with all due respect to the well-meaning abolitionists in the northern sections, simple abolition would not do. Charles Carroll of Carrollton, that representative southern abolitionist, would no more have considered setting free his slaves, without making elaborate provision for their future, than he would have thought it a kindness to open Cousin Rachel's wicker cage of tropical finches, setting them at liberty to fend for and warm and feed themselves in the cold Maryland winter.

Carroll knew, of course, that it was not reasonable to expect slave-holders all over the south to rise as one man and free their slaves on purely moral grounds. Slaves had a monetary value just as actually as horses and furniture and acreage did, and setting them free meant throwing good money away. Most slave-holders did not find money plentiful enough to throw away. They might disapprove of the institution of slavery, but when they had to choose between hard cash and self-sacrificing idealism they showed themselves just as human as anybody else.

Every once in a while some high-minded southern gentleman would prove himself the exception to the rule and, washing his hands clean of the detestable institution, would free every one of his slaves. More often, gentlemen manumitted not all of their slaves but a chosen few — negroes who for some outstanding service or special faithfulness seemed to merit a reward, or who seemed particularly well fitted to make a success of life as "free niggers."

Carroll was one of those who manumitted some of his people from time to time. In 1817, for example, he manumitted thirty of them at once.[15] Apparently he left no comment on how these negroes used their freedom, or how it used them,

[15] Certificates of Freedom (Hall of Records, Annapolis), Liber C, 24-9.

but other kind-hearted gentlemen have put it feelingly on record that manumission was not always a success. It was not the cost so much as it was the upkeep. After they had taken money out of their own pockets to set their people free, the people remained a moral responsibility. The young, able-bodied negroes might be independent enough in good times — though times were not very good when these newly freed workers came in competition with the slave labor which had already reduced the poor white's scale of living to a pitiable level — but as soon as they met misfortune they would be right there at the back door, confidently expectant of food or rent-money or medicine or a layette for the new baby. The unemployables, of course, would never have left the shelter of the warm kitchen. Almost every slaveholder had an Aunt Lucy who, though she was in her second childhood, had been a good faithful nurse thirty years ago, or an Aunt Maria who had never been quite right in her head since she got religion at the Sugar Creek revival, or an Uncle John who was just naturally worthless. It was not humanly possible — certainly not possible to an ex-master who had been kind enough to set his negroes free in the first place — to keep from throwing good money after bad. And most of them were not rich enough to go in for large-scale philanthropy.

Charles Carroll of Carrollton was. That was why he repeatedly concerned himself with the idea of manumitting all his slaves, long after his neighbors had dismissed the scheme as crackbrained and impractical. The richest man in America would not have needed to beggar himself to set free his slaves, and to do the thing properly. He could have well afforded to establish the employables on little farms of their own, make charity allowances to the old and the sick and the incapable, and pay good wages to the ones he hired back to work for him. Because certain abolitionists knew that he was financially able to free and provide for the future of his slaves they interpreted his failure to do so as upholding the institution of slavery; and they did not hesitate to air their views in the public prints. It always made Carroll furious. He would have preferred to have people think almost anything else about him. Every time such a personal attack was launched against him he was seriously tempted to give the lie to his critics by promptly manumitting all his slaves. At least three different times he nearly lost his temper to the extent of doing so. But, worrying over his problem, considering all the facets of the hard situation as was his lifelong habit, he found he could not conscientiously take such a step. It would have been self-indulgence, he said. It would have been, too, the arrogant flaunting of wealth in the face of the neighbors whose problem was the same as his and who could not afford to follow his example. It would have solved Carroll's own personal problem at the cost of making his neighbors' problem worse — and that had never been Carroll's way. He had never yet considered his own welfare before his state's and his country's. He had never yet run away from a situation. Certainly half a century had not changed much the young man who had been unwilling to solve his personal religious problem by disregarding what became of the rest of Catholic Maryland.

Along with all the other progressive abolitionists, Carroll got a jolt when Eli Whitney invented the cotton gin. In a few years it had revolutionized the cotton situation in the south. The slow and tedious process of separating cotton fiber from seed went into the discard, and the south enjoyed a magnificent boom. But this boom had the unfortunate incidental effect of giving slavery a new lease on life. Gentlemen who had hitherto advocated the gradual abolition of slavery, along the lines that Mr. Carroll was always suggesting, now hesitated to upset the whole economic system of the prosperous agricultural south; and the fabric of social self-consciousness, so carefully upreared by such men as Jefferson in Virginia and Carroll in Maryland, appreciably weakened. Further importation of slaves was constitutionally at an end in 1808, but the question of whether slavery should be extended into the newly opened United States territories remained dangerously at issue. The dispute became sectional. Slavery flourished in the south and resentment in the north. The scheme of gradual, volun-

270 CHARLES CARROLL OF CARROLLTON

tary abolition was admittedly a failure; things went from bad
to worse; and by 1820 that dyed-in-the-wool abolitionist,
Charles Carroll of Carrollton, was writing: "Why keep alive
the question of slavery? It is admitted by all to be a great evil;
let an effectual mode of getting rid of it be pointed out, or let
the question sleep forever. . . ." [16]

He did not stay discouraged long. In 1816 the National
Colonization Society of America had been organized, and an
attempt made on Sherbro Island, off the west coast of Africa,
to colonize a group of free American negroes. The first colony
failed, but in the following year a treaty was successfully
concluded with the native princes, and within a few years
more the project seemed fairly headed for success. The
modern result of these beginnings is the negro republic of
Liberia.

Carroll became as enthusiastic about the Colonization Society as he had been about gradual abolition. He thought that,
with a colony established in Africa, the prospect of a south
purged of slavery became more than an idealist's dream. More
personally, he saw opening before him the way in which he
could free all his own slaves without creating the problem of
discontent and double standards and possible uprising in his
community. To "the Society," as he always called it, he gave
his time and energy without stint, and the undeniable prestige
of his name; and when Bushrod Washington died he became
its president. The northern abolitionists were hard put to it to
find room for criticism, but some of them managed to rise
above their difficulties. Mr. William Lloyd Garrison went on
record as exclaiming in amazement that in spite of Mr. Carroll's nefarious connection with the society to ship negroes to
Africa "he is lauded beyond measure as a patriot, a philanthropist, and a Christian!" [17]

People who knew Mr. Carroll, however, did not find hard
to explain the esteem in which he was held by his neighbors.
Even in the bitterest political campaigns few people had both-

[16] To Robert Goodloe Harper, April 23, 1800; Rowland, *Life*, II, 321.
[17] Horace Greeley, *Thoughts on African Colonization* (1832).

ered to throw mud on his motives. Many people — including, to a man, the members of the Republican Party — thought him misguided and pig-headed, but even these recognized his obvious sincerity. Anybody who had ever had business dealings with him said feelingly that age had failed to mellow him — there was still nothing slipshod about his methods and he still accounted for every penny due him. His employees still complained that he expected them to work as hard as he did. But almost anybody would have told you that, whatever his faults, Mr. Carroll was a good and a truly religious man, a practicing as well as a professing Christian.

Since he had got older, and especially since his mind had been relieved of public worries, he had given more thought to religion. Remembering how his father had concerned himself with the spiritual destiny of his only child, he conceived it his duty to concern himself with that of his own children and their children. He asked his cousin John Carroll, now Archbishop of Baltimore but still as intimate a friend as he had been nearly seventy years ago at Bohemia Manor Academy, to draw up for him a list of books. Then he drew up a list of his own. He knew very well that John Carroll's list would be a nice orthodox one, all the books written from the Roman Catholic point of view. He knew nearly enough about the Roman Catholic religion; he had been brought up in it. Now he wanted to compare it, point for point, with the other religions of the world. Some of the books on his own list were far from orthodox. A good many of them he had read before, for he had never been one to shut his ears to other people's opinions. The Roman Catholic Church, for instance, had branded Voltaire as a dangerous and sacrilegious man, and put his books on the Index. Yet Voltaire, through the years, had been one of Charles Carroll's favorite authors; his friends abroad had instructions to send him each new volume of irreverencies as soon as it came off the press. Now he read these books over again, with many others — not as literature, but as theology. He read his old Latin books, comparing the beliefs of the ancients with those set forth by the Deists, the Presbyterians, the Mohammedans, the Roman Catholics, and so on. It was an absorbing study. It occupied his spare time for nearly three years straight. Incidentally, he found no reason to change his religion for another one, but he felt better for having looked around. "The great number in every religion not having the leisure or means to investigate the truth of the doctrines they have been taught, must rest their religious faith on their instructors," [18] was his considered opinion; and he emphasized that he thought such people would have as good a chance of heaven as those who did have the opportunity to "investigate." He added, however, "but they who, from liberal education, from understanding, from books, not written by one party only, and from leisure, have the means of examining into the truth of the doctrines they have been taught as orthodox, are in my opinion bound to make the examination, nor suffer early instructions and impressions or habits or prejudices to operate against the conviction of what is right. . . ."

All this brings us, of course, to the subject of Charles Carroll's own personal religion — no subject for discussion, for how can any outsider pretend to know how a man feels about God? Nevertheless the religious belief and practice of this particular great man have been pawed over as thoroughly as have the fine points of Alexander Hamilton's illegitimacy or George Washington's love affair with the Low Land beauty. And at any time it would have been quite sufficient to say: "Charles Carroll of Carrollton was a good and a religious man, who all his life subscribed to the doctrines of the Roman Catholic Church."

This simple fact has been embroidered by everybody who ever wrote as much as a paragraph about Charles Carroll. It shouldn't and needn't have been done in the first place. But, since it has become an issue, it has to be dealt with.

Carroll, as we have seen, was born of parents who were Roman Catholics. So many Irish people were. They brought him up in their own faith and sent him to schools and colleges

<hr>

[18] To Harriet Chew Carroll, August 29, 1816; Gurn, *Charles Carroll*, p. 191.

which were conducted by Jesuit priests. Naturally, he grew up to be a Roman Catholic too.

He was a normal little boy and so he accepted rather than dissected what he was taught. By the time he was grown, however, he had formed a fairly clear idea of his religion and was able to put it in words. He was just twenty-one when he replied to a letter full of fatherly good advice: "If I practised what you teach, I Shoud not only be a compleat gentleman but a good Christian, which is much ye most important of ye two. A good conscience & a virtuous life are certainly ye greatest blessings we can enjoy on earth. I don't aim nor never did at connonization; I detest served up devotion, distorted faes & grimace. I equally abhor those, who laugh at all devotion, look upon our religion as a fiction, & its holy misteries as the greatest absurdities." [19] He lived seventy-four years longer and never in any essential changed this thesis.

He was not of a particularly religious temperament, as his father was. There is a story that his father had, at one time in his youth, wanted to become a priest. A good thing he did not, with that temper of his! He had a definite religion which was an essential part of him, but he did not spend very much time meditating about it. Under ordinary circumstances he would probably not even have thought about it very often.

The circumstances, however, were not ordinary. His religion was constantly and forcibly being brought to his attention. He knew, in the first place, that he had been sent to school in Europe, separated from his parents for many years, because little Catholic boys might not be educated as such in Maryland. He knew that there were various laws which made Maryland an unpleasant place for grown-up Catholics to live in: that they were not permitted to vote, or hold public office, or practice law; that they were not only forbidden to attend their own church but were taxed for the support of an entirely different one; and that they paid general taxes which were exactly twice as high as those which non-Catholics were expected to pay. He had heard all this and more from his father, who

[19] January 17, 1759; Carroll Papers, I, 38.

felt very strongly about it. He had heard all about the persecutions the Irish Catholics had suffered back in the old country
— with family anecdotes. He had heard how his grandfather,
Charles Carroll the Attorney-General, had come to America
with a new motto on his coat-of-arms — "Anywhere, so long as
it be free!" — how he had left the old country he loved only to
meet bitter disappointment in the new; how he had gone to jail
because of his stubborn convictions and his impudent tongue;
how he had been succeeded by a son — Charles Carroll's
own father, Charles Carroll of Annapolis — who had never
known anything but frustration. He knew that his father had
lived to be an old man without the chance to live a normal life
as a citizen and be of use to his country; that he had, like the
Attorney-General, served some time in jail; that he had wanted
to leave Maryland and the domination of the British crown and
found a new colony in New France.

All this he knew or had been told. When he came home
from England, grown up and educated, Charles Carroll of
Carrollton had tasted the bitterness for himself. No use going
into all that again. He thanked God that he had been able to
do something about it. "When I signed the Declaration of
Independence," he wrote many years later, "I had in view not
only our independence of England but the toleration of all
sects, professing the Christian Religion, and communicating to
them all great rights. Happily this wise and salutary measure
has taken place for eradicating religious feuds and persecution,
and become a useful lesson to all governments. . . ." [20] He
had got religious freedom for Maryland in 1776 and religious
freedom for the whole country had followed it in 1789. He
was glad of an opportunity to relax, not to worry about it any
more. Religion, he had always felt, was hardly a decent sub-

[20] To G. W. P. Custis, February 20, 1829. Guilday, quoting this in his
Life and Times of John Carroll, p. 82n, adds, "One is at liberty to suspect
that the great Catholic patriot was reading this laudable motive into his
part of the Revolution a half-century before. . . ." He says further, on
pages 86–7, that this "sentiment . . . may be the mellowed reflection of an
old man of ninety, whose words at this time were always couched in the
pious accents of religion and of peace." I expect Charles Carroll would want
me to refrain from comment.

HOMEWOOD

BALTIMORE, MARYLAND

ject for contention or even discussion; his own religion had been contended about and discussed far too often to suit him.

People had urged him, before the Revolution, to change his church affiliation before it entirely ruined his promising career. He always refused, politely, but so unmistakably that the friends who had with the best intentions in the world introduced the unfortunate subject never mentioned it again. He had three good reasons for refusing, any one of them, from his point of view, entirely adequate. In the first place, his defection would have broken his father's heart, and he cared more for his father than for any other human being. He said on one occasion that he would not leave the Roman Catholic Church "even if my filial love did not restrain me — for I can truly say, *Nequeo lachrymas perferre parentis*." [21] In the second place he was Irish and stubborn, like his father and grandfather and innumerable other ancestors before them; he could not be forced into any uncongenial action "merely to humour the prejudices of fools," [22] and he would do his own thinking, thank you. "I have too much . . . pride," [23] he said himself, speaking of leaving the Roman Catholic Church. And in the third place his Church suited him. "Upon conviction only a change of religion is desirable," he said; "on a concern so seriously interesting to all of us no worldly motives should sway our conduct." [24]

The last reason was, of course, the one Carroll considered most important. Undoubtedly, there were parts of the doctrines which he saw through a glass darkly — he spoke himself of the "holy misteries" of the Roman Catholic Church [25] — and which he accepted on faith, as they are supposed to be accepted. He never criticized other people's religions or urged them to give up their own for his. "I feel no ill will or illiberal prejudices against the sectarians which have abandon[ed]

---

[21] To William Graves, August 15, 1774; *Maryland Historical Magazine*, XXXII, 223.

[22] *Ibid*.

[23] *Ibid*.

[24] To Harriet Chew Carroll, August 29, 1816; Gurn, *Charles Carroll*, p. 191.

[25] To Charles Carroll of Annapolis, January 17, 1759; Carroll Papers, I, 38.

that faith [the Roman Catholic]; if their lives be conform-
able to the duties and morals prescribed by the Gospel, I . . .
hope and believe they will be rewarded with eternal happiness. . . ." [26] Plain enough. As to his own Church, he never
discussed its teachings in detail, and he never attempted to
explain or defend them. Why should he? The Roman Catholic religion is an excellent religion. It may suit only a part of
the Christianized world, but it suited Charles Carroll and he
was always unswervingly loyal to its teachings.

He was not always so loyal to his Church's organization.
Though he found no fault with it in point of theology he was
not blind to certain abuses which had crept into its administration. "I execrate ye intolerating spirit of ye Church of
Rome," he wrote plainly on one occasion.[27] "No one has a
greater regard for the Jesuits than myself," he said too; "I
revere the virtue, I esteem the learning, I respect the apostollic
labours of individuals but am forced to acknowledge their in-
stitute & plan of government liable to great abuses. . . ." [28]
Speaking of the Jesuits again (he had no particular prejudice
against that order, but because he had been educated in Jesuit
schools and colleges he was more familiar with it than with
any other) he mentioned "the extensive too extensive privileges confer'd by former Popes on that order," [29] and he
judged "dangerous to the State a body of men who implitully
believe the dictates of one Superior, & are *carried on to ye execution of his orders with a blind impetuosity of will & eager-
ness to obey without the least enquiry or examination.*" [30] The
italics were his own. "Reason was not given to man merely to
restrain his passions, or merely to regulate his own actions, but
to weigh & examin wether the actions he is sollicited or commanded by others to perform, are such as can stand the scrutiny

[26] To Harriet Chew Carroll, August 29, 1816; Gurn, *Charles Carroll*, p. 191.
[27] To William Graves, August 15, 1774; *Maryland Historical Magazine*, XXXII, 223.
[28] To Charles Carroll of Annapolis, October 22, 1761; Carroll Papers, I, 71 [sic].
[29] *Ibid.*
[30] *Ibid.*

& sentence of an unerring, if unprejudiced, Judge. . . ." [31]
He criticized individual priests of his acquaintance, too. Respect for the cloth did not make him hesitate to say: "I really wish we never sent for a priest; they are troublesome animals in a family. . . ." [32]

Possibly a good Catholic would not have expressed such sentiments. Yet no communicant was ever more loyal to what he called "the true spirit & discipline of the Catholic Church." [33] Various historians have given widely varying opinions of Carroll's religion, one of them devoting a whole book to his life as a Catholic, and making him appear lopsided, a man whose religion made everything else subordinate; others have said plainly that he was not a good Catholic or even a good Christian, but had been infected in his youth by the atheistic tendencies of the France in which he was educated. His present biographer — a Protestant, and not too churchgoing a Protestant at that — is not prepared to say how good or how bad a Catholic he was, being no judge. From the point of view of most of us it does not matter. He was a good Christian, a good man. No need to take anybody's word for it. He could speak for himself, and did, in almost all of the letters he wrote in his old age. Read, for example, this letter to his son, who thought as little about religion as most young men do:

"In writing to you I deem it my duty to call your attention to the shortness of this life, and the certainty of death, and the dreadful judgment we must all undergo, and on the decision of which a happy or a miserable eternity depends. The impious has said in his heart, 'There is no God.' He would willingly believe there is no God; the passions, the corruptions of the heart would fain persuade him there is none. The stings of conscience betray the emptiness of the delusion; the heavens proclaim the existence of God, and unperverted reason teaches that He must love virtue and hate vice, and reward the one and punish the other.

[31] *Ibid.*
[32] To Charles Carroll of Annapolis, October 30, 1769; *ibid.*, II, 122B.
[33] To Charles Carroll of Annapolis, October 22, 1761; Carroll Papers, I, 71 [sic].

"The wisest and best of the ancients believed in the immortality of the soul, and the Gospel has established the great truth of a future state of rewards and punishments. My desire to induce you to reflect on futurity, and by a virtuous life to merit heaven, have suggested the above reflections and warnings. The approaching festival of Easter, and the merits and mercies of our Redeemer copiosa assudeum redemptio have lead [sic] me into this chain of meditation and reasoning, and have inspired me with the hope of finding mercy before my Judge, and of being happy in the life to come, a happiness I wish you to participate with me by infusing into your heart a similar hope. Should this letter produce such a change, it will comfort me, and impart to you that peace of mind which the world cannot give, and which I am sure you have long since ceased to enjoy. . . .

"God bless you, from yr. aff. father

"CH. CARROLL OF CARROLLTON" [34]

One more letter, though belonging to a later period of his life, ought to be quoted in this connection. "On the 20th of this month I entered into my eighty ninth year," the old Signer wrote in September 1825: "this in any country would be deemed a long life, yet . . . if it has not been directed to the only end, for which man was created, it is a meer nothing an empty phantom, an indivisible point, compared with eternity.

"Too much of my time & attention have been misapplied on matters to which an impartial Judge, penetrating the secrets of hearts, before whom I shall soon appear, will ascribe [no] merit deserving recompense. On the mercy of my redeemer I rely for salvation, and on his merits; not on the works I have done in obedience to his precepts, for even these, I fear, a mixture of alloy will render unavailing, and cause to be rejected." [35]

He meant his charities, of course. A "Charity Acct" had al-

[34] April 12, 1821; Rowland, *Life*, II, 327–8.
[35] To Charles W. Wharton, September 27, 1825; "1800 Carroll MSS Ac. 422," in Library of Congress, p. 3.

ways been part of his budget, as it had been part of his father's. The name of Charles Carroll of Carrollton had for years headed every subscription list; he had acquired considerable reputation as a philanthropist. Schools and colleges were his most frequent beneficiaries, as they had been his legislative pets back in his political days. It was his favorite theory that the whole future of the country depended upon "the proper instruction of youth." He liberally contributed also to certain orphanages run by the Catholic Church, and supported priests in Annapolis and at Doughoregan Manor, to serve those communities. There were not very many organized charities in Carroll's time; people were only just beginning, a generation and a half after the Declaration of Independence, to see the gilt wear off the splendid theory "that all men are created equal" and to feel that something had to be done about the appalling actuality underneath. In the absence of community-supported welfare organizations, Carroll had for many years acted as a one-man social agency. The greater part of his "Charity Acct" had always gone for "annuities & gifts to different servants and poor" around him. He handled this sort of thing nicely and sensitively, with a technique that was, again, far in advance of his times. If he had not made himself loved in his business dealings he did succeed in making poor people sure that, whether or not it would avail Mr. Carroll of Carrollton anything to venerate the Pope and supplicate the saints and go without meat on Fridays, his works would admit him to any heaven worth going to.

He was a good man, yes; but it is not well to dwell too long upon his virtues. Some of his biographers have done that. It is necessary to remember that, for all his charities, Charles Carroll of Carrollton never mixed charity with his business; that, right after writing a beautiful religious letter, he could sit down and write to a debt-ridden widow:

"Madam/

"I am sorry that I was out of the way when you called at my house this morning — you need not give yourself ye trouble of another visit, if you will please to inform me by a line, when I may expect yr husband's debt will be discharged. Unless the Judgt is satisfied by next Provincial, & a time assigned for the payment of ye other bond, I shall be obliged to put it in suit." [36]

Besides his love of money, which he kept to an age when, according to his own admission, he ought to have been thinking exclusively about the world where there is neither moth nor rust nor thievery, he retained a very human bitterness about party politics. During these first years of his political inactivity Carroll reminds us of nothing quite so much as a die-hard present-day Republican suffering (and far from silently) life under the New Deal. His criticisms of the administration were practically the same criticisms that we have heard in our time — "too theoretical and fanciful a statesman," "experiments," "fantastic tricks," [37] "turbulent and disorganizing spirits," inducements "held out to the indolent and needy, but not really intended to be executed," and so on.[38] Like the present-day political underdogs, he never tired of sharpening his tongue on the many "foibles" of the administration under which he had to live.

None of the presidents after Washington met with his approval. He expected too much, undoubtedly. But he knew John Adams too well to think him a worthy successor to his admired old friend, although he politely "set a great value on his services," and felt "a sincere regard for all who stood firm in the most dangerous and critical situation of our affairs." [39] That last was a smooth bit of political *double-entendre*, though. Adams had nearly always stood firm, but he had certainly missed his footing at the time of the Conway Cabal, and so he forfeited Carroll's support in the campaign of 1796. Carroll favored in preference General Pinckney of South Carolina,

---

[36] To an unnamed person, and undated. This is a letter presented to the Maryland Historical Society in 1934 by L. W. Green, and at the time I copied it was in a folder of miscellaneous Carroll letters, all of them of the nineteenth century.
[37] To Alexander Hamilton, April 18, 1800; Hamilton, *Works of Alexander Hamilton*, VI, 434–5.
[38] To Alexander Hamilton, August 27, 1800; *ibid.*, 467.
[39] To John Henry, December 16, 1792; Rowland, *Life*, II, 193.

the first of several unlikely candidates who got the compliment, at least, of the uncompromising old Signer's backing. After Pinckney had been eliminated as a possibility Carroll did half-heartedly support Adams in preference to the dreaded Jefferson; but after four years of the Adams type of administration he found himself speaking of the "present critical situation of this country" and saying, "The President remarks that we are fallen upon evil times; I fear a great part of the evil may be attributed to his shifting conduct, his passions, his indiscretion, vanity & jealousy — I had a high opinion of Mr. Adams, and I still believe him to be an honest man, but his integrity cannot compensate for his weaknesses, which unfit him for his present station. Were a competition for places and power between the friends and opposers of the administration the only object of the contest, it would be a matter of indifference to me by what party the governt. should be administered: If Mr. Adams should be reelected, I fear our constitution would be more injured by his unruly passions, antipathies, & jealousy, than by the whimsies of Jefferson. . . ."[40] Up to the last minute, however, he hoped that somebody, even though that somebody were Aaron Burr, whom he suspected of being "not less a hypocrite than Jefferson,"[41] to get in ahead of his particular abomination the Sage of Monticello. Outlining the horrors he expected from any administration of Jefferson's, he ended his gloomy prediction, ". . . and so will terminate the Union, if Jefferson should continue President for eight years. . . ."[42]

Jefferson's term of office did not, of course, terminate the Union, any more than Franklin Roosevelt's has. But Mr. Carroll of Carrollton sat through that quite unrevolutionary administration on the edge of a mental volcano. He momentarily expected the grimmest worst. It would not be charitable to say that, when the United States under Jefferson went for-

[40] To James McHenry, November 4, 1800; Steiner, *Life and Correspondence of James McHenry*, p. 473.
[41] To Charles Carroll of Homewood, February 8, 1801; Rowland, *Life*, II, 249.
[42] *Ibid.*

ward pretty prosperously, he was disappointed; but certainly he did not find it pleasant to find his gloomy predictions unrealized. It is much to be feared that he held Jefferson's quiet administration against him to the end of his days.

Carroll's attention was drawn away from presidential foibles, however, by the really alarming situation in Europe. Napoleon was far more of an ogre than any candidate the Republican Party — Mr. Carroll still called it that, out of pure stubbornness, though almost everybody else now spoke of the Democratic Party — could produce. A president who sufficiently disliked Napoleon, no matter what his other faults, was suddenly quite acceptable to the old Federalist. (And again there is a parallel. As this book is being written there is another ogre in Europe, like Napoleon less hated for his principles than for his appalling efficiency in getting what he wants; and people who once could say nothing too uncomplimentary about Mr. Roosevelt's impudent pretensions to a third term have shelved for the duration their fears for American democracy at his hands.) To Charles Carroll of Carrollton, who had never had even a normal amount of personal ambition, Napoleon was nothing less than a monster. Anxiously he followed the young Corsican's meteoric career from first consul to emperor in the space of less than five years. Nothing in that career roused his admiration, but as one by one the kingdoms of Europe fell victim to Napoleon's military dictatorship he began to feel a lively fear for the destiny of the United States. This country was still very young and defenseless, and Napoleon was known to have dreams of an American empire. And most of Napoleon's dreams seemed to have a flair for coming true. Charles Carroll of Carrollton, always ready to expect the worst of the Democratic administration which had always been Francophile and had condoned more terrible excesses than the ambitions of Napoleon, was ready to make choice between evils. He wrote on June 23, 1803: "I am of opinion it would be good policy to unite with Great Britain against France and her allies, seize upon all the Country to the east of the Mississippi, and under cover of the British fleet land

30,000 men in the province of Yucatan, march into Mexico, then to Peru, and to declare the Spanish colonies independent, and their independence to be guaranteed by Great Britain and the United States. If we enter into the war I am not for doing things by halves. . . ." [43] Obviously not. He had always been a visionary. If there had ever been any doubt that he had thrown his weight for independence less because he valued the principles of liberty than because he as an Irishman hated the English, here in his old age was the answer. He still had little love for the English. But anything was better than the threat of dictatorship.

Along with other respectable citizens of Baltimore, Carroll had a personal grudge against the upstart Corsican, quite apart from his aspirations to world power. Tradition has always had it that it was Charles Carroll of Carrollton who in 1803, in Baltimore, had presented to Miss Betsy Patterson Napoleon's dashing young brother Jerome. Anyway, whether he did or not, it is certain that Miss Betsy's father was a good friend of the Carroll family, that she herself was an intimate of the Caton girls, and that her brother Robert would later marry the eldest of them, Mary Ann. Society took it as a personal insult when, Betsy and Jerome having married after a rapid courtship that left Baltimore breathless with interest, Napoleon took it on himself to announce that the marriage was of no force. "Miss Patterson," Baltimore heard that he had called Betsy, when he sent her a message that she would not be allowed to land with her husband in France. He tried to secure a divorce from the Pope, but when the Pope to his credit refused, Napoleon promoted the divorce himself, in 1806. This without regard for the fact that "Miss Patterson," turning the other cheek, had named her baby Jerome Napoleon Bonaparte. She was not good enough, he said, for his younger brother. Not good enough! Baltimore society seethed. Who were these upstart Bonapartes anyway? Corsican riffraff! They ought to be honored by an alliance with the Maryland Pattersons. And who did this Napoleon Bonaparte think he was, specifically, to set

[43] To R. G. Harper; Rowland, *Life*, II, 255.

aside a marriage made by Cousin John Carroll, Archbishop of Baltimore? And so on, and on. Napoleon was the technical winner of the controversy: poor young Betsy, refused permission to enter France, soon saw the last of her spineless husband, whom his brother married later to a homely German princess. But Betsy won a signal moral victory. She is one of the romantic characters in American history; they are still writing plays and novels about Betsy, and in Baltimore there are still plenty of people who welcome a chance to call Napoleon names on her behalf.

America teetered on the brink of war for years. There was never much prospect of an alliance with England, except in the hopes of certain Federalists; on the contrary, the constant friction between England and the United States, which was not relieved by a series of administrations consistently hostile to the British, presaged another war with the enemy of thirty years before. In 1807 the British ship *Leopard* impressed four sailors from the defenceless American *Chesapeake*, after an attack in which three Americans were killed and eighteen wounded. A "paper" blockade (considered by the United States illegal) and objectionable Orders in Council followed. The Western Indians defended their lands against American settlement with British guns and powder; the Battle of Tippecanoe, in which nearly two hundred frontiersmen were killed, afforded the War Hawks (a younger generation of Republicans whom the election of 1810 sent to Congress) another *casus belli*. Die-hard Federalists, however, continued to disapprove. "The Administration of this country has got us into a miserable hobble, from which nothing can extricate us but England's declaring war against us," Carroll wrote to his son-in-law in January 1812. "Notwithstanding the manifold provocations given by our government, and its manifest partiality for France, the English cabinet is too wise to help our rulers out of the scrape by declaring war against the Unted States." [44]

Though England made public atonement for the *Chesapeake-Leopard* affair and was just on the point of repealing

[44] To R. G. Harper, January 21, 1812; Rowland, *Life*, II, 289.

the Orders in Council, the United States declared war on June 19, 1812. Carroll, taking his perennially gloomy view of things, could not say too much about the misery "our present wicked Administration" had brought upon the United States.[45] "Is the war to go on?" he wrote to his son-in-law in 1813. "Can it be prosecuted without the means, and against the general bent of the nation? In consequence of the President's recommendation, an entire stop, I suppose, will be put to exports from this country. Will the people long submit to such privations? Their folly or corruption in the re-election of Mr. Madison must now be manifest." [46] After the riot in Baltimore, following an attack on the newspaper, *The Federal Republican*, he wrote: "The late occurrences in Baltimore, and the temper of this government render a residence insecure in this State, and I may want all the sums I can command to enable me to move out of it, if the state of politics does not grow better, and men be suffered to speak their sentiments on the measures of the present rulers of our country and to take what newspapers they please." [47] He was very bitter and very discouraged. He was seventy-five, too old for another fight, but the motto on the seal he used was still *Ubicumque cum Libertate*. Had American liberty been worth all the work and worry? Would it have been better if, after all, he had left his home nearly fifty years ago?

Maryland had had no battles fought on her soil thirty-odd years ago, in the American Revolution, but now her good luck failed to hold. The town of Washington — which Marylanders still thought of as being part of Maryland, as indeed it had been at the time of the other war — fell into the hands of the British in August 1814 and its public buildings were burned. Charles Carroll of Carrollton reported on the twenty-fifth: "The fire at Washington was plainly seen by several of my people about ten o'clock last night." [48] From Washington it

---

[45] To Charles Carroll of Homewood, December 5, 1813; Rowland, *Life*, II, 298.　　　　[46] To R. G. Harper, March 4, 1813; *ibid.*, II, 295.
[47] To Charles Carroll of Homewood, August 5, 1812; *ibid.*, II, 291–2.
[48] To Charles Carroll of Homewood, August 25, 1814; Rowland, *Life*, II, 304.

was only a step to Baltimore, interesting to the British not only as an important commercial center but as a "nest of privateers." The famous Baltimore ships had done their part in making the British navy uncomfortable. The British had had no difficulty taking Washington; they expected that Baltimore would be easy too. But when on September 11, 1814, the decorous church-bells forgot it was Sunday and rang out a frantic message that the British fleet had been sighted off North Point, Baltimoreans snapped into action as if they had been defending Baltimore all their lives. They met the British next morning on Patapsco Neck, fought them all day, killed their commanding officer, and drove them back to their ships. The Britishers — no mean antagonists, for they were the men who had fought under Wellington in the Peninsular Campaign — were baffled but far from beaten. About two o'clock on the morning of September thirteenth the enemy ships opened fire on Fort McHenry, south of Baltimore, the namesake of Charles Carroll's old colleague in the United States Senate. All day long and most of the night the firing continued, but the lighter cannon of Fort McHenry drove the British ships back whenever they ventured within range. About one o'clock in the morning of September fourteenth the British, while keeping up a heavy fire, attempted a surprise attack on the fort from the rear. They sent in small boats twelve hundred picked men equipped with scaling ladders. They were nearly there when the Americans saw them and opened fire. The next few minutes were nearly hot enough to make up for Maryland's lack of battles during the Revolution. The noise was deafening, and the glare so intense that one of the occupants of the fort, a rooster, thought daylight had come and sent forth a lusty crow from the top of a parapet. But, as things turned out, this patriotic American did not crow much too soon.

During the bombardment, a young Marylander watched from one of the British ships, which he had boarded in order to try to effect the release of a friend. Francis Scott Key was not then famous, though Baltimoreans knew him as a promising lawyer and Annapolitans remembered the boy who had lived with his uncle, Charles Carroll's old friend Dr. Upton Scott, while he was a student at St. John's College. Young Mr. Key had an aptitude for verse-making; now he reached into his pocket for something to write on and scribbled hurriedly, before he should forget the words that came into his mind: "O say can you see, by the dawn's early light. . . ."

On December 24, 1814, England and the United States signed a treaty of peace which was unsatisfactory from many points of view, since it added no territory to the United States and did not even mention, much less settle, the question of impressment which had been one of the chief causes of war. But it was more than satisfactory, to men who had gone through both the wars with England, to know that the mother country had failed again. The successful Revolution, then, had not been just a flash in the pan. The United States had shown that she could hold her own against all comers. England, it was to be hoped, had learned her lesson in that respect. And when, a few months later, Napoleon met his final defeat at Waterloo and lost his status as a world menace, there was nothing to be feared from France either. Yes, there would be peace, with the United States "likely to become at no distant period, populous, flourishing and powerful," — thus Charles Carroll of Carrollton; "how long it will continue so, depends on the adherence to the principles which laid the foundation of its growing prosperity; the confederation of these States, sovereign and independent within the powers not delegated to the general confederacy, their incorporation with that surviving and controlling government, also sovereign and independent as to the powers devolved on it by the confederacy, is a curious and complicated piece of mechanism of which the world has had no example; time will discover how long it will go on without derangement." [49]

This was the nearest he ever came to putting into words his views on states' rights. It was one subject on which he never

[49] To Elizabeth Caton Stafford, February 26, 1828; Field, *Unpublished Letters*, pp. 210–1.

could make up his mind. On most other subjects he had very definite views and expressed them strongly; thus, not long after the treaty of 1814, he set down his considered opinion of war: "War I consider as a great calamity, and having a stronger influence in corrupting the morals of a nation even than a long peace, and therefore most weighty and just should be the cause to justify engaging in it; I think with Cicero, nullum bellum justum, nisi necessarium. . . . Again, a few thoughts on war and its causes; they are frequently concealed from the public, springing more from low intrigues, antipathies, ambition of individuals, and plausible pretences of violated national honor, than from the ostensible and alleged reasons and topics set forth in declarations. Collisions of interests and real grounds of quarrel, will, no doubt, sometimes arise, especially between maritime and commercial nations envious and jealous of each other. But if rulers were wise they would, at least ought, to resort before the sword is drawn, to pacific negotiations, carried on with good faith, free from irritation and in the spirit of peace, avoiding hatred and mutual reproaches. . . ." [50]

A man is not necessarily behind the times because he has been dead more than a hundred years. "If ever there was a purist in politics and religion," Jefferson's most partisan biographer says of his subject's bitter enemy, Charles Carroll of Carrollton, "it was this old Roman of Maryland." [51]

[50] To R. G. Harper, April 17, 1816; Rowland, *Life*, ii, 310.
[51] Thomas E. Watson, *The Life and Times of Thomas Jefferson* (1927), p. 390.

CHAPTER X

De Senectute

1817–1832

H E KNEW HOW to grow old gracefully. In 1817 he was
eighty, an age which few gentlemen of his gouty
era attained. Those who did were usually groaning
about with some ailment or other and were far from enjoying
life — how can anyone expect to enjoy life on a regimen of
milk-toast and soft-boiled eggs? — but Charles Carroll of Carrollton was the exception to every rule. In the first place, he
took a cold plunge every morning at Doughoregan Manor,
where he had had a "limestone bath" built. What was more,
he plunged in head first. Then he rode around his estate, or
called on some of his neighbors. It was nothing for him to ride
twenty miles in the course of a morning; and the horses he
rode were not worn-out, gentle old mares, either. He took as
much pride as ever in being superbly mounted. He still kept
open house, frequently entertaining a dozen or more guests at
dinner. After dinner (at which there had been no specially
prepared mushy dishes for Mr. Carroll of Carrollton, but
the same Madeira and Maryland ham the others enjoyed) the
guests would retire for naps and their host would retire to his
library to catch up on his reading. Cicero, Theocritus, the
elder Pliny — he felt the need for reading as other people feel
the need for sleep — Molière, Racine, Voltaire; the newspapers; the new books sent from England. His eyesight was
still excellent, and his mind found its accustomed fare as easily
digestible as ever. Later in the afternoon he would ride again,

perhaps, or play with his younger grandchildren; in the evening there would be more guests or, if one of his older granddaughters were visiting him, even a ball. Mr. Carroll of Carrollton had long since lost his taste for dancing — though nobody doubted that he was physically quite able to lead every figure — but he still enjoyed watching it over his chessboard. If, that is, he had been able to get any of the guests to take him on. But Mr. Carroll had been playing brilliant chess for nearly sixty years now; most of them knew his reputation, and nobody likes to be beaten every game. Fairly early in the evening, he would courteously excuse himself to the company and go to bed. But not because he was tired; rather because he expected to be up "before day" in the morning.

People in Baltimore and in Anne Arundel County could have told you years before that Mr. Carroll of Carrollton was a remarkable person, but the country at large was only beginning to realize it. Even back in the days when he had held public office he had been more prominent in Maryland affairs than in national ones; he had never been nationally known in the sense that Washington and Franklin and Jefferson were. It was his own fault; instead of eagerly accepting (but with a proper show of reluctance, of course) every honor that came his way, he had refused several important posts which would have brought him into the public eye.[1] On top of that he had deliberately made himself unpopular. He had clung to certain principles of the Federalist Party at a time when most of its members were finding it expedient to modify their views. For a long while most of the United States paid no attention to him. The administration was unfriendly in self-defense,

---

[1] Perhaps even Molly would have hesitated to quote Ogden Nash on Charles Carroll of Carrollton. Yet the frivolous great man has summed up the serious-minded great man more neatly, I think, than anybody else has:

> "Yes, fatal handicaps in life are fortunately few,
> But the most fatal of all is the faculty of
>   seeing the other person's point of view,
> . . . . genius won't get you as far as everyday
>   facility
> Unless it is accompanied by a conviction of
>   infallibility . . . ."

and, anyway, what of it if Mr. Carroll of Carrollton chose to disapprove? He no longer held public office. But presently a new political generation was in power, a generation which neither remembered nor cared that Mr. Carroll of Carrollton had subscribed to the old Federalist Party. It was more interested in remembering the country's earlier history, and the fact that Charles Carroll had been one of the men, their faults forgotten in the passage of time, who had signed the Declaration of Independence. Only a few of them were left, and fame sought them out.

At first Mr. Carroll found it a pleasant change, after the years of public ostracism, to receive testimonials from the newspapers and verses from amateur poetesses and visits from tourists he had never heard of before. Eventually it became a burden. The era was one in which people enjoyed public occasions, complete with orations and garlands and a Personage who would lend dignity and grace by his presence; and there was no great man in America who lent more elegance to an assemblage than the venerable Charles Carroll of Carrollton. He was all that a statesman should have been and too seldom was, one whom the populace could cheer without a twinge of regret at his failure to look the part and act it. This fortunate circumstance, coupled with the fact that there was a good deal of genuine patriotic feeling in America, after the successful ending of the second war with England, flooded Mr. Carroll's mail with invitations to ride in a barouche in this or that procession, or to deliver the oration of the day on such and such an occasion, or simply to sit on a flag-draped platform while somebody else invoked the Muse.

He refused all the invitations that came from a distance, pleading his great age; but even those which came from Baltimore and Washington would have proved onerous if he had accepted them all. Each of itself was tiresome enough. At a typical Fourth of July celebration, in Baltimore in 1820, Carroll rode in a long procession through the streets, flanked by Colonel John Eager Howard and General Samuel Smith, to a rostrum erected at the foot of the Washington Monument;

there he delivered to the orator of the day, a Doctor Watkins, the copy of the Declaration of Independence which he had carried in the procession, and received from him in turn the typical tribute: "Few, very few, of those whose hearts swelled with the triumph of patriotism when this *declaration* first received the sanction of *a nation's will*, now survive to participate in the blessings of their own creation. *One* of these few, *our own representative*, silvered o'er indeed and trembling with age, but still cherishing in his heart the remembrance of that proud day when his name was first enrolled among the guardians of our infant independence, *now sits in the midst of us*: — The same hand which, *forty-four years ago*, traced upon this immortal scroll the name of CHARLES CARROLL, of *Carrollton*, now presents it to me. Who could witness such a scene unmoved? Who could stand in the presence of the venerable patriot, and not catch the influence of that holy flame which filled, illumined, and inspired *him*, in '76?" [2]

It was characteristic of Charles Carroll of Carrollton that he always sat through such oratorical flourishes with acute discomfort. He did not like to hear himself praised and when he got home from public affairs he frequently said as much to his family.

But he really enjoyed taking part in the public ceremonies which celebrated Lafayette's visit to America in 1824. The two men had had little enough in common back in the war days when, with all their children broken out with smallpox, Charles and Molly Carroll had entertained the marquis at dinner. But the passage of time had made less formidable the twenty years' difference between their ages, and Lafayette's mind was no longer that of the immature boy who had found it romantic to enlist for American liberty. Carroll was proud to be the friend of this man who had opposed the violence of the Jacobins, had counseled and tried to enforce moderation, and had lost his immense personal popularity in doing so. He was tremendously interested to hear now at first hand how Lafayette had been imprisoned for his sympathy with the con-

[2] *Niles' Weekly Register*, July 8, 1820.

servatives, and how Napoleon had finally seen to it that he was freed; he was especially glad to hear, at long last, something good about Napoleon.

Lafayette, coming by water from his resplendent receptions in New York and Philadelphia — he was visiting America as the guest of Congress, and America was leaving nothing to the imagination — landed at Fort McHenry October seventh. Charles Carroll was there to meet him, along with the other notables. "The meeting of LaFayette with the venerable Charles Carroll, col. Howard, generals Steuart, Stricker, Reed, Benson, and other revolutionary soldiers, in the *tent of Washington*, had a most powerful effect on the feelings of all," the newspaper reported. "He grasped their hands, he folded them in his arms, and, with his eyes brimful of tears, and others who, like him, had fairly stood in the hottest of the fight in many battles, were dissolved by the pressure of the recollections that thickened upon them. . . ." [3] Lafayette and Carroll rode from Fort McHenry into Baltimore in the same barouche, accompanied by General Samuel Smith and Colonel John Eager Howard. They passed under a civic arch draped with flags, French and American, of course, and, in honor of Charles Carroll of Carrollton, to whom Baltimore would always accord special notice even on Lafayette's day, the flag of Ireland too. Lafayette stayed in Baltimore five days, and on October ninth Carroll attended an elaborate ball given in his honor.

Yorktown was the next stop in the distinguished guest's triumphal journey, for there the forty-third anniversary of Cornwallis' surrender was to be celebrated October seventeenth. Carroll had to refuse the invitation to join the party; he would have enjoyed the company of Lafayette but he was, after all, eighty-seven years old and the roads were no better than they had ever been. The other signers of the Declaration had to refuse as well. There were only two of them left, John Adams of Massachusetts and Thomas Jefferson of Virginia, and they were old men too. Everybody was getting very old.

[3] *Niles' Weekly Register*, October 16, 1824.

It had been a shock to see that boy, Lafayette, with his hair whitened.

Adams and Jefferson died two years later, on the same day, the Fourth of July which marked the semicentennial of the Declaration of Independence. Carroll had refused an invitation to take part in the celebration in nearby Washington not because he, at eighty-nine, was unable to make the trip, but because he had just refused a similar invitation from New York and could not "with propriety" accept a later one.[4] He was as meticulous about his manners as ever. But when he heard the news of the deaths of Adams and Jefferson he agreed promptly to take part in the magnificent memorial services which the City of Baltimore was arranging for July twentieth. Although he had disapproved of the politics of both men and was violently opposed to some of Jefferson's views, it was characteristic of Carroll that he in no way let the past interfere with his paying just tribute to their services. On the other hand it was equally characteristic that he did not suddenly begin to heap them with extravagant praise. "Though I disapproved of Mr. Jefferson's administration and was dissatisfied with a part of Mr. Adams', both unquestionably greatly contributed to the Independence of this country," was the way he put it; "their services should be remembered, and their errors forgotten and forgiven. This evening I am going to Baltimore to attend tomorrow the procession and ceremonies to be paid to the memories of those praised and dispraised Presidents. . . ."[5]

Now that he was the Last of the Signers — people pronounced the title solemnly, as if it were written in capitals — Charles Carroll of Carrollton found himself more than ever a national figure. He received an increasingly large number of delegations; a newspaper was named after him; he had more invitations than he could have accepted if he had wanted to; he was visited by every tourist who could obtain an introduc-

[4] *Niles' Weekly Register*, July 8, 1826.
[5] To Charles H. Wharton, July 19, 1826; Rowland, *Life*, II, 340–1. It should be Charles W. Wharton.

tion; he was showered with ridiculous but kindly meant little presents of the type that still go to the White House. One man, for instance, sent him an "American Box" made of thirteen different kinds of wood on the outside alone ("symbolic of the original states," the proud craftsman said) and twenty-four altogether. "The main frame is old Hickory which Binds and unites Together the Balance, emblematic of the firmness of which the Twenty four United States will Be Bound Together By the administration of our Modern Hickory Should he be Elected." [6] Carroll never failed to write graceful little notes of appreciation for these gadgets; this particular "American Box," he wrote with every appearance of gratitude, had arrived on his birthday and he made a point of showing it "to a large company . . . assembled to celebrate the day." [7] He did not think much of Andrew Jackson, but he had not forgotten his political training and wrote Jackson's partisan smoothly: "Let the most distinguished citizens be chosen presidents. . . ."

A compliment more to his liking than most of those he received was the franking privilege conferred on him by Congress.[8] Not only did he feel real appreciation every time he wrote on the outside of an envelope "Ch. Carroll of C — free," he still liked to save money on little things like postage. It was one of the family characteristics which had made him as well as his father the richest man in America, and which led young Charles Carroll Harper, by this time at school in the high-postage zone of France, to write to his grandfather: "I beg you to frank & have forwarded the enclosed letter for Mrs. Chissell. The other is from Emily to Aunt Caton; the third, for Mr. Gilmor, from Charlotte." [9]

The most unpleasant thing about being the Sole Surviving Signer was the tendency toward being regarded less as a human

[6] To one of his tenants (unnamed), September 22, 1828; Carroll Papers, VIII, 711.

[7] Ibid.

[8] John Barney, from the House of Representatives, to Charles Carroll of Carrollton, May 19, 1828; Carroll Papers, VIII, 709A.

[9] October 16, 1830; ibid., VIII, 715A.

being than as a subject for orations. In his young days Charles Carroll had wanted to live in a tub, like Diogenes, in order to avoid having to play cards; [10] but at no time in his life had he wanted to live on a pedestal like Simon Stylites. He hated being praised, as he considered, "too much." He wrote once to his daughter Mary: "I am too deeply impressed with the knowledge of my defects to be elated by the praises bestowed on me in the public prints and funeral eulogies; God only knows the heart of man and if he is deserving of praise; whoever is unworthy in his sight, must be mortified by praises, which, conscience says, are not merited. . . ." [11]

Besides, some of the encomia were enough to make anybody mad. Hear, just as an example, the sonorous roll of Daniel Webster: "Of the illustrious signers of the Declaration of Independence there now remains only Charles Carroll. He seems an aged oak, standing alone on the plain, which time has spared a little longer after all its contemporaries have been levelled with the dust. Venerable object! We delight to gather around its trunk, while it yet stands, and to dwell beneath its shadow. Sole survivor of an assembly of as great men as the world has witnessed, in a transaction one of the most important that history records, what thoughts, what interesting reflections, must fill his elevated and devout soul! If he dwell on the past, how touching its recollections; if he survey the present, how happy, how joyous, how full of the fruition of that hope, which his ardent patriotism indulged; if he glance at the future, how does the prospect of his country's advancement almost bewilder his weakened conception! Fortunate, distinguished patriot! Interesting relic of the past! Let him know that, while we honor the dead, we do not forget the living. . . ." [12] And so on. Mr. Webster probably meant well, but it was obvious that he had never been one of those

[10] Charles Carroll of Carrollton to Charles Carroll of Annapolis and Elizabeth Brooke Carroll, August 10, 1758; Carroll Papers, I, 33.

[11] Undated; Field, *Unpublished Letters*, p. 194.

[12] "Adams and Jefferson, A Discourse in Commemoration of the Lives and Services of John Adams and Thomas Jefferson, delivered at Faneuil Hall, Boston, on the 2d of August, 1826," *The Works of Daniel Webster* (1858), I, 146–7.

who had gathered around Charles Carroll's trunk — what a
way to speak of a gentleman's person! "Venerable object,"
indeed! "Interesting relic of the past!" And finally, of all
things, "weakened conception!"

The people who had met Charles Carroll of Carrollton told
an entirely different story. Everybody who could visited the
Signer when he went to Baltimore, just as he visited Fort
McHenry and the Washington Monument; and everybody
was sufficiently impressed to make a record of the meeting.
The comments do not appreciably vary in the course of many
years. Contrast James K. Paulding's in 1816 with Philip Hone's
in 1830.

"I dined with old Carroll of Carrollton," Paulding recorded,
"who is a little old fellow almost eighty, but active sprightly
and intelligent in a most extraordinary degree, and almost as
good a laugher as Adam Drummond." Whoever he was. "I
never saw a finer old fellow, and we took to each other
hugely." [13]

"I paid this morning a visit, which I had long been wishing
for, to the venerable Charles Carroll, the only surviving signer
of the Declaration of Independence," wrote Hone. "He will
be ninety-four years of age next September. His faculties are
very little impaired, except his sight, which within the last
few months has failed a little, and deprives him of the pleasure
of reading at all times, which he has heretofore enjoyed. He is
gay, cheerful, polite, and talkative. He described to me his
manner of living: he takes a cold bath every morning in the
summer, plunging headlong into it; rides on horseback from
eight to twelve miles; drinks water at dinner; has never drunk
spiritous liquors at any period of his life, but drinks a glass or
two of Madeira wine every day, and sometimes champagne
and claret; takes as much exercise as possible; goes to bed at
nine o'clock, and rises before day." [14]

The anecdotes of other visitors help fill in the picture of
Charles Carroll in his old age. Josiah Quincy, who visited him

[13] William I. Paulding, *Literary Life of James K. Paulding* (1867), p. 76.
[14] *Diary of Philip Hone*, edited by Bayard Tuckerman (1889), I, 13.

in 1826, recorded: "I paid two visits to Charles Carroll (the signer of the Declaration of Independence), and dined with him and Mr. Gallatin at Mr. Caton's, where the service, though the most elegant I had ever seen, in no wise eclipsed the conversation. . . . Old Mr. Carroll, courtly in manners and bright in mind, was the life of the party. He was then in his ninetieth year,[15] but carried himself as if thirty years younger than his contemporary, John Adams. I have never seen an old man so absolutely unconscious of his age. One reason may have been that Carroll was very spare in his person, and had no surplus pound of mortality to weigh down the spirit. On terminating my first call upon this very active patriarch, he started from his chair, ran downstairs before me, and opened the front door." The stairs in the Caton house are circular and fairly steep. Mr. Carroll's present biographer tried running down them, by way of scientific experiment, and nearly broke her neck. "Aghast at this unexpected proceeding, I began to murmur my regrets and mortification in causing him the exertion." But Mr. Quincy need not have bothered. " 'Exertion!' exclaimed Mr. Carroll. 'Why, what do you take me for? I have ridden sixteen miles on horseback this morning, and am good for as much more this afternoon. . . .' "[16]

John H. B. Latrobe, who knew him well, described him as he appeared a few years before his death. "In my mind's eye I see Mr. Carroll now, a small, attenuated old man, with a prominent nose and somewhat receding chin, small eyes that sparkled when he was interested in conversation. His head was small and his hair white, rather long and silky, while his face and forehead were seamed with wrinkles. But old and feeble as he seemed to be, his manner and speech were those of a refined and courteous gentleman, and you saw at a glance whence came by inheritance the charm of manner that so eminently distinguished his son, Carroll of Homewood, and his daughters Mrs. Harper and Mrs. Caton."[17]

[15] Actually, only in his eighty-ninth.
[16] Josiah Quincy, *Figures from the Past* (1926), p. 246.
[17] Rowland, *Life*, II, 359.

Most of the people who visited and were impressed by the
old Signer were pleasantly impressed with his family as well.
Some of his children and grandchildren were always visiting
him when he stayed at the Manor in the summertime, and he
no longer spent the winter months in Annapolis as he and his
father had used to do. Poor old Annapolis had had its day.
By the first quarter of the new century it had already atrophied
into the dreariness which would distinguish it for many years,
and those who remembered it in its brilliant heyday, as Charles
Carroll did, found it depressing as well as dull. Baltimore was
now the Maryland metropolis, the interesting place to be.
Mary, the elder daughter and favorite child, the one who had
married Richard Caton, lived in Baltimore, and Charles Carroll
was finally persuaded to spend the winter months at her house.
But he insisted on paying Mary board.

Mary and Richard Caton were still living in the big brick
mansion, on the corner of Front and Lombard Streets, which
Charles Carroll of Carrollton had built for them at the time
of their marriage. They gave him the nicest room in the house,
the big corner one over the drawing-room. From his front
windows he could see over the roofs of lesser houses clear out
to the water, and frequently he amused himself watching the
boats through a spyglass. He brought several cases of favorite
books from the Annapolis house and turned the room into a
bed-sitting-room, where he often received his intimate friends.
Quite aside from the strangers who came to see him out of
curiosity, he had more company — or so they used to say —
than anybody in Baltimore.

His favorite visitors (for he was clannish like all the Carrolls) were the members of his own family. It was a big family
by this time; men who have reached their nineties have not
only grandchildren but great-grandchildren. Among others,
Charles Carroll of Carrollton had held in his arms — but gin-
gerly, for he still thought precious little of holding howling
infants — Charles Carroll the Sixth, the Attorney-General's
great-great-great-grandson.

But Charles Carroll of Homewood was gone. He had died

in 1825, a few months after the death of Kitty's husband, General Harper. The cherished only son, who had cost his gay young mother her health and been considered well worth it, had never amounted to much. He had inherited the full measure of the famous family charm — everybody commented on that — but the family vein of iron was conspicuously absent. And Charles Carroll of Carrollton had never got over his not enjoying *De Senectute* and *Le Malade imaginaire*. He had no idea of the value of money, either, and that was in the Carroll lexicon a cardinal fault. If he had been anybody else's son Charles Carroll of Carrollton would have called him spoiled and lazy. As it was, he never lost patience, and no outsider ever knew from him that he was the least bit disappointed in his son. But he worried about him. Particularly he was distressed by Charles's showing not the slightest interest in his own or any other church. It was true that, on the occasion of his marriage to Harriet Chew, he had made rather a scene by having a fit of religion at the last moment and insisting that the ceremony be performed by a priest; but after that flare-up he lapsed into his usual indifference. Later he desired that his little daughters be brought up as Catholics. This was infraction of a prearranged agreement, but "unfortunately," Charles Carroll of Carrollton wrote, "though at present he has little religion himself, he is quite in earnest." [18] But his apathy about his own spiritual welfare worried his father to the end.[19]

He worried about Mary and Kitty, too. Not along the same lines; but Mary did have a habit of "lolling on the bed, and reading romances," and Charles Carroll of Carrollton was fully "persuaded that the frequent lecture of novels unfits the mind for solid improvement. . . ." [20] But Mary was not interested in solid improvement. Her father was concerned over the fact that she thought too much about Social Position and the Correct Thing — earlier Carrolls had never considered this necessary — and he did not hesitate to tell her about it. Kitty, for her

[18] To Harriet Chew Carroll, August 29, 1816; Gurn, *Charles Carroll*, p. 191.
[19] January 30, 1801; Rowland, *Life*, II, 247–8.
[20] Undated; Field, *Unpublished Letters*, p. 168.

part, was extravagant. Kitty as a matron was irresponsible as
she had been as a girl. He did not hesitate to tell Kitty about
that either.

All this must have been a little trying for those dignified
ladies Mrs. Caton and Mrs. Harper, middle-aged women now
and venerated grandparents in their own right. But they bore
very patiently with Papa. They adored him and they understood him. If he criticized now it was because he still blamed
himself for giving his children, in the years following Molly's
death, too little of his time. He was still trying to make it up
to them.

And, anyway, Papa always criticized in a nice way. He always apologized for mentioning his children's faults, and
beyond mentioning them he never did anything toward cor-
recting them. He had always been over-indulgent; he knew
it, but it was always too late to stop. Even when he was most
disgusted at his son's recklessness with money it never occurred
to him to cut down his allowance. Altogether the three children cost him a pretty penny. Charles Carroll of Homewood
received from his father in the course of twenty-four years
$130,500 in cash.[21] Catherine Carroll Harper, though she had
a husband to support her, received $86,958 in twenty-three
years.[22] Mary Carroll Caton, whose husband was a well-to-do
man in his own right, received $88,025 in twenty-two years.[23]
When the grandchildren came along, Charles Carroll of Carrollton continued to shoulder the financial burden. He sent
girls as well as boys to school in Europe, and when they grew
up and married well he continued to send them checks. Once
he sent one of his married granddaughters a draft for ten
thousand dollars.[24]

Naturally Carroll's favorite granddaughters were the four

[21] Memorandum in the Library of Congress' folder labeled "Charles
Carroll of Carrollton Miscellaneous papers regarding his estate and the suit
brought by his son and others." This label is, of course, in error; the suit
in question was brought by Carroll's grandson, after his death. His son had
predeceased him.
[22] *Ibid.*   [23] *Ibid.*
[24] Charles Carroll of Carrollton to Mary Ann Caton Wellesley, September
12, 1830; Field, *Unpublished Letters*, p. 212.

Caton girls whom he knew most intimately. Mary Ann, the eldest and prettiest — though all of them were pretty — married Robert Patterson, brother to the glamorous Betsy who had married Napoleon's brother Jerome Bonaparte, and went to Europe with him. Louisa and Elizabeth Caton went along. Robert was trying to keep an eye out for Betsy and her interests, a wearing business which had its social compensations for the Caton sisters in the famous people they incidentally met. (All three of them were a good deal like their mother.) Also, the young ladies bore letters of introduction to other prominent people and they found that Grand-papa, who in addition to being the Sole Surviving Signer was the richest man in America and the descendant of a good old Irish family, had a name to conjure with even in Europe. What with one thing and another, they soon found themselves moving in the most dazzling circles. In Paris they were presented to the King and the Royal Family; in London the Prince Regent and the Duke of Wellington were definitely attentive. Louisa, — "always," according to her father, "a proud and saucy puss "—[25] promptly got herself engaged to Colonel Sir Felton Bathurst Hervey, who had served Wellington as aide-de-camp at the Battle of Waterloo, and married him without returning to America. Charles Carroll of Carrollton professed himself delighted with the match, even though he hated to see Louisa settle down so far away from home. He was not narrow enough to be prejudiced against her husband as an Englishman and a Protestant, and was otherwise pleased that she was marrying into the excellent Hervey family. Besides, the colonel had made a a good impression by bothering to set down a detailed account of the Battle of Waterloo for his grandfather-in-law elect.[26]

The three Caton sisters — called in English society the "Three American Graces" — received enough attention to turn the heads of much more experienced ladies, and their grandfather was more than a little concerned about them. He

[25] *Maryland Historical Magazine*, XVI, 312.
[26] Undated; Field, *Unpublished Letters*, p. 176.

remembered the London of his own young days — the wicked city whose temptations were so manifold that he had prudently failed to guarantee his good behavior because "I never like to promise unless morally certain of being able to fulfil my promise. . . ." [27] And the reports sent home by the Caton granddaughters indicated that if London had changed in sixty years it had not been for the better. "What a dissipated life the fashionable in London lead!" wrote Grand-papa to Mary Ann Caton Patterson; "what time have they for reflection? the nights consumed in a variety of entertainments and amusements, and a large portion of the day in bed. Their manners are most agreeable and fascinating, and no doubt their tempers are amiable. Yet, to me, used to a comparatively retired life, such a whirl of pleasure appears incompatible with real happiness; for that depends on the love of God, a good conscience, and the exact and faithful discharge of the duties we owe to God and man." [28]

Yet he continued to make it possible for the Caton girls to stay in England and move in the most expensive social circles. Soon all three of them were entirely lost to their family in America, for a few years later Robert Patterson died and his widow married old Lord Wellesley, the Duke of Wellington's elder brother and lord lieutenant of Ireland. Lady Hervey's husband died too, and she married another Englishman, the Marquis of Carmarthen who was heir to the Duke of Leeds. Elizabeth, the third sister, did less brilliantly but well enough when she married the eighth Baron Stafford. Titles, anyhow, for three of her four daughters — surely society-minded Mary Caton had reason to be pleased.

Her other daughter, Emily, is always made to sound the Cinderella of the lot. "The fourth sister, Emily, married a MacTavish," is the customary way of dismissing the youngest Caton after much going-on (snobbishness, Charles Carroll of Carrollton would have called it) about the brilliancy and beauty and social position of her celebrated sisters. But Emily

[27] To Charles Carroll of Annapolis, January 29, 1760; Carroll Papers, I, 47.
[28] October 16, 1816; Field, *Unpublished Letters*, p. 183.

was the old Signer's favorite grandchild and repaid his affection, in her turn, more lavishly than any member of the family.[29]

It must not be supposed that Charles Carroll of Carrollton in his old age got all his social excitement vicariously, from the gaieties of his grandchildren. He maintained a distinct social life of his own. Most of the friends of his own age had, it is true, predeceased him; but they would have been in any case too old for him now. For Mr. Carroll had stayed young in spite of his years. Younger people — even quite young people — found that he was only too glad to meet them on their own level, and was perfectly able to do so. Though old-fashioned in his dress he was modern in his point of view. He still kept up with world politics, and when President Jackson and his cabinet came to dinner on his ninety-fourth birthday he surprised some of the gentlemen by his ability still to discuss current events as knowledgeably as any of them. Visitors were generally attracted by the way "his tact and skill in conversation lead him to the subjects most familiar to his hearer; while he is so well read that he appears to have considered each himself." [30]

[29] Carroll's affection for all his children and grandchildren blinded him, as I have said, to their faults. And they, knowing that Grand-papa when aroused was not averse to speaking his mind, made a definite effort to conceal from him the jealousies that love of money — still the family failing — bred among them. I do not think that the old Signer knew, for instance, that the Harpers and MacTavishes were at odds over the educations given the children of those branches of the family. He did foresee the possibility of the discreditable suit which followed the filing of his will for probate, for he "remarked that he wished to protect . . . all his gifts to Mrs. MacTavish, as he did not wish to get his affairs into the hands of the lawyers as they would afford them fine pickings. . . ." According to Father Chanche, "Not one of the members of the other branches of the family" took such care of the old man as Mrs. MacTavish did; also, he was especially fond of her husband, a Scotchman who had been sent from Canada as consul to the port of Baltimore. John MacTavish was one of those to whom, in his extreme old age, Charles Carroll issued a power of attorney. Father Chanche further deposed, in the case of *Charles Carroll et al. vs. Emily MacTavish*, that Mr. Carroll had said, of the gift of a house and land to Mrs. MacTavish, "it was strange, that if he could give twelve thousand acres to his grand Son from pride, he could not give one thousand acres to his grand daughter from affection."

[30] George Ticknor to E. Ticknor, March 1, 1815; S. Hilliard and others, *Life, Letters and Journals of George Ticknor* (1880), I, 41.

Young people who came to call on the Caton family found themselves returning to call on Mr. Carroll of Carrollton. No reflection on the Catons, either, but there was no doubt as to who was best qualified to be the center of attraction.

A constant flow of company, however, was not enough to occupy the good and well-used mind which still distinguished the last surviving Signer. Nor were his other diversions: the autograph collection he had started when he was ninety, the basketful of "beautiful puppies" [31] his old favorite Flora had contributed to the liveliness of his bedroom, or even the instruction of his great-grandchildren in the French language. (This last he enjoyed most of all, and visitors were politely reconciled to listen while the infant prodigy warbled a little "french song," [32] Grand-papa beating out the time with an encouraging forefinger.) He had been busy all his life, working hard at something or other, and found himself too old to break the habit. Idleness in a nonagenarian, he considered, was no less reprehensible than in a youth. So he set regular working hours for himself. He mapped out elaborate courses of reading — the three-year comparative study of religions was only one of them — and made notes as conscientiously as if he had some chance of using them later. In his spare moments he still kept the "plantation books," the personalized record of all the colored people who lived on his estates. He did much of the work connected with the American Colonization Society. He still took care of all his own charities, which were numerous enough to take a good deal of his time, especially as his mail was flooded with begging letters and he insisted on carefully investigating every one. Most of his business affairs were out of his hands — he had executed a power of attorney to his son-in-law Richard Caton, his grandson Charles Carroll, and his grandson-in-law John MacTavish — but he did con-

[31] Charles Carroll of Carrollton to Mary Ann Caton Wellesley, September 12, 1830; Field, *Unpublished Letters*, p. 213.

[32] M. J. Joussand (?)'s memorandum, "My reminiscences of the late Venerable Charles Carroll of Carrollton," enclosed in a letter to the Reverend John M. Chanche, September 27, 1833; Carroll Papers, VIII, 717A-D.

tinue to take an active interest in those businesses which seemed to him connected with the growth of America. He sat on the Board of Directors of the Baltimore and Ohio Railroad Company and was connected also with the Chesapeake and Ohio Canal Company with which the old Potomac Company had merged in 1823 and which would also lay its tracks into the middle west. When in 1828 he laid the cornerstone for the B & O he remarked that it seemed to him an occasion second in importance only to his signing the Declaration of Independence.

"Two fine youths," startlingly dressed in flesh-colored tights and winged helmets to represent Mercuries, rather stole the show from Mr. Carroll of Carrollton, supposed to be the chief attraction. Still the old Signer was impressive enough as, erect and animated in his ninety-first year, he broke ground for the railroad which was "to unite the east to the west, for the commencement of this great work which will commemorate an epoch in the history of the internal improvements of our beloved country." [33] It was far from being his last public appearance, but many were seeing for the last time the Charles Carroll who had become a Maryland legend.

The 1830's brought with them the realization that perhaps, after all, old Mr. Carroll of Carrollton was not going to live forever. People had got so used to thinking of him as an American Institution, the Last Surviving Signer of the Declaration of Independence, that they had quite discarded the idea that he was mortal flesh instead of immortal marble. Middle-aged persons who had not been born at the time Charles Carroll signed the Declaration were too used to making pilgrimages to see him, as they made pilgrimages to see Bunker Hill and Independence Hall, to realize that he was a man instead of a symbol. Even his family, who saw him without the expression of serious dignity which he wore when he sat on flag-draped rostra, or the formal graciousness with which he acknowledged the cheers of street crowds, found it hard to believe that

[33] William Baer to Charles Carroll of Carrollton, July 14, 1826; Carroll Papers, VIII, 710B.

CHARLES CARROLL OF CARROLLTON
BY CHARLES WILLSON PEALE

Grand-papa was in failing health. But by 1831 the signs were unmistakable.

A strange gentleman who met him a short time before his death found, however, that he was still a commanding personality. "Entering his drawing-room . . . I found him reposing on a sofa and covered with a shawl, and was not even aware of his presence, so shrunk and shrivelled by the lapse of years was his originally feeble frame. Quot libras in duce summo! But the little heap on the sofa was soon seen stirring, and, rousing himself from his midday nap, he rose and greeted me with a courtesy and grace which I shall never forget.

"In the ninety-fifth year of his age, as he was, and within a few months of his death, it is not surprising that there should be little for me to recall of that interview save his eager inquiries about James Madison, whom I had just visited at Montpelier, and his affectionate allusions to John Adams, who had gone before him. . . ." [34]

Carroll's mind was still as clear as crystal about the events and the men of the American Revolution. It was his favorite topic. He could still repeat passages from speeches which he had heard in the Continental Congress and thought particularly fine; he could still work himself up to a pitch of enthusiasm or indignation as he described the state of the country at the time of the Revolution; he could still dwell on the details of those affairs which had come within his province as a member of the Board of War. "Were I to enter the Hall at this remote period," he said once, "and meet my associates who signed the instrument of our independence, I would know them all, from Hancock down to Stephen Hopkins." [35] But on more recent

[34] A Mr. Winthrop, very probably Senator Robert Charles Winthrop (1809–94), as quoted by Senator George Frisbie Hoar in *Proceedings in the Senate and House of Representatives upon the Reception and Acceptance from the State of Maryland of the Statues of Charles Carroll of Carrollton and of John Hanson, Erected in Statuary Hall of the Capitol* (1903). This is a nice example of Carroll's lifelong ability to make himself pleasant to anybody he met. It is not likely that his allusions to John Adams were "affectionate." But he still knew how to manage a conversation so gracefully that his visitor, an admirer of Adams, actually thought Carroll had committed himself.

[35] Gurn, *Charles Carroll*, p. 288.

events his memory was increasingly dim. He forgot, for example, that he was president of the American Colonization Society.[36] He frequently forgot the name of the person he was talking with, if it were a fairly recent acquaintance; and he frequently repeated the same question which he had just asked a few moments before, and which had already been answered. However, "It is proper to add," said one conscientious gentleman, "that in conversing with a Member of the Family, I observed that I was struck with the singularity of his asking the same Question several times, in a short space, as to indifferent matters — but that as to the amount of his Credit at the Bank in Baltimore — he made only Enquiry once. It was remarked to me at the time, that on that subject his faculties were firm and a single answer was sufficient in Money Matters." [37] This circumstance did not seem so remarkable to the people who knew Mr. Carroll well. His mind would be failing indeed when it no longer concerned itself with finances.

But even when he asked the same questions over again "the questions in themselves were always sensible and well put." [38] Roger Brooke Taney declared roundly that "he was capable of reasoning soundly on any subject properly presented to his mind, & any suggestion immediately recalled to his mind the considerations connected with it." [39]

This is borne out by the fact that he enjoyed his books — which were not light literature — as much as he ever had. Unfortunately, his eyesight had begun to fail and this disability weighed heavily upon him. "I have always taken great delight in reading," he had written several years before to Judge Richard Peters, his old associate on the Board of War; "the weakness of my eyes deprives me of that pleasure. Conversing with the dead we are amused and instructed, and not flattered; to be excluded from their conversation at my time of life is a

[36] Memorandum of evidence given by Elliott Cresson, in Library of Congress' folder labeled "Charles Carroll of Carrollton Miscellaneous papers. . . ."
[37] James Baker to Charles Carroll Harper, January 14, 1833; Jonathan Meredith Papers, Library of Congress.
[38] M. J. Joussand (?) 's memorandum; Carroll Papers, VIII, 717B-D.
[39] Deposition in "Charles Carroll of Carrollton Miscellaneous papers. . . ."

serious misfortune. . . ." [40] For a time he had stubbornly refused to be read aloud to. It was not the same. But finally he yielded gracefully to the realization that his eyes would never be any better. His friends were very kind about coming in the mornings to read to him, and his granddaughter Emily Caton MacTavish was always ready to take her turn. Emily wrote his family letters for him, too, nursed him when he was ill — he was ill more often now — and saw to it that his company was amusing but not overtiring. Mr. Carroll frequently said that he did not know what he would do without her.[41]

He was not well all during the year 1831, but he made a remarkable recovery and in the spring of 1832 Philip Hone, revisiting Baltimore, was amazed to find Carroll again able to ride considerable distances on horseback. They rode all around Baltimore, visiting Doughoregan Manor and another country seat besides. Even so, Hone could not fail to see that he had aged greatly in the last two years. "Mr. and Mrs. Caton having called this morning to invite us, we passed an hour or two delightfully at their house in the evening," he wrote in his diary. "The family were all present. Mr. Carroll was cheerful and talkative, and enjoyed himself very much until nine o'clock, when, according to his uniform practice, he took the arm of Mrs. MacTavish, and quietly left the room. I feel while in the presence of this venerable man as if I were permitted to converse with one of the patriarchs, revisiting the land which, in days long gone, he had enriched with his patriotic counsels. He is in his ninety-sixth year; [42] his hearing is defective, and his memory of recent events imperfect; but he presents a beautiful example of the close of a well-spent life, — serene, cheerful, and happy; prepared, it would seem, 'to take his rest, with all his country's honours blest.' It is very probable I shall never see him again after the present visit, and this reflection enhanced the value of the delightful hour I have just passed in

[40] June 25, 1827; Rowland, *Life*, II, 355–6.
[41] Deposition of the Reverend John M. Chanche; "Charles Carroll of Carrollton Miscellaneous papers. . . ."
[42] Actually, only in his ninety-fifth.

his company. I made Mary take a seat by his side, and she has it to say that she conversed some time with the last surviving signer of the immortal Declaration of Independence." [43]

This was in March. Mr. Carroll was well enough during the warm summer months, but when the time came for him to celebrate his ninety-fifth birthday he was gravely ill, so ill that the Reverend John M. Chanche was called in to administer the Sacrament. "Emily sent you to me," Mr. Carroll greeted him, "She takes care of both my body and my soul." [44] During these last months Mrs. MacTavish had given almost all her time to his care and entertainment. She and Mrs. Caton shared the nursing. The doctors, one of them Dr. Richard Steuart, whose family had been old friends of the Carrolls in Annapolis, came in every day, but there was nothing they could do. Mr. Carroll was not in pain; he was simply very old, too old to go on living. His body had grown pitifully frail — he weighed now less than a hundred pounds — but his spirit was as indomitable as ever. He still insisted on being propped up on a couch or in an easy-chair, rather than go ignominiously to bed, and he was unbelievably cheerful. He could still make little jokes about his doctors, his Aesculapiuses, as he called them [45] (no one had ever "enjoyed" a classical education more richly than Charles Carroll had) and it was he who comforted his daughter Mary and his granddaughter Emily when they could no longer wipe away tears without his seeing them. He fully realized that he was dying; he realized as fully that dying did not matter.

They called the priest for the last time on November thirteenth, late in the afternoon. It was very cold weather, and there was a great fire in the big corner bedroom which Charles Carroll had not left for some time. His daughters and some of his grandchildren were with him, together with a few intimate friends and, of course, Doctor Steuart. When Father

[43] Tuckerman, *Diary of Philip Hone*, 1, 50.
[44] Deposition of the Reverend John M. Chanche; "Charles Carroll of Carrollton Miscellaneous papers. . . ."
[45] *Oration in Honor of the Late Charles Carroll of Carrollton, before the Philodemic Society of Georgetown College, December 13, 1832* (1832).

Chanche arrived and prepared to administer the last rites of the Church three or four old colored servants tiptoed into the room to kneel behind the white folks who were forming a semicircle in front of the fireplace. Old Mr. Carroll had been placed in 'a large easy-chair; before him the blessed candles, a crucifix, and a silver bowl of holy water stood on a little table. A daughter and grandchildren knelt on either side of his chair. Doctor Steuart, kneeling too out of courtesy, was profoundly impressed by the scene: "The ceremony proceeded. The old gentleman had been for a long time suffering from weak eyes, and could not endure the proximity of the lights immediately before him. His eyes were three-fourths kept closed, but he was so familiar with the forms of this solemn ceremony that he responded and acted as if he saw everything passing around. At the moment of offering the Host he leaned forward without opening his eyes, yet responsive to the word of the administration of the Holy Offering. It was done with so much intelligence and grace that no one could doubt for a moment how fully his soul was alive to the act."

The rites completed and the tears wiped away from black faces as well as white — for Mr. Carroll had been as kind a master as a father — his physician suggested that he take a little nourishment, for he had been fasting all day. "Thank you, Doctor, not just now," Charles Carroll answered him gently; "this ceremony is so deeply interesting to the Christian that it supplies all the wants of nature. I feel no desire for food." [46]

They got him into bed and he thanked them with his usual courtesy. He continued to refuse food and a little later fell into a light sleep; but he appeared to be lying in an uncomfortable position, and his granddaughter Emily asked the doctor to move him a little. Charles Carroll roused long enough to say again, "Thank you, Doctor," and again slept. He died quietly in his sleep, some time after midnight.

[46] *Appleton's Journal*, 1874.

BIBLIOGRAPHY

BIBLIOGRAPHICAL NOTE

THE author to whom I am chiefly indebted is, of course, Charles Carroll of Carrollton himself. Because he lived to be ninety-five years old, and was always taking his pen in hand, I have been able to get my knowledge of him in the best possible way, from his many letters. I am almost equally indebted to his father, who wrote almost as many, and whom I must thank also for the fact that the Carroll of Carrollton letters are as revealing as they are. Charles Carroll of Annapolis was about the only person who could strike sparks from the calm and self-contained Charles Carroll of Carrollton, and I appreciate his doing it often.

The best collection of original Carroll letters is in the Maryland Historical Society. Happily for the student, it is in good and usable shape. It is this collection to which I refer when I say "Carroll Papers," though, of course, there are Carroll papers in several other libraries. It is a poor manuscript collection that does not have at least a few letters from Charles Carroll of Carrollton. The Pennsylvania Historical Society, for instance, has a very nice collection; the Pierpont Morgan Library has several items; the New York Public Library has a folder of miscellaneous Carroll letters in addition to those to be found in the Emmet Collection. The Manuscripts Division of the Library of Congress has some very interesting scrapbooks. A number of invaluable letters are in private collections, but although I have had access to several such collections I found little or nothing of interest that Miss Rowland had not already quoted. Scattered Carroll letters and other materials appear from time to time in the non-Carroll Maryland collections which I shall list presently.

When you remember that the first three Charles Carrolls were prominently associated with the town of Annapolis for nearly a hundred and fifty years it is easy to see why almost all Annapolis and Anne Arundel County material is, to a certain extent, Carroll material as well. I have read with profit to this book wills, deeds, records of manumissions, accounts, inventories, judgments, and proceedings of the mayor's court. All these materials were to be found in the Hall of Records, at Annapolis. In the Anne Arundel County Court House there were more deeds and wills. In the Land Office there were still more deeds, land grants, chancery and provincial court proceedings, and maps. In the Baltimore County

Court House, at Towson, I read the wills and deeds that touched Charles Carroll's later life.

There are files of the *Maryland Gazette*, which came into being just about the time Charles Carroll of Carrollton did, in both the Maryland Historical Society and the State Library at Annapolis. These two are by far the most complete, though several other libraries have scattered issues. And, by the way, I recommend the *Maryland Gazette* most enthusiastically to the general reader. Much of my research was as tiresome as it was necessary — testamentary papers, for instance, — but the *Maryland Gazette*, especially in the years of Jonas Green's editorship, was pure recreation.

In the Manuscripts Division of the Library of Congress and in the Maryland Historical Society I did my most interesting reading, the letter-books and family papers of the Annapolitans and Baltimoreans who were Charles Carroll's neighbors and friends. The former had the sixty-volume Galloway-Maxcy-Markoe Papers, the Jonathan Meredith Papers, and the Robert Goodloe Harper Papers; the latter, the Calvert Papers (valuable chiefly as background), the Dulany Papers, the Bordley Papers, the Eden Correspondence, the Gilmor Papers, the Letter-Books of Dr. Charles Carroll and of Charles Carroll the Barrister, the Boucher Correspondence, and the Otho Holland Williams Papers. The Dulany and Gilmor collections, containing in part such interesting non-Dulany and non-Gilmor material as the Homony and Tuesday Club records, are especially worth the notice of the social historian.

Having told you where I found all these original-source materials, I must warn you that you may find them somewhere else. Ever since the new Hall of Records was built in Annapolis, papers which had been charitably sheltered under other roofs, before the State made suitable provision for housing them in a building of their own, have been finding their way there. The first archivist, the late Dr. James A. Robertson, was extremely zealous in the matter of accessions and I have traveled to Annapolis with more than one of his truckloads of material. ("You may never get another chance at an escort of state police" — and I never have.) I do not know to what extent this sort of thing has been going on, in the last few years, but I should certainly advise the student of official or semi-official material to try the Hall of Records first.

Because footnotes are supposed to facilitate matters for the zealot who likes to look things up, rather than to put him to unnecessary trouble and expense, I have thought it better in most cases to refer to the printed *Archives of Maryland* rather than to the original manuscripts. These volumes, published under the auspices of the Maryland Historical Society, have been most carefully prepared and are checked and rechecked before publication; if they contain any inaccuracies I have not been smart enough to find them. By the same token, I have quoted with all confidence from Miss Kate Mason Rowland's *Life and Correspondence of Charles Carroll of Carrollton*; she is accuracy itself, and some of the letters are inconvenient to refer to because the originals are in private hands. I could not with the same proof or even feeling of confidence quote Mr. Thomas M. Field's *Unpublished Letters*; I quoted it nevertheless because I suspected him of nothing worse than carelessness, and some of the letters, so important and interesting that I felt I ought to use them, I had not been fortunate enough to see the original.

In appending a list of printed books I am not including, by any means, all of those I read. These are the ones that helped me — most of them a little, but some of them very greatly. And I have not been able to resist marking a few with asterisks; these are not necessarily the most valuable, but they are the ones that I especially liked.

Abbott, Wilbur C., *New York in the American Revolution* (New York: Charles Scribner's Sons, 1929).

*Adams, John, *The Works of John Adams, with the Life of John Adams*, edited by Charles Francis Adams. 10 vols. (Boston, 1850–56).

Adams, Randolph G., *Headquarters Papers of the British Army* (Ann Arbor: University of Michigan Press, 1926).

*Alexander, Holmes, *Aaron Burr: The Proud Pretender* (New York: Harper Brothers, 1937).

American Archives, edited by Peter Force. Published by act of Congress. 9 vols. (Washington, 1837–53).

Andrews, Charles M., *The Colonial Background of the American Revolution* (New Haven: Yale University Press, 1924).

Andrews, Matthew Page, *The Founding of Maryland* (Baltimore: Williams and Wilkins Co., 1933).

Andrews, Matthew Page, *History of Maryland: Province and State* (Garden City: Doubleday, Doran & Co., 1929).

Anthony, Irvin, *Decatur* (New York: Charles Scribner's Sons, 1931).

Appleton's Journal, 1874.

Archives of Maryland, edited by William Hand Browne (Baltimore: 1883–   ).

Bacon, Thomas, *Laws of Maryland* (Annapolis, 1765).

Beard, Charles A., *Economic Origins of Jeffersonian Democracy* (New York: The Macmillan Co., 1915).

Beard, Charles A., *An Economic Interpretation of the Constitution of the United States* (New York: The Macmillan Co., 1925).

Beard, Charles A. and Mary R., *The Rise of American Civilization.* 2 vols. (New York: The Macmillan Co., 1927).

Bemis, S. F., *The Diplomacy of the American Revolution* (New York: D. Appleton-Century Co., 1935).

Beveridge, Albert J., *Life of John Marshall.* 4 vols. (Boston, 1919).

*Boucher, Jonathan, *Reminiscences of an American Loyalist, 1738–1789; Being the Autobiography of the Revd. Jonathan Boucher* (Boston: Houghton Mifflin Co., 1925).

*Bowers, Claude G., *Jefferson and Hamilton* (Boston: Houghton Mifflin Co., 1925).

Boyd, Thomas, *Mad Anthony Wayne* (New York: Charles Scribner's Sons, 1929).

Boyle, Esmeralda, *Biographical Sketches of Distinguished Marylanders* (Baltimore, 1877).

Brent, Daniel and John C., *Biographical Sketch of the Most Rev. John Carroll* (Baltimore, 1843).

Browne, William Hand, *George Calvert and Cecilius Calvert* (New York, 1890).

Browne, William Hand, *Maryland: the History of a Palatinate* (Boston, 1912).

Burnett, Edmund C., *Letters of Members of the Continental Congress.* 5 vols. (Washington: Carnegie Institution, 1921–31).

Chastellux, Marquis de, *Voyages de M. le Marquis de Chastellux dans l'Amérique Septentrionale.* 2 vols. (Paris, 1788).

Creel, George, *Tom Paine: Liberty Bell* (New York: Sears Publishing Company, 1932).

Cresson, W. P., *Francis Dana* (New York: Lincoln MacVeagh, The Dial Press, 1930).

*Culver, Francis Barnum, *Blooded Horses of Colonial Days* (Baltimore: published by the author, 1922).

Deane, Silas, *The Deane Papers*, edited by Charles Isham. 5 vols. (New York, 1886–90).

Delaplaine, Edward S., *Life of Thomas Johnson* (Frederick H. Hitchcock, The Grafton Press: New York, 1927).

Delteil, Joseph, *Lafayette* (J. Ferenczi et Fils: Paris, 1930).

Dickinson, John, *Letters from a Farmer in Pennsylvania to the Inhabitants of the British Colonies* (New edition, New York, 1903).

Dictionary of American Biography, edited by Allen Johnson and Dumas Malone. 20 vols. (Charles Scribner's Sons: New York, 1928–36).

Doniol, Henri, *Histoire de la participation de la France à l'établisse-ment des États-Unis d'Amérique.* 5 vols. (Paris, 1886–1900).

Drinkwater, John, *Charles James Fox* (New York: Cosmopolitan Book Corporation, 1928).

*Eddis, William, *Letters from America, Historical and Descriptive; Comprising Occurrences from 1769–1777 Inclusive* (London, 1792).

Edgar, Lady, *A Colonial Governor in Maryland: Horatio Sharpe and His Times, 1753–1773* (London: Longmans, Green & Company, 1912).

Farrand, Max, *The Records of the Federal Convention.* 3 vols. (New Haven, 1911).

Faÿ, Bernard, *Franklin, the Apostle of Modern Times* (Boston: Little, Brown & Company, 1929).

Field, Thomas M., *Unpublished Letters of Charles Carroll of Carroll-ton, and of his Father, Charles Carroll of Doughoregan* (New York, 1902).

*Fisher, Sidney George, *The Struggle for American Independence.* 2 vols. (Philadelphia, 1908).

Fiske, John, *The American Revolution.* 2 vols. (Boston, 1891).

Fiske, John, *The Critical Period in American History, 1783–1789* (Boston, 1892).

*Fiske, John, *Old Virginia and Her Neighbors.* 2 vols. (Boston, 1897).

Fitzpatrick, John C., *George Washington Himself* (Indianapolis: Bobbs-Merrill Company, 1933).

Franklin, Benjamin, *The Life of Benjamin Franklin, Written by Him-self*, edited by John Bigelow. 3 vols. (Philadelphia, 1884).

Franklin, Benjamin, *"My Dear Girl": The Correspondence of Ben-jamin Franklin with Polly Stevenson, Georgiana and Catherine Shipley*, by James Madison Stifler. (New York: George H. Doran Company, 1927.)

Franklin, Benjamin, *The Writings of Benjamin Franklin*, edited by Albert Henry Smyth. 10 vols. (New York, 1905–07).

Frischauer, Paul, *Beaumarchais: Adventurer in the Century of Women* (New York: Viking Press, 1935).

Galloway, Joseph, *Letters to a Nobleman in the Conduct of the War* (London, 1779).

Gerry, Elbridge, Jr., *The Diary of Elbridge Gerry, Jr.* (New York: Brentano's, 1927).

Greeley, Horace, *Thoughts on African Colonization* (New York, 1832).

Griffin, Martin I. J., *Catholics and the American Revolution.* 3 vols. (Philadelphia, 1907–11).

Griswold, Rufus Wilmot, *The Republican Court; or, American Society in the Days of Washington* (New York, 1867).

Grove, William J., *History of Carrollton Manor* (Frederick: published by the author, 1928).

Guilday, Peter, *Life and Times of John Carroll, Archbishop of Baltimore* (New York, 1922).

Gurn, Joseph, *Charles Carroll of Carrollton 1737–1832* (New York: P. J. Kenedy & Sons, 1932).

Hall, Basil, *Travels in North America*. 2 vols. (Philadelphia, 1829).

Hamilton, John C., *The Works of Alexander Hamilton*. 7 vols. (1850–51).

Harlow, Ralph Volney, *Samuel Adams, Promoter of the American Revolution* (New York: Henry Holt & Co., 1923).

Harper, Robert G., *Observations on the Dispute between the United States and France* (London, 1798).

Hilliard, S., and others, *Life, Letters and Journals of George Ticknor*. 2 vols. (Boston, 1880).

Hockett, Homer C., *Political and Social History of the United States 1492–1828* (New York: The Macmillan Company, 1931).

Hodgson, Adam, *Letters from North America*. 2 vols. (London, 1824).

Hollister, Paul M., *Famous Colonial Houses* (Philadelphia: David McKay Company, 1921).

*Hone, Philip, *Diary of Philip Hone*, edited by Bayard Tuckerman. 2 vols. (New York, 1889).

Hudleston, F. J., *Gentleman Johnny Burgoyne* (Indianapolis: Bobbs-Merrill Company, 1927.

Hughes, Rupert, *George Washington*. 4 vols. (New York: William Morrow Company, 1926 et seq.).

Hungerford, Edward, *The Story of the Baltimore & Ohio Railroad, 1827–1927* (New York: G. P. Putnam's Sons, 1928).

Jefferson, Thomas, *The Writings of Thomas Jefferson*, edited by Albert Ellery Bergh. 20 vols. (Washington, 1905–07).

Jefferson, Thomas, *The Writings of Thomas Jefferson*, edited by H. A. Washington. 9 vols. (Washington, 1853–4).

Johns Hopkins University Studies in History and Political Science (Baltimore: The Johns Hopkins University Press, and later the Oxford Press, 1898–   ).

Johnson, H. P., *The Yorktown Campaign and the Surrender of Cornwallis, 1781* (New York, 1881).

Journals of the American Congress from 1774 to 1788, The. 4 vols. (Washington, 1823).

Laurens, Henry, *Correspondence of Henry Laurens*, edited by Frank Moore. (New York, 1861).

Lee, Charles, *Memoirs and Letters of Major General Charles Lee* (London, 1792).

*Lee, Henry, *Memoirs of the War in the Southern Department of the United States* (Washington, 1827).

*Little, Shelby, *George Washington* (New York: Minton, Balch & Company, 1929).

*Loth, David, *Alexander Hamilton: Portrait of a Prodigy* (New York: Carrick and Evans, 1939).

*Maclay, William, *Journal of William Maclay: United States Senator from Pennsylvania 1789–91* (New York: Albert and Charles Boni, 1927).

Maryland Gazette, Annapolis, 1728–34, edited by William Parks; 1745–1800, edited by Jonas Green and later members of his family.

Maryland Historical Magazine (Baltimore, 1905–   ).

Mayer, Brantz, *Journal of Charles Carroll of Carrollton,. During his Visit to Canada in 1776, As One of the Commissioners from Congress; with a Memoir and Notes* (Baltimore, 1876).

Minnigerode, Meade, *Jefferson Friend of France* (New York: G. P. Putnam's Sons, 1928).

Murray, Elizabeth Hesselius, *One Hundred Years Ago or the Life and Times of the Reverend Walter Dulany Addison 1769–1848* (Philadelphia, 1895).

McCaffrey, John, *Eulogy on Charles Carroll of Carrollton* (Baltimore, 1832).

McCoy, Samuel, *This Man Adams* (New York: Brentano's, 1928).

McSherry, James, *History of Maryland* (Baltimore, 1904).

Niles' Weekly Register. 75 vols. (Baltimore, 1811–49).

Osborn, Lucretia Perry, *Washington Speaks for Himself* (New York: Charles Scribner's Sons, 1927).

Paine, Thomas, *Common Sense.* Published anonymously. (Philadelphia, 1776).

Palmer, Frederick, *Clark of the Ohio* (New York: Dodd, Mead & Co., 1930).

Parton, James, *Life and Times of Benjamin Franklin.* 2 vols. (New York, 1864).

Partridge, Bellamy, *Sir Billy Howe* (New York: Longmans, Green & Co., 1932).

Paulding, William I., *Literary Life of James K. Paulding* (New York: Charles Scribner's Sons, 1867).

Perkins, J. B., *France in the American Revolution* (Boston, 1911).

Pise, C. C., *Oration in Honor of the Late Charles Carroll of Carrollton before the Philodemic Society of Georgetown College December 13, 1832* (Georgetown, 1832).

*Pleasants, J. Hall and Howard Sill, *Maryland Silversmiths 1715–1830* (Baltimore: Lord Baltimore Press, 1930).

Preston, John Hyde, *Gentleman Rebel: The Exploits of Anthony Wayne* (New York: Farrar & Rinehart, 1930).

Preston, John Hyde, *Revolution 1776* (New York: Harcourt, Brace & Co., 1933).

Proceedings in the Senate and House of Representatives upon the Reception and Acceptance from the State of Maryland of the Statues of Charles Carroll of Carrollton and of John Hanson, Erected in Statuary Hall of the Capitol (Washington, 1903).

Reed, W. B., *Life and Correspondence of Joseph Reed.* 2 vols. (Philadelphia, 1847).

Ridgely, David, *Annals of Annapolis* (Baltimore, 1841).

Riley, Elihu S., *The Ancient City. A History of Annapolis, in Maryland, 1649–1887* (Annapolis, 1887).

Riley, Elihu S., *Correspondence of "First Citizen"* — Charles Carroll *of Carrollton, and "Antilon"* — Daniel Dulany Jr., *1773, With a History of Governor Eden's Administration in Maryland 1769–1776* (Baltimore, 1902).

Riordan, M. J., *Cathedral Records* (Baltimore, 1906).

Rivington's Gazette.

Roosevelt, Theodore, *Gouverneur Morris* (Boston, 1888).

*Rowland, Kate Mason, *Life and Correspondence of Charles Carroll of Carrollton.* 2 vols. (New York, 1898).

Rowland, Kate Mason, "Maryland Women and French Officers," *Atlantic Monthly*, November 1890.

*Russell, Charles Edward, *Haym Salomon and the Revolution* (New York: Cosmopolitan Book Corporation, 1930).

Russell, Phillips, *Benjamin Franklin, the First Civilized American* (New York: Brentano's, 1926).

Russell, Phillips, *The Glittering Century* (New York: Charles Scribner's Sons, 1936).

Sanderson, John and Joseph M., *Biographies of the Signers.* 9 vols. (1817 and later 1823–27).

Scharf, J. Thomas, *History of Maryland.* 3 vols. (Baltimore, 1879).

Sellers, Charles Coleman, *Benedict Arnold: The Proud Warrior* (New York, Minton, Balch & Co., 1930).

Semmes, John E., *John H. B. Latrobe and His Times* (Baltimore, 1917).

Semmes, Raphael, *Crime and Punishment in Early Maryland* (Baltimore: The Johns Hopkins Press, 1938).

Sherman, Frederic Fairchild, *Early American Painting* (New York: The Century Company, 1932).

Smertenko, Johan J., *Alexander Hamilton* (New York: Greenberg, 1932).

Somerville, Charles W., *Robert Goodloe Harper* (Washington, 1899).

Steiner, Bernard C., *The Institutions and Civil Government of Maryland* (Boston, 1899).

Steiner, Bernard C., *Life and Correspondence of James McHenry* (Cleveland, 1907).

Stevens, B. F., *Facsimiles of Manuscripts in European Archives Relating to America, 1773–83*. 25 vols. (Washington, 1889–98).

*Stockett, Letitia, *Baltimore: A Not Too Serious History* (Baltimore: Norman, Remington Co., 1928).

Stryker, W. S., *The Battle of Monmouth* (Princeton: Princeton University Press, 1927).

Sullivan, Kathryn, *Maryland and France 1774–1789* (Philadelphia: University of Pennsylvania Press, 1936).

Van Doren, Carl, *Benjamin Franklin* (New York: Viking Press, 1938).

Van Tyne, Claude H., *The Loyalists in the American Revolution* (New York, 1902).

Wallace, David D., *Life of Henry Laurens* (New York, 1915).

*Walpole, Horace, *Memoirs of the Reign of George the Third*, edited by Sir D. le Marchant. 4 vols. (London, 1845).

Wandell, S. A. and Minnigerode, Meade, *Aaron Burr*. 2 vols. (New York: G. P. Putnam's Sons, 1925).

Washington, George, *The Diaries of George Washington*, edited by John C. Fitzpatrick. 4 vols. (Boston, 1925).

Washington, George, *The Writings of George Washington*, edited by John C. Fitzpatrick. c. 30 vols. (Washington, 1931–   ).

Washington, George, *The Writings of George Washington*, edited by W. C. Ford. 14 vols. (New York, 1889–1893).

Washington, George, *The Writings of George Washington*, edited by Jared Sparks. 12 vols. (New York, 1846).

Watson, Thomas E., *The Life and Times of Thomas Jefferson* (New York: Dodd, Mead & Company, 1927).

Wellesley, Marquess of, *The Wellesley Papers*. 2 vols. (London, 1914).

Wheeler, Joseph Towne, *The Maryland Press, 1777–1790* (Baltimore: Maryland Historical Society, 1938).

Whitlock, Brand, *Lafayette*. 2 vols. (New York: D. Appleton & Company, 1929).

Wilson, P. W., *William Pitt, the Younger* (Garden City, New York: Doubleday, Doran & Company, 1933).

*Wilstach, Paul (editor), *Correspondence of John Adams and Thomas Jefferson* (Indianapolis: Bobbs Merrill Company, 1925).

Wilstach, Paul, *Tidewater Maryland* (Indianapolis: Bobbs Merrill Company, 1931).

Winsor, Justin, *Narrative and Critical History of America.* 7 vols. (Boston, 1888).

Winterich, John T., *Early American Books and Printing* (Boston: Houghton Mifflin Company, 1935).

Woodward, W. E., *George Washington: The Image and the Man* (New York: Horace Liveright, Inc., 1926).

*Woodward, W. E., *Lafayette* (New York: Farrar & Rinehart, 1938).

*Wroth, Lawrence C., *A History of Printing in Colonial Maryland 1686–1776* (Baltimore: Williams & Wilkins Company, 1922).

INDEX

INDEX

Page references to mentions in the text, by name, or otherwise obviously, are listed here in roman type. Page references to indirect mentions in the text are listed in italics. Page references to mentions in the notes only (nothing either direct or indirect in the text above) are followed by n.

Baltimore, George Calvert (first) Lord, 5–6, 96
Baltimore, Jane Lowe, Lady (wife of the fifth Lord Baltimore), see Jane Lowe
Baltimore, Mary Janssen, Lady (wife of the fifth Lord Baltimore), see Mary Janssen
Baltimore and Ohio Railroad, 306
Baltimore Furnace, 167
Baltimore Iron Works, 89, 217–8, 218n
Bank of the United States, see United States Bank
Barbados, 207n
Barney, John, 295n
Barrington, Daniel, 54, 79
Barrington, Lord, 54
Bath (England), 60–2
Bath (Virginia), 195
Batson, ———, 12
Beanes, (Doctor) William, 286
Beaumarchais, Pierre-Augustin Caron de, 190–1, 205
Bedlam, 192
Belgium, 58
Belvedere, 260
Benson, (General) ———, 293
Bill of Rights, see United States Constitution
Bird, ———, 54
Bird, Christopher, 54, 81n, 83–4
Bird(?), Esther (Mrs. — Browne), 54, 81–2, 91
Bladen, Anne (Mrs. Benjamin Tasker), 55
Bladen, Barbara, 55–6
Bladen, Harriet, 55–6
Bladen, Thomas, 55–6
Bladen, Mrs. Thomas, see Barbara Janssen
Bladen, William, 55
Bloody Assizes, 7
Board of War, 158–9, 166–7, 175–6, 180, 307–8
Bohemia Manor Academy, 29–30, 138, 271
Bonaparte, Jerome, 283–4, 302
Bonaparte, Mme. Jerome, see Elizabeth Patterson
Bonaparte, Jerome Napoleon, 283
Bonaparte, Napoleon, see Napoleon I

Bonhomme Richard's victory over Serapis, 201
Bordley, Stephen, 69n
Boston, Massacre, 95–6; Port Bill, 119–20, 130; Tea Party, 117–9, 127
Boucher, (Reverend) Jonathan, 88, 98, 109, 112, 132
Bourges, 34, 40, 42–5
Bradshaw, ———, 67n
Brandywine, Battle of the, 173
Brice, John, III, 83, 88
Bristol, 152
British West Indies, 224, 227
Brogden, (Reverend) William, 83
Brooke, Clement, 26
Brooke, Mrs. Clement, see Jane Sewall
Brooke, Elizabeth (Mrs. Charles Carroll of Annapolis), mentioned, 39, 52, 65–6, 68–9, 217, 220, 272–3; characterized, 51; parentage, 26; marriage and birth of son, 26; affection for him, 27–8; sends him to school, 30; failing health, 40; reluctance to leave Maryland, 50; illness, 50; death, 51; letters from son, see under Charles Carroll of Carrollton
Brooke, Rachel (Mrs. Henry Darnall), 68–9, 89–90, 108, 215, 232, 267
Brooke, (Reverend) Robert, 16
Brooklandwood, 260
Browne, (Mrs.) Esther, see Esther Bird(?)
Brownists, 6
Bunker Hill, 306
Burgoyne, (General) John, 173–4, 191
Burke, Edmund, 75
Burning of the Peggy Stewart, The (painting in Maryland State House), 127
Burr, Aaron, 231, 257, 281
Butler, (Senator) Pierce, 241

Caesar, 71, 168
Calvert, Caroline (Mrs. Robert Eden), 86, 98, 112, 131–2
Calvert, (Secretary) Cecilius, 68n, 69n, 73n
Calvert, (Governor) Charles, 20
Camden, Battle of, 201

265; goes to the theater, 53, 87, 265; refuses to play cards, 43–5, 48, 87; death of mother, 51; friends in London, 53–4; in love with Louisa Baker, 58–63, 81–2; returns to Annapolis, 63, 64–7; assumes title, 67; affection for Cousin Rachel Darnall, 69, 86, 215; interest in Stamp Act, 70–80; engaged to Rachel Cooke, 80–4; her death, 83–4; engaged to Molly Darnall, 84; marriage, 85, 106n; early married life, 86–91; birth of children, 90, 130–1, 162; joins Homony Club, 87–8; business interests, 89, 161, 217–8, 305–6; meets Daniel Dulany, 102, 106; challenged by Lloyd Dulany, 107; writes "First Citizen" letters, 103–12; influences 1773 election in Maryland, 112; thanked for patriotic services, 113–4; on first Committee of Correspondence, 119–20; refuses to be a delegate to First Continental Congress, 120–1; in unofficial contact with it, 121; refuses to change religion for political reasons, 122–3; advocates separation from England, 123; connected traditionally with Peggy Stewart Tea Party, 126–7; attends Lloyd Dulany's party, 127–8; on various patriotic committees, 129–30; entertains Washington, 132; goes to Philadelphia for Second Continental Congress, though not a member, 132–3; on mission to Canada, 133, 136, 137–52; keeps journal, 139–40; forms friendship with Franklin, 140; influences Maryland to vote for independence, 153–4; accepts seat in Congress, 156–7; on Board of War, 158, 166–7; signs Declaration, 159; returns to Maryland Assembly, 160; connection with Maryland Bill of Rights and Constitution, 160–2; obtains leave on account of wife's health, 162, 166, 177–8, 202; elected to first Maryland Senate, 163; at odds with father over Tender Bill, 164–6; boards with Mrs. Yard, 166; part in Conway Cabal, 176–80; goes to

Valley Forge, 178–80; resigns from Congress, 183–4, 188; part in French alliance, 184–5; suggested for presidency of Congress, 185–6, 204; vacations at the Springs, 194–7; characterized in state politics, 193, 200; refuses election to Congress on account of religious prejudice, 202–4; suggested as minister to France, 202, 253–4; entertains Lafayette, 206–7; urges ratification of Articles of Confederation, 210; celebrates victory at Yorktown, 212; deaths of members of his family, 215–7; entertains community in celebration of treaty of peace, 218–9; present at Washington's resignation, 219; education of and relations with children, 219–20, 235, 247–8, 299–301; their marriages, 220–2, 261–4; refuses to go to Constitutional Convention, 226–9; defeats Chase plan for emission of paper money, 228; associates self with Federalist Party, 229; urges ratification of Constitution, 231; elected to U. S. Senate, 231; service in Senate, 232–4, 236–42; reelected, 242; resigns seat, 243–4; retains seat in Maryland Assembly, 243–4; refuses commission to Indians, 244–5; mentioned as presidential candidate, 245–7; in Federalist party politics, 249–51, 253–5; retirement from politics, 258–61; designs houses, 262–3; life in retirement, 264–5, 289–90; takes part in patriotic functions, 291–2, 294; charities, 278–9; welcomes Lafayette, 293–4; receives franking privilege, 295; moves to Baltimore, 299; affection for grandchildren, 264, 301–4, 309; old-age hobbies, 271–2, 305; lays Baltimore and Ohio cornerstone, 306; failing health and memory, 306–10; failing eyesight, 308–9; receives last communion, 310–1; death, 311

Carroll, Mrs. Charles, of Carrollton, *see* Mary Darnall

Carroll, Charles, of Homewood, mentioned, *157*, 162 232, 292, 298;